Liberalism and Value Pluralism

POLITICAL THEORY AND CONTEMPORARY POLITICS

Series Editors: Richard Bellamy, University of Reading, Jeremy Jennings, University of Birmingham, and Paul Kelly, London School of Economics and Political Science

This series aims to examine the interplay of political theory and practical politics at the beginning of the twenty-first century. It explores the way that the concepts and ideologies that we have inherited from the past have been transformed or need to be rethought in the light of contemporary political debates. The series comprises concise single-authored books, each representing an original contribution to the literature on a key theme or concept.

Also published in this series:

Love and Politics
Fiona Mackay

Political Morality: A Theory of Liberal Democracy
Richard Vernon

Forthcoming titles:

Defending Liberal Neutrality
Jonathan Seglow

Democracy and Global Warming
Barry Holden

War, Law and Global Order
Danilo Zolo

Liberalism and Value Pluralism

George Crowder

LONDON • NEW YORK

Continuum

The Tower Building, 11 York Road, London SE1 7NX
370 Lexington Avenue, New York, NY 10017–6503

First published 2002

© George Crowder 2002

All rights reserved. No part of this publication may be reproduced or transmitted in any form or by any means, electronic or mechanical, including photocopying, recording or any information storage or retrieval system, without permission in writing from the publishers.

British Library Cataloguing-in-Publication Data
A catalogue record for this book is available from the British Library.

ISBN 0–8264–5048–2 (hardback)
     0–8264–5047–4 (paperback)

Library of Congress Cataloging-in-Publication Data
    Crowder, George.
        Liberalism and value pluralism / George Crowder.
            p. cm. — (Political theory and contemporary politics)
        Includes bibliographical references and index.
            ISBN 0–8264–5048–2 (hardback) — ISBN 0–8264–5047–4 (paper-
back)
            1. Liberalism—Philosophy. 2. Liberalism—Moral and ethical aspects.
    3. Social values. 4. Pluralism. I. Title. II. Series.
        JC574 C768 2002
        320.51—dc21   2001042204

Typeset by YHT Ltd, London
Printed and bound in Great Britain by Biddles Ltd, Guildford and King's Lynn

Contents

	Preface and Acknowledgements	vii
1	Introduction	1

Part I   Liberalism and Value Pluralism

2	Liberalism and its Justification	21
3	Value Pluralism	44

Part II   Pluralist Arguments: Liberal and Anti-Liberal

4	From Pluralism to Anti-Utopianism: Berlin's Case	78
5	Pluralism against Liberalism? Conservatism and Pragmatism	103

Part III   From Pluralism to Liberalism

6	From Pluralism to Liberalism I: Diversity	135
7	From Pluralism to Liberalism II: Reasonable Disagreement	158
8	From Pluralism to Liberalism III: Virtues	185
9	Pluralist Liberalism	217
10	Conclusion	258
	References	263
	Index	274

Preface and Acknowledgements

I came to the subject of value pluralism through the unlikely medium of the classical anarchist thinkers of the nineteenth century, who were all monists. Attempting to understand the anarchist concept of freedom in terms of Isaiah Berlin's distinction between negative and positive liberty, I was led to an interest in Berlin's thought in general. Berlin's work in turn led me to the writings of John Gray. It was Gray's critical interpretation of Berlin that opened up for me the question of how Berlin's commitment to liberty and liberalism on the one hand could be reconciled with his value pluralism on the other. For Gray, Berlin's pluralism implied that choices among competing incommensurable values, such as liberty and equality, were fundamentally non-rational. Particular rankings of such values could be the result only of subjective preference or cultural inheritance. It seemed to follow that the universal priority accorded by Berlin and other liberals to such goods as liberty and toleration could not be defended in the rational and universal terms characteristic of the liberal tradition. If this was true, then, as Gray pointed out, much of traditional liberal theory was undermined, indeed much of conventional political philosophy. But was it true?

It seemed to me initially that Gray was correct. In an article, 'Pluralism and liberalism', in 1994, I argued that (1) all of the existing arguments linking pluralism and liberalism, including Berlin's, were faulty. I concluded that (2) value pluralism does not support liberalism, and more speculatively that (3) pluralism positively undermines any rational case for liberalism. My argument

vii

PREFACE AND ACKNOWLEDGEMENTS

received a reply from Berlin and Bernard Williams which persuasively attacked (3) but failed to address (1) or (2). I was impressed by the force of their argument that a reasoned case for liberalism was *compatible* with pluralism – although in the case of Berlin this came as a genuine surprise in the light of some of his published remarks. But it seemed to me that Berlin and Williams had done nothing to show that such a case could be *generated* by pluralism, and this had been my main concern. Nevertheless, they stimulated me to rethink my views.

It now seems to me that not only (3) but also (2) was mistaken. I still believe that the arguments hitherto offered to ground liberalism in pluralism are unsuccessful, but it does not follow that no successful argument of the kind is possible. Indeed I now believe that such a case can be made, and this book is an attempt to make that case.

Of the many debts I have accumulated in writing the book, the first I wish to acknowledge is to those who have thought and written about value pluralism before me. I have already mentioned the late Isaiah Berlin and John Gray. I should add John Kekes as a third philosopher whose influence has been especially important for me. In the course of my argument I disagree with much that they say (in the cases of Gray and Kekes, especially their political conclusions), but I want to make clear at the outset my great respect for their pioneering contributions without which I could not have written this book. Other writers whose work on pluralism or liberalism I have found especially fruitful include Richard Bellamy, William Galston, Will Kymlicka, Charles Larmore, Stephen Macedo, Martha Nussbaum, John Rawls and Joseph Raz.

Drafts of various parts of the work were read and commented on by Rick De Angelis, Henry Hardy, Chandran Kukathas, Charles Larmore, Lionel Orchard and Andrew Parkin. My thanks to them all. I am especially grateful to Richard Bellamy, Martin Griffiths and Norman Wintrop, who read most of the manuscript and gave me a great deal of astute advice. Thanks also to Caroline Wintersgill and Neil Dowden at Continuum, to Daphne Trotter for copy-editing, and to Anne Gabb and Julie Tonkin for advice on wordprocessing. Flinders University funded some of the research expenses through its system of Establishment Grants administered by the University Research Board. This funding made possible, among other things, my first experience of research assistance, ably

PREFACE AND ACKNOWLEDGEMENTS

provided by Jane Abbey and Stacey Rowse. Also valuable were the outside studies leave granted me by the University for one semester and the part-time teaching release for another semester funded by the Faculty of Social Sciences.

Parts of the book draw on previously published articles or chapters. I am grateful to the Political Studies Association for permission to use 'Pluralism and liberalism', *Political Studies*, 42 (1994), 293–305, and 'Communication: Isaiah Berlin and Bernard Williams, "Pluralism liberalism: a reply"', *Political Studies*, 44 (1996), 649–50; to the Society for Applied Philosophy for 'John Gray's pluralist critique of liberalism', *Journal of Applied Philosophy*, 15 (1998), 287–98; and to Frank Cass for 'From value pluralism to liberalism', *Critical Review of International Social and Political Philosophy*, 1(3) (1998), 2–17.

For Sue

CHAPTER 1

Introduction

This book is a defence of liberalism on the basis of value pluralism.[1] Some recent theorists have argued that if values are plural in the relevant sense, then the traditional claim of liberalism to represent the best political order universally must be rejected. Under value pluralism, these theorists claim, desirable political forms vary along with local traditions or the demands of political pragmatism. I shall argue that this view is mistaken, and that if value pluralism is true, then we ought, so far as practicable or prudent, to endorse a liberal form of politics universally. Moreover, we ought, with the same proviso, to support a strong form of liberalism that is 'perfectionist' in the sense that a liberal state should promote liberal forms of the good life. A liberal state should accommodate many such forms, but should not attempt to be wholly neutral among conceptions of the good. Finally, pluralist liberalism will be redistributive and moderately multicultural, and is likely to temper democracy with constitutional safeguards.

In this introductory chapter, I lay out the basic question for liberalism raised by value pluralism, sketch my answer to that question, and indicate the main steps by which I construct my argument.

1.1 The Problem

I begin by offering a preliminary account of value pluralism,

INTRODUCTION

separating out its constituent elements and contrasting it with certain other ideas with which it is often confused. I then start to draw out the issues concerning its moral and political implications, before presenting an overview of my case.

Value pluralism is the view, associated in particular with the late Isaiah Berlin, that fundamental human values are irreducibly plural and 'incommensurable', and that they may, and often do, come into conflict with one another, leaving us with hard choices.[2] The idea has four main components: universality, plurality, incommensurability and conflict. First, pluralists claim that there are certain fundamental *universal values*, the enjoyment of which contributes to human flourishing. These values range from the satisfaction of survival needs, such as the need for food and shelter, to benefits required for any human life to count as a good life, such as friendship and intimacy, to the social and political values that frame the potentialities and limits of individual lives, including values such as justice, liberty and equality. Such values may be understood or instantiated in different ways in different cultural or material circumstances. They are also objective in the sense that these things make any human life go better than it would otherwise, even though particular human goods may be neglected or denied by a particular society or individual.

Second, the things that are valuable for human beings – including both universal and local values – are *plural* or several. Many different goods are required for human flourishing, not just one or a few – unless this is a trivial or empty category such as 'happiness' understood as meaning no more than 'what is good for human beings'. Furthermore, values are themselves internally complex, containing distinct components (also subject to material and cultural variation in particular instantiations) that add further to moral diversity. The broad value of 'liberty', for example, may be thought of as containing distinct 'negative' and 'positive' elements – the idea of non-interference and the idea of self-government.

The third component of pluralism is the most distinctive. This is that values are not only plural but may be radically so: they may be *incommensurable* with one another. The good of justice is a radically different thing from the good of adequate nourishment: each makes its own distinctive claim. The one cannot be subordinated to the other in an absolute hierarchy of values (i.e. that applies in all cases), and they share no common denominator in terms of which they can be measured along the same dimension. For the value pluralist, no

2

INTRODUCTION

basic value is inherently more important or authoritative or weightier than any other, and none embraces or summarizes all other values. In contrast with classical utilitarians, for example, value pluralists will regard pleasure as merely one value among others, a value grounding claims of its own which are no more fundamental or authoritative than claims based on liberty and equality. (More accurately, on the value-pluralist view there will be no single good of 'pleasure', but many different pleasures, each with its own character and ethical force.)

Fourth, these plural and incommensurable values may in particular cases come into *conflict* with one another. That is, they may be incompatible or mutually exclusive, such that one is realizable only at the cost of sacrificing or curtailing another – as for example if positive liberty (self-government) may be increased only by sacrificing some degree of negative liberty (non-interference). It is in such cases of conflict among incommensurables, as I shall argue in a moment, that we are faced with the kind of problematic choice that is a central implication of the pluralist outlook.

Before discussing the implications of pluralism for choice, however, it is important to contrast value pluralism with other ideas that are often insufficiently distinguished from it. Three such contrasts will be crucial to my later arguments, namely contrasts between value pluralism and, respectively, plurality of belief, relativism and monism. First, value pluralism is not mere 'plurality of belief', the idea that different people or groups of people believe different things. This latter is the usual sense attached to the word 'pluralism' in contemporary political theory. But value pluralism in the sense that concerns me is not an empirical claim about the nature of current belief. Rather, it is a claim about the true nature of morality independently of what some people may happen to believe. It is a meta-ethical theory of the real features of moral (and other) value. Consequently my argument that value pluralism grounds a case for liberalism should not be confused with the familiar claim that liberalism is justifiable as the most sensible response to modern divergence of belief about the good life. In a moment I shall point to the shortcomings of this latter claim, and later I shall argue that even in its most sophisticated form, in the work of John Rawls (1971, 1993), the argument from plurality of belief needs to be reinforced by reference to value pluralism (Chapter 7).

Second, value pluralism is not relativism. To say that values are plural and incommensurable is not to say that they are valid only

3

INTRODUCTION

from a particular cultural or epistemological perspective. Some plural values may be merely local, but it is an essential component of the pluralist outlook that there are at least some universal values, generic goods that contribute to any good life. Moreover, relativists may believe that a particular morality, although only locally valid, is internally harmonious such that all moral questions receive a single unambiguous answer from the rules of that moral system. Pluralists, by contrast, insist that any set of values may have, probably will have, plural and incommensurable elements, making hard choices inescapable for all moralities – whether or not such choices are acknowledged as hard in the relevant sense. Later I shall argue that one of the problems with recent anti-liberal interpretations of pluralism is that they illegitimately collapse pluralism into relativism (Chapter 5).

The third contrast is the most important of all: between value pluralism and its opposite, ethical monism. Roughly speaking, ethical monism is the view that a single value or narrow range of values overrides or provides a common denominator for all others. For the ethical monist, all goods can be comprehended within a single harmonious system either subject to or in terms of the super-value. Although our everyday ethical experience is one of frequent conflict among different moral considerations, such conflicts could all be resolved, once and for all, if only we could reach a full understanding of morality's monist structure. This has been the dominant view of the nature of value, in one version or another, throughout the history of Western thought. In one version the monist structure of morality is thought to be contained in the will of God or the fabric of the universe, yielding a natural law that human beings can discover by the use of their reason. Alternatively, a monist system might be implied by the nature of human wants or preferences: classical utilitarianism is a modern form of monism, in which all values can be ordered according to the super-value of utility, classically understood as pleasure, the one thing wanted for its own sake. What is common to all monist views is the idea that in some sense human morality forms a unified or harmonious whole. Its practical implication is that all moral conflicts can be solved, at least in principle, by reference to a single ranking of values that applies in all cases.

For pluralists like Berlin, ethical monism is false because moral conflict goes deeper than this. 'The world that we encounter in ordinary experience is one in which we are faced with choices

4

INTRODUCTION

between ends equally ultimate, and claims equally absolute, the realization of some of which must inevitably involve the sacrifice of others' (Berlin, 1969: 168). Values, including moral values, are not monistic in structure but plural. Value pluralism is a view of the nature of morality that claims to take seriously, more seriously than monism, the conflictual nature of our moral experience. Monism need not deny moral conflict altogether. But according to value pluralists, monist views underestimate the depth of moral conflict, regarding it as a superficial or temporary phenomenon, or as at least in principle surmountable by a clearer conception of the essential unity of moral values and principles. Value pluralism, on the other hand, takes actual ethical conflicts as an accurate sign that the moral fissures we regularly experience run all the way down.

In our personal life, for example, we are often confronted with situations in which we are torn between the rival demands of apparently equally weighty moral or prudential considerations. Should I lie to help a friend? This question has no clear answer if it is conceived as a demand for a general judgement, one that mediates decisively across a generality of cases, between the abstract values of honesty and friendship. Honesty and friendship each make their own distinctive claims, and neither outranks the other in all or most cases. Even in a particular case it may be unclear which value and course of action has the prior claim. My friend is important to me, but so is my personal integrity and sense of justice towards others who would be manipulated by a lie. Each value possesses its own characteristic force, and it may not be possible to determine with confidence that one value should come first all things considered, even in this particular case. The idea of value pluralism reflects our sense of the depth of moral conflicts of this kind. The difficulty of many of our moral choices seems to stem from the deeply fragmented nature of the ends we pursue.

Similarly, the idea of value pluralism captures the apparently intractable nature of many questions of public policy. As William Galston writes:

> My experiences dealing with policy disputes while in government greatly fortified my belief in value pluralism. In case after case, I encountered conflicting arguments, each of which seemed reasonable up to a point. Each appealed to an important aspect of our individual or collective good, or to deep-seated moral beliefs. Typically, there was neither a way

5

INTRODUCTION

to reduce these considerations to a single common measure, nor an obvious way to give one moral claim priority over the others. The most difficult public choices, I came to believe, are not between good and evil, but between good and good. (1999a: 880)

On the value-pluralist view, the conflicts with which we are familiar are not all ultimately resolvable, at least not in the way that monists suppose, but are the permanent, inevitable result of the deep structure of moral experience. The best explanation of such conflicts is that they result from the diversity of goods, each of which makes its own claims on us, claims that cannot be translated into any other terms.

Many people will find this picture of the nature of values persuasive and even attractive. It fits with salient aspects of modern moral experience, in particular with our sense of the multiplicity of genuine values, and of the distinctness of those values which is highlighted by those cases where we have to choose among them. And here we come to the central problem. If goods are plural and incommensurable, then how can we decide what to do in cases where they conflict?

Some philosophers go so far as to say that on the value-pluralist view we cannot decide such cases rationally at all.[3] The conflicting values will confront one another like contending sovereigns, beyond whose authority there is no further appeal. If negative and positive liberty are incommensurable, a proponent of this view will say, each value generates its own reasons for action, but there can be no reason to choose one value rather than the other all things considered, even in a particular situation. Where a decision must be made in such cases it can only be made intuitively or arbitrarily.

Given this extreme, irrationalist interpretation of its implications for choice, value pluralism would appear to be a threat not only to liberalism but to the whole enterprise of Western political philosophy as traditionally conceived. If the plurality and incommensurability of values really did rule out rational choice in the ethical realm, then it would be impossible to justify any political position, liberal or otherwise, by giving decisive reasons for it. Fortunately there is no need, as I shall show (Chapter 3), to accept such an extreme reading of the implications of value pluralism for action. Consistently with recognizing the plurality and incommensurability of values, we can choose among such values for good reason.

6

INTRODUCTION

However, even if rational choice is compatible with value pluralism, the question remains, *which* moral and political choices are rational under pluralism? There is reason to believe that such decisions will still be 'hard choices', in two senses. First, to choose one good is necessarily to forgo another genuine good, and the loss of the latter can not wholly be compensated by the gain of the former. Second, we must choose without the guidance of any overriding super-value or ranking system such as that proposed by the classical utilitarians and other monist thinkers. If so, it may seem that value pluralism prevents us from appealing for guidance to general rules. On the pluralist view, no single value or limited range of values will always override others, and no single value or limited range of values is capable of representing or commensurating all others. At best, some values will have priority in some cases, other values at other times: sometimes justice will be more important than friendship, sometimes the opposite. What we should do would seem to be purely a matter for judgement in the particular case, and there appears to be no possibility of arriving at a rule requiring the pursuit of some values rather than others across a generality of cases. This presents a serious problem for both individuals and whole societies. Should I lie to help a friend? If value pluralism teaches that we must proceed in such cases without the guidance of general rules, it may seem that our personal choices will be unsatisfactorily arbitrary. The problem is more disturbing still at the social or collective level. Most people believe that public policy ought to be guided by coherent and consistent rules or principles rather than proceeding ad hoc. If value pluralism is true and the general ranking and measurement of values is problematic, then how can we justify any set of general moral and political principles capable of guiding public policy?

How, in particular, might *liberal* public policy be justified? Must hard choices always be liberal choices? The principles of liberalism imply the ranking of certain values, including personal autonomy and religious toleration, ahead of alternative lists of values, for example those of socialists or conservatives, as a general guide for legislation and policy. But if values are plural and incommensurable in the sense described, then how can such a liberal ranking be rationally defensible? Must a consistent pluralist not insist that whether personal autonomy should be ranked ahead of, say, reverence for tradition is a question that can only be rationally determined in a particular case rather than as a matter of general

INTRODUCTION

principle? But if that is so, then pluralism would seem to undermine any reasoned defence of a general political position such as liberalism. Liberals do not want to be liberals in some situations and non-liberals in others. The reasoned defence of liberalism surely requires the justification of a liberal ranking not just in some cases but across a generality of cases. But that is precisely what pluralism appears to rule out.

On this issue a debate has developed between two schools of thought, respectively liberal and anti-liberal.[4] The former view, that of Berlin and others, is that the political form best fitted to the pluralist point of view will be broadly liberal.[5] A number of arguments have been advanced for this position, and in subsequent chapters I shall be examining several of these and proposing some new ones. Here I discuss two of the more straightforward in order to give some idea of how liberals may respond or actually have responded to value pluralism, and some idea of the kind of criticism to which those responses are vulnerable.

First, liberals may be tempted to mount what I shall call the 'argument from indeterminacy'.[6] If values are plural and incommensurable, so this argument goes, then so must be ways of life. Many conceptions of the good life will be equally legitimate, and none will be rationally determinate or compelling for all persons. If so, it is unreasonable for governments to impose any particular conception of the good on their citizens. Rather, individuals and groups should be left alone to decide for themselves how to live. Value pluralism thus leads to the liberal doctrine of limited government or state neutrality by way of moral indeterminacy.

This argument may seem superficially attractive, but at least in this simple form it relies on a radical degree of indeterminacy which is neither supportive of liberalism nor an implication of pluralism. The pivotal claim is that if values are plural and incommensurable then no account of the good life is more rationally compelling than any other. But if that is so it does not help the cause of liberalism, which ranks certain goods, like individual liberty, above others and so amounts itself to an account of the good. If all solutions to the question of the good are on a moral par, then illiberal solutions have as much claim to respect as liberal. In any case, value pluralism does not lead to such blanket indeterminacy or relativism. If values are plural in the relevant sense it does not follow that all (or even many) ways of life are on a moral par. Among other things, value pluralism involves the idea, as we have seen already, that at least some values

8

INTRODUCTION

are universal. Respect for universal values will therefore be a critical standard applicable to all ways of life and it will not necessarily be the case that all will meet the standard equally (see 5.3 below). Indeed, pluralism implies several such critical standards, as I shall argue later. Pluralism does not entail radical moral indeterminacy, nor would such radical indeterminacy support liberalism in any case. For these reasons, pluralism does not imply a case for liberalism by way of the simple argument from indeterminacy.[7]

A second argument from pluralism to liberalism is contained in the following passage from Michael Walzer, who is defending Berlin's claim that value pluralism and liberalism are connected:

> Concretely, there are many connections between pluralism and liberalism, and they work both ways. The experience of pluralism (as in the years after the Protestant Reformation) is likely to generate among some people – how many is a question – a commitment to toleration, respect, freedom of choice, and these are the people we most admire, the enemies of cruelty and oppression. And the institutions and practices of liberalism are likely to open public space to previously repressed and invisible groups, turning a merely theoretical or potential pluralism into an actual, on-the-ground pluralism – hence freeing individuals to live the lives they value without coercion, humiliation, or fear. Liberalism is a way of accommodating or enabling pluralism; pluralism provides the critical occasions when liberal values matter. (1995: 30)

As an account of how value pluralism is connected with liberalism, this suffers from two serious problems. First, its starting point is actually not Berlinian value pluralism at all, but plurality of belief. The 'experience of pluralism' in the wake of the Reformation was the experience of diverging religious beliefs, not a sudden realization that values are irreducibly plural and incommensurable. Second, how does the fact of divergent beliefs connect with the justification of liberalism? Even if people recognize the plurality of beliefs as a fact, it remains open to them to decide how to respond to that fact. Toleration is one option, the liberal option, but the imposition of orthodoxy is another – indeed, the pursuit of orthodoxy is more amply represented by historical precedent than is toleration. What *justifies* the liberal option? Walzer avoids this question with his claims of probability: 'The experience of pluralism ... *is likely to* generate ... a commitment to toleration' (my

9

INTRODUCTION

emphasis). But is the experience of plural beliefs so likely to have that effect if we do not, or cannot, give people reasons to be tolerant? Indeed, Walzer's claim here is empirically false. The experience of plural beliefs led immediately to the wars of religion. It was only when people began to see reason to behave differently that the movement for religious toleration began to gain ground. The bare fact of plurality of belief does not justify (and is not even likely to lead to) liberal toleration.

The failure of the two arguments discussed is symptomatic of the shortcomings of past attempts to argue from value pluralism to liberalism. Two general problems have been especially prominent. First, there has been a tendency to slide off the idea of value pluralism into some other view. In the two arguments reviewed we have seen pluralism conflated with, respectively, indeterminacy and plurality of belief. One thing we can learn from these cases, then, is the need to stay strictly focused on what is most distinctive of the value-pluralist view. In particular, we have to face up to the central pluralist notion of incommensurability and its implications.

This suggests the second recurring problem with past liberal interpretations of pluralism. Given the plurality and incommensurability of values, why privilege the values of liberalism (toleration and personal autonomy, for example) over the alternatives? This is the central question for any attempt to build a bridge from value pluralism to liberalism. In the case of Walzer's argument for a tolerant response to post-Reformation plurality of belief, the implicit answer is perhaps that liberal values are to be preferred because the alternatives are, in effect, violence and cruelty. But from a value-pluralist point of view this answer merely begs the same sort of question, in this case why privilege the opposing values of peace and humane treatment? No doubt these are important values, but may there not be cases in which other values – justice, liberty, the truth – are even more important? The problem value pluralism presents for reasoned argument in general is that of why one should rank one particular value ahead of another, or more broadly how one can choose rationally among options given value incommensurability. The problem for liberal argument in particular is that of why one should privilege specifically liberal values under pluralism. Past attempts to connect value pluralism and liberalism have been unpersuasive because they have provided no convincing answer to this question.

In recent years the shortcomings of the existing liberal arguments

10

INTRODUCTION

have been exploited to the full by a second major school of thought on the political implications of value pluralism. Broadly anti-liberal critics such as John Gray and John Kekes argue that value pluralism and liberalism are profoundly at odds. For Gray (1993b, 1995a, 1995b, 2000a, 2000b), the message of value pluralism is that there can be no universal ranking of human values for good reason. It follows that the ranking implied by orthodox liberalism, the universal privileging of goods such as personal autonomy, rights and toleration, is at best only one such proposal among others, no more objectively grounded or compelling than alternative configurations. The traditional claim of liberalism to constitute a political order universally superior to the alternatives is therefore untenable. At most it can claim to represent one possible form of modus vivendi, appropriate to some circumstances but not others.

Indeed, in the light of value pluralism liberalism may seem not merely to lack the universal superiority it claims for itself, but to be universally illegitimate and unethical. This is the view of Kekes (1993, 1997, 1998). Liberalism, Kekes argues, imposes a general ranking of goods where there can be no rational warrant for such a ranking without reference to the kind of background tradition that liberalism undermines. Such an imposed ranking denies the true nature – the incommensurability and particularity – of the goods it tries to rank. Kekes insists on this point even if the privileged liberal values are ostensibly 'procedural', that is, setting out rules that purport to be instrumental to the pursuit of various good lives rather than informed by any particular substantive conception of the good life. As Kekes puts it, states or individuals that regard such rules as overriding 'would regularly have to subordinate the values that make life worth living to abstract and impersonal procedures' (1993: 212). In setting certain goods above others in a permanent hierarchy, and perhaps in suppressing some goods altogether, liberalism seems to neglect the full pluralist range and force of human ethical experience. Rather, Kekes believes, it is the conservative outlook, according to which value conflicts are resolved by reference to a conception of the good life based on tradition, that best accommodates the demands of pluralism.

Do liberals have to accept these conclusions? I argue that they do not. Indeed, value pluralism is itself the ground of a powerful case for liberalism. I agree with the critics that previous attempts to argue from value pluralism to liberalism have been unconvincing. Despite that, and despite the difficulties attaching to all such

11

INTRODUCTION

attempts, it is a liberal rather than non-liberal form of politics that fits best with value pluralism. Pluralism implies a distinctive case for liberalism.

That case, as I present it, is directed to establishing three principal claims. First, value pluralism leaves room for various sorts of *particularist* argument for liberalism – that is, arguments that justify liberalism within particular cultural or historical limits. Pluralism is compatible with reasoned choice within a context, and that context may be favourable to liberalism. But particularist justifications represent a retreat from the universality of the traditional liberal project, and many liberals will want to press towards a more universal case.

That pluralism also allows a *universal* case for liberalism, indeed that such a case can be grounded in the idea of value pluralism itself, is my second principal claim. This is the most controversial component of my overall thesis, and I shall spend most of my time on it. How can we arrive at general principles recommending liberal values in the face of value pluralism? My answer is, by reflecting on the conceptual elements of pluralism itself and drawing out their normative implications. I argue that the formal features of value pluralism imply certain normative principles that are best satisfied by a liberal form of politics. There are five such principles: (1) universal values must be respected in all cases; (2) the incommensurability of values has certain implications that ought to be recognized; (3) a 'diversity' of values and ways of life must be promoted; (4) 'reasonable disagreement' about the good life should be accommodated; (5) practical reasoning under pluralism requires the practice of certain virtues, especially personal autonomy. The first two of these principles, universality and incommensurability, have the effect of ruling out, or at least weighing against, liberalism's ideological rivals, such as Marxism, anarchism and conservatism. But a positive case for liberalism emerges from the last three in particular: diversity, reasonable disagreement and the pluralist virtues.

Third, the pluralist arguments I construct recommend a certain form of liberalism. Pluralist liberalism will be universalist in the scope of its claims, and predominantly 'perfectionist' in Rawls's sense that it promotes a liberal conception of the good rather than aspiring to complete neutrality concerning the good. In the key policy areas of economic distribution and culture, the pluralist liberal polity will take a social or egalitarian form, redistributionist

INTRODUCTION

and moderately multicultural, in contrast with classical or laissez-faire and monocultural models. In its method of collective decision making, pluralist liberalism is likely to place constitutional restraints on democracy rather than relying wholly on political processes, however 'deliberative'.

I do not claim that the case I set out is the only way to argue for liberal conclusions or for these particular liberal conclusions. However, I try to show that the value-pluralist approach is a distinctive and powerful form of liberal argument, and one that has definite advantages over alternatives such as Rawlsian neutrality.

1.2 Plan of the Book

My general strategy is to bring out the political implications of value pluralism by a series of steps, each of which brings me closer to the particular form of liberalism I intend ultimately to defend, and each of which helps to eliminate opposing views. I proceed as follows.

Part I lays out working accounts of liberalism and value pluralism. In Chapter 2, I set out my understanding of what liberalism is, why we should be concerned with its justification, and how that justification is usually attempted in the existing literature. I distinguish a number of standard approaches to liberal justification generated by two central debates, first between universalist and particularist arguments, secondly between neutrality and perfectionist arguments. This analysis provides a typology of liberal argumentation which I refer to later in order to position the pluralist case. Those already familiar with this literature might skip this chapter and go directly to the next.

In Chapter 3, I develop my account of value pluralism. I begin by looking more closely at the main elements outlined earlier: universal values, plurality, conflict and incommensurability. I then ask how far choice among plural values can be rational, arguing that rational choice among plural values, and therefore among rival political systems, is possible in accordance with two kinds of guideline, respectively particularist and universalist. First, reasons to rank plural values can be generated by attention to the particular context of decision. Second, certain normative principles for ranking plural values are implicit in the formal components of value pluralism itself. These are the five principles listed in the previous section:

13

INTRODUCTION

universality, incommensurability, diversity, reasonable disagreement and the pluralist virtues. They come progressively into play in subsequent chapters, first to weigh against liberalism's rivals, and later to commend liberalism directly. In the final section of Chapter 3, I examine the question of why one should believe that value pluralism is true. I argue that while the truth of pluralism cannot be demonstrated absolutely, the case for it is persuasive on balance.

In Part II, I pursue the debate between the rival liberal and anti-liberal interpretations of pluralism introduced earlier. First, in Chapter 4, I examine the most significant attempt in the existing literature to link value pluralism with liberalism, the case presented by Isaiah Berlin. The best of the arguments that can be extracted from Berlin emphasizes the pluralist commitment to the recognition of incommensurability, hence to the inevitability of fundamental moral conflict. The effect of this is to eliminate as 'utopian' two of liberalism's most prominent historical rivals, namely classical Marxism and anarchism, which project a perfected social world free of such conflict. Liberalism, by contrast, conforms with the lessons of pluralism in its acceptance of significant social conflict as a permanent feature of human experience, a feature that can only be managed rather than transcended. However, Berlin does not provide a complete pluralist case for liberalism because his anti-utopianism is also consistent with conservatism and pragmatism.

Chapter 5 assesses the conservative and pragmatic interpretations of pluralism advanced by Kekes and Gray respectively. The assumption common to these anti-liberal writers is that rational choice among conflicting plural values is possible only by reference to a particular context. Context is identified by Kekes with local tradition, by Gray with circumstances inviting a pragmatic modus vivendi. Both argue that pluralist particularism requires us to reject liberal universalism. I respond that neither Kekes's narrow traditionalism nor Gray's vague modus vivendi offers a defensible interpretation of the pluralist outlook. On the other hand, pluralism allows, and even grounds, a case for liberalism along particularist lines. Moreover, the pluralist principle of respect for universal values, as well as undermining anti-liberal traditionalism, hints at the possibility of a case for liberalism that is more universal.

How does value pluralism entail a universal case for liberalism? This is the subject of Part III. In Chapter 6, I set out the first of my three main arguments from pluralism to liberalism, namely the argument from *diversity*. Pluralism implies a commitment to the

14

INTRODUCTION

promotion of a diversity of goods and (secondarily) ways of life. 'Diversity' here includes the idea not only of a multiplicity of values but also of a degree of coherence among those values, at least to the extent that these do not become self-defeating or self-destructive. Pluralist diversity is best realized under liberalism, because the 'approximate neutrality' of which liberalism is capable permits the accommodation of a greater range of values than possible under alternative forms of politics. Liberalism gives political effect to the balanced goal of multiplicity and coherence through its maintenance of a framework of individual rights and liberties. The maintenance of a liberal framework is not without costs, but these are outweighed by gains in the diversity internal to societies, which will in turn generate diversity among societies.

The second of my principal arguments from pluralism to liberalism is set out in Chapter 7. This is another version of the 'approximate neutrality' defence of liberalism, this time by way of a pluralist commitment to the accommodation of *reasonable disagreement* about conceptions of the good life. The argument is brought out through a critical comparison between the pluralist approach to liberal justification and Rawls's 'political' argument for liberal neutrality in *Political Liberalism* (1993). I am especially concerned to meet a serious objection to my pluralist argument advanced from a Rawlsian perspective by Charles Larmore (1996: Chapter 7), who argues that pluralism cannot ground a case for liberalism as neutral among conceptions of the good because pluralism is itself a controversial conception of the good. I reply that the pluralist approach is no more controversial than the political liberalism of Rawls and Larmore, in part because the most fundamental assumption of political liberalism, that of 'reasonable disagreement', actually presupposes value pluralism. Moreover, the pluralist case for liberalism is in certain key respects superior to the Rawls–Larmore argument. It makes explicit the kind of 'metaphysical' assumptions the latter relies on but tries to conceal, it rehabilitates the traditional liberal goal of universality in contrast with particularism, and it recovers the traditional philosophical goal of truth in contrast with consensus.

In Chapter 8, I shift away from neutralist justifications of liberalism towards a 'perfectionist' approach by way of a pluralist theory of *virtues*. This is the third of my principal arguments from pluralism to liberalism. My starting point is the last of the normative principles implied by the formal features of pluralism,

15

INTRODUCTION

namely our need for skills in particularistic practical reasoning if we are to cope successfully with conflict among plural values. To cope well with value pluralism, that is, to choose for good reason among incommensurable goods, people need certain virtues of the kind implied by Aristotelian accounts of practical reasoning. Among the various links between pluralist and liberal virtues, the most important for my case is that between pluralist 'flexibility' in decision making and liberal personal autonomy. Since the emphasis on individual autonomy is so distinctive of liberalism, to show that pluralist practical reasoning requires autonomy is to provide a powerful pluralist argument in favour of liberalism against its rivals. Building on the work of Joseph Raz (1986) and Stephen Macedo (1990), I argue that an ideal of strong autonomy is implied by the relatively demanding nature of rational choice under pluralism. The effect of this argument is to present liberalism as not merely a political framework for a society characterized by diversity and disagreement, but also an ethical framework for the best human lives, whatever substantial content these may have.

Having set out the value-pluralist case for liberalism, my final major task is to consider what kind of liberalism this will be: the subject of Chapter 9. My first move will be to capture the general character of pluralist liberalism by examining the relation between the neutrality and perfectionist arguments that have so far been developed separately. I argue that the two can be reconciled to a degree, but that ultimately the perfectionist argument has priority. The liberal state justified along pluralist lines will tend more to the active promotion of liberal values, especially personal autonomy, than to neutrality among conceptions of the good life which may include some that are illiberal. I then explore the implications of this view in two key areas of public policy, namely economic distribution and the treatment of cultural minorities. On the issue of economic distribution I consider and reject the classical or laissez-faire liberalism exemplified by Hayek (1944) and Nozick (1974) as too narrow in its effective subordination of all other values to the values of the market. Rather, pluralism implies a positive case for a social or egalitarian form of liberalism. I go on to argue that pluralism implies the rejection of laissez-faire as much in the cultural as in the economic field. Pluralist liberalism will acknowledge special rights for cultural minorities, although these will be subject to liberal limits. Finally, I examine the implications of value pluralism for the process by which public policy is formulated:

16

INTRODUCTION

should this involve constitutional protections insulated from ordinary politics, or should it emphasize democratic deliberation? Here I argue that although collective decision making under pluralism may take the form of 'deliberative democracy', this will probably be subject to constitutional restraints. These and the other central claims and arguments in the book are summarized in Chapter 10.

Notes

1. Throughout this book I shall use the terms 'value pluralism' and 'value pluralist' interchangeably with 'pluralism' and 'pluralist'. 'Pluralism' therefore means 'value pluralism' unless otherwise qualified. 'Plural values' refers to values that are both plural and incommensurable in the value-pluralist sense.
2. For Berlin's account of value pluralism, see especially Berlin (1969, 1980, 1981, 1992a, 1996, 1997, 2000). This is not to say that Berlin invented the idea. Intimations of value pluralism have been detected in the thought of Aristotle, and in pagan polytheism in general, with its picture of a world divided into many different spheres, each ruled by its own deity in rivalry with the others (Nussbaum, 1990: 226). In modern times a pluralist understanding of value may have been approximated, or at least hinted at, by thinkers such as Machiavelli, Montaigne, Hume, Vico, Herder, Weber and Oakeshott (Kekes, 1993: 12; Berlin, 1997). Only since Berlin, however, have some philosophers explicitly positioned themselves as value pluralists. These contemporary thinkers are the most important sources, apart from Berlin himself, for my understanding of value pluralism and its implications: Bellamy (1999, 2000), Chang (1997), Galston (1999a, 1999b), Gray (1993a, 1993b, 1995a, 1995b), Hampshire (1983), Kekes (1993, 1997, 1998), Nagel (1991), Nussbaum (1986, 1990, 1992a, 1992b, 2000a, 2000b), Raz (1986, 1995), Richardson (1997), Stocker (1990), Williams (1979, 1980, 1985), Berlin and Williams (1994). Recent collections of articles on the subject of pluralism include G. Dworkin (1992), Mack (1994), Archard (1996), Chang (1997). See also the list of contemporary pluralists given by Kekes (1993: 12).
3. Versions of this view seem to be held, at least in some moods, by Berlin (1969), Hampshire (1983), Raz (1986) and Gray (1993b, 1995a).
4. Surveys of the debate are provided by Crowder (1998), Dzur (1998), Galston (1999b) and Gray (1998).
5. Apart from Berlin's work, and Berlin and Williams (1994), explicitly liberal interpretations of pluralism can be found in Williams (1980), Hampshire (1983), Raz (1986, 1995), Lukes (1991), Walzer (1995),

17

INTRODUCTION

Crowder (1998, 1999), Bellamy (1999, 2000) and Galston (1999a, 1999b).

6. I shall come to particular instances of the argument from indeterminacy later. In one case it is attributed to Berlin (4.1.1 below), in another, pursued by Hayek (9.2).

7. Compare the argument from 'reasonable disagreement', which I support (Chapter 7). The latter can be seen as a more sophisticated version of the former, allowing indeterminacy among competing conceptions of the good life, but restricting this within a set of limits implied by value pluralism itself.

PART I

Liberalism and Value Pluralism

CHAPTER 2

Liberalism and its Justification

It is only when we have some grasp of the general terrain of contemporary liberal theory that we shall be in a position to see how value pluralism bears on that theory. In this chapter I give an account of what liberalism is, why it needs to be justified and how that justification is usually attempted. I engage here with a huge literature which cannot, of course, be treated comprehensively in a single chapter. My purpose is to provide a context of debate for my more specialized arguments regarding value pluralism, and to introduce certain concepts, questions and themes which I shall refer to in those arguments.

I present the main contemporary strategies for the justification of liberalism as turning on two debates, first between universalist and particularist approaches, second between neutrality and perfectionism. The principal positions in liberal theory can be understood as permutations of these views: universalist neutrality, particularist neutrality, universalist perfectionism, particularist perfectionism. I argue that the debate among these rival approaches to liberalism has reached something of an impasse. All these views exhibit strengths and weaknesses, and it is hard to conclude that any has a clear edge over its competitors. Later, in Part III, I shall ask whether a value-pluralist approach might break the deadlock.

2.1 Liberalism and its Justification

2.1.1 What is liberalism?

The idea of liberalism is, of course, complex and contested, but there is general agreement that liberalism involves a commitment to the following four main values or principles: the equal moral worth of individuals (issuing in a principle of equal treatment), individual liberties and rights, limited government and private property.[1]

The starting point for liberal argument is concern for the human individual. Whether this is seen as a claim about what human beings actually are or about how they ought to be seen for the purposes of political settlement, the foundational liberal principle is *equality of moral worth* (Vlastos, 1962). This is the notion, most famously expressed by Kant, of the human individual as possessing a special moral status among the things of this world (Kant, 1956). In virtue of their unique capacity for rational and moral self-direction, individual persons possess a moral value or worth that nothing else has. Moreover, since individual persons are equally human, the special moral worth that attaches to their humanity attaches to each individual equally: 'Liberal theories assume that all human beings possess whatever features make us worth counting in roughly equal measure with all other human beings' (Johnston, 1994: 21). From this follows the most fundamental liberal commitment, in Ronald Dworkin's formulation, to treat all persons with 'equal concern and respect' (Dworkin, 1977, 1985).

What is involved in treating all persons with equal concern and respect? Liberals disagree about this. Indeed, the major divisions within liberalism (and between liberals and other inheritors of the ideals of the Enlightenment, notably socialists) may be traced to different interpretations of this basic requirement (Kymlicka, 1990: 4–5). However, all liberals agree that equal concern and respect involves some standard of *equal treatment* understood as treatment that does not discriminate irrationally. In virtue of their equal humanity, individual persons should be treated in the same way unless there is good reason to treat them differently. For example, racial and sexual differences are not good reasons to decide who may vote and who may not. This does not mean that racial and sexual differences, or the broader differences of circumstance with which these are typically intertwined, may never provide good reasons for differential treatment. Some, although not all, liberals hold that

LIBERALISM AND ITS JUSTIFICATION

where such differences have resulted in systematic injustice or disadvantage, that is good reason for the state to intervene to remove the disadvantage or to compensate its victims (Rawls, 1971; Dworkin, 1977, 1985; Kymlicka, 1989, 1990, 1995).

All liberals interpret equal concern and respect as involving a commitment to some conception of *individual liberties*, and most understand these liberties in terms of *rights*. This is the second of the four defining liberal commitments. If liberals are asked what it is about human beings that is so special and deserving of respect, a common response will be Kant's notion of the individual person's capacity for moral autonomy, that is, the potential of human beings to decide for themselves how they ought to act, in accordance with rationally self-imposed ethical constraints. To honour this capacity in social and political practice will be, for most liberals, to allow the individual a substantial sphere of liberty within which to exercise the ability to pursue, as John Stuart Mill expresses it, 'our own good in our own way', subject only to constraints that all reasonable persons can accept (1974: 72). This will be a sphere of liberty from interference by other people and by government, even democratic government. The claim of the individual to be free, within limits, even from democratic or majoritarian constraints is customarily captured by the notion of individual rights, or entitlements independent of the wishes of the majority. Equal concern and respect issues, in short, in a liberal commitment to the values of *personal autonomy* and *toleration*.

The liberal commitment to individual autonomy and toleration suggests the third major component of the liberal outlook, namely the idea of *limited government*. Although far from the sole source of repression of individuals, governments have historically been among the most potent (Shklar, 1989). Consequently, liberal conceptions of liberties and rights have as their corollary the idea that the authority of the state must be bounded by recognized limits. As John Locke puts it: 'Though the *Legislative*, whether placed in one or more, whether it be always in being, or only by intervals, tho' it be the Supream Power in every Common-wealth; yet, *First*, It is *not*, nor can possibly be absolutely *Arbitrary* over the Lives and Fortunes of the People' (1988: section 135). Governments, even democratic ones, may not treat individuals just as they please, but must observe constraints that are enforceable at the suit of the individual.

Exactly where the boundary should lie between state authority and individual rights is the principal issue that separates different streams of liberalism. More precisely, the principal issue is over attitudes to *private property*, the fourth salient feature of the liberal outlook. Locke can again be taken to speak for the basic commitment common to all liberals: 'The great and chief end therefore, of Mens uniting into Commonwealths, and putting themselves under Government, is the Preservation of their Property. To which in the state of Nature there are many things wanting' (ibid.: section 124).[2] For all liberals, individual freedom includes the freedom to own property. As John Gray expresses it: 'Private property is the embodiment of individual liberty in its most primordial form and market freedoms are indivisible components of the basic liberties of the person' (1986: 62).

However, while all liberals are agreed that some recognition of private property is an essential entry in the list of fundamental individual rights, the liberal spectrum includes many shades of opinion as to how far private property should be protected. The reason is that the institution of property is arguably ambivalent in its effects on personal autonomy. Property may be an instrument and expression of autonomy both as a positive resource for the pursuit by individuals of their various plans of life and, consequently, as a check on the power of government. Exclusive property rights may also be, for those with no capital of their own, a serious limitation on personal autonomy, constituting a barrier to self-development as severe as any presented by government interference. At this point the liberal tradition divides into its two great streams. Classical or laissez-faire liberalism (Locke, Adam Smith, Friedrich Hayek, Robert Nozick) emphasizes individual rights of non-interference with private property and market outcomes, and consequently insists on a minimal or highly restricted role for government. Social or egalitarian liberalism (T.H. Green, L.T. Hobhouse, John Rawls, Ronald Dworkin) connects personal autonomy with redistribution and consequently with a more interventionist role for goverment. One issue I shall eventually have to consider is whether the liberalism supported by value pluralism is closer to the laissez-faire or the redistributive variety.

A second major division within contemporary liberalism is of more recent origin but roughly follows the contours of the classical–social split. This is the question of the proper liberal attitude to cultural traditions, especially those of minority groups. Classical liberals on the one hand generally stand for non-interference and strictly identical treatment for all citizens regardless of cultural background (Kukathas, 1992, 1998). Social liberals are more inclined to authorize state intervention in order to preserve cultural identities that are under threat (Kymlicka, 1989, 1995). Here, too, I shall have to consider, in due course, which of these views is more strongly indicated by a case for liberalism based on value pluralism.

2.1.2 Why does liberalism need justification?

Why should we be concerned with the question of whether and how far liberalism thus understood can be justified? In view of the de facto political dominance of liberal–democratic regimes in the contemporary world, it might be tempting to regard such a task as unnecessary. No prominent liberal holds such a view unequivocally, but some come close. Francis Fukuyama (1992), for example, is often read as asserting that the pre-eminence of liberal values and institutions is now assured following the collapse of the Marxist alternative embodied by the Soviet Union. Richard Rorty argues that under current conditions liberals do not need to justify their position philosophically, but can simply rely on a 'historico-sociological description of the way we live now' (1991: 185).[3]

To claim that a reasoned defence of liberalism is unnecessary exhibits a complacency both out of keeping with liberal tradition and unwarranted by historical experience. Questions of justification remain of central importance to liberals no less than to others, and although philosophical analysis may not be the only way of investigating such questions, it is surely among the most penetrating. Why is the philosophical justification of liberalism important? First, even if we can suppose that liberal values and institutions are secure from the threat of illiberal alternatives, live questions persist, of the kind noted above, as to what form of liberalism these ought to reflect: laissez-faire or redistributive, monocultural or multicultural? These are large and complex questions with more than merely academic significance; they deeply affect the lives of millions of people. They are questions of justification. We may reasonably expect that the answers that should be given to these questions will be strongly influenced, if not determined, by the kinds of justification that are offered for liberalism as a whole. Second, it is in any case far from obvious that the future of liberal politics is secure. On the intellectual plane

LIBERALISM AND VALUE PLURALISM

alone, liberal principles are still subject to many challenges, both from outside Western traditions of thought (Islam, Confucianism), and from within (Marxism, participatory democracy, and some versions of communitarianism, feminism, ecologism and post-modernism).[4] Third, liberalism's own principles mandate constant attention to the grounds of its legitimacy. Given their fundamental commitments to equality of moral worth and personal autonomy, liberals are obliged to ask, at every stage, how far the institutions and practices of a society are justifiable to all its citizens, indeed to all reasonable persons (Rawls, 1971; Dworkin, 1985; Waldron, 1987).

To adapt the words of Locke, that person ill-deserves the name of liberal who has no concern for questions of rational justification. However, it is one thing to see the need for justification, another to provide it. I now turn to the question of how exactly liberalism might be defended on reasoned grounds.

2.2 Liberal Justifications

Attempts to justify liberalism have taken many different forms, and the treatment I offer is inevitably selective and contestable. What I take to be the leading types of liberal justification in the contemporary literature emerge from responses to two central issues, first whether such justification should be universalist or particularist, second whether it should be neutralist or perfectionist.

On the first of these questions, liberals might argue on 'universalist' grounds, claiming that liberal principles and institutions are rationally and ethically superior to all alternatives regardless of time or place. On this reasoning a liberal political order is presented as the best possible for all human beings, mandated by universal reason; other political forms may be commendable in certain respects but are inferior to liberalism all things considered. Alternatively, however, liberals might make a more qualified, 'particularist' claim, namely that liberalism is to be justified not universally but only within particular historical and cultural conditions. Rather than binding every rational being, the principles characteristic of liberalism might be seen as having force only for those who share the basic value commitments – the cultural and historical outlook – in which the principles are grounded. What is at stake in this debate as regards practical policy is whether liberal

LIBERALISM AND ITS JUSTIFICATION

programmes (e.g. to promote human rights) are to be encouraged, or even enforced, cross-culturally and universally, or whether liberals ought to be more modest in their claims, addressing only those whose traditions are in some degree sympathetic to liberal values and forbearing to criticize those whose traditions are not.

The second major issue in the literature is whether liberalism should be defended on 'perfectionist' or 'neutralist' grounds. To defend liberalism on perfectionist grounds is to recommend it as a substantive conception of the good life involving the privileging of certain characteristic values and virtues rather than others. The neutrality argument for liberalism, on the other hand, presents liberalism not as a substantial conception of the good life in competition with others but as a purely instrumental political settlement which avoids judgements about the good in order to accommodate several such conceptions. In practical terms, perfectionist liberals are likely to authorize the state to take positive steps to promote and even enforce a characteristically liberal morality. Neutralists, on the other hand, will be more inclined to accommodate the wishes of local communities and religious or cultural groups whose practices (e.g. censorship) run counter to liberal values like personal autonomy.

These two issues, universalism versus particularism and neutrality versus perfectionism, cut across each other. Universalist defences of liberalism may be either neutralist or perfectionist, and the same is true of particularist defences. Conversely, if liberalism is seen on the perfectionist model, then it might be upheld universally as representing the best conception of the good for all human beings, or merely locally as the conception of the good favoured by a particular culture or civilization. A liberalism that aspires to neutrality may be promoted as a political framework able to accommodate all or most cultures, or merely a procedural settlement for the different streams within a common political culture. The two-issue matrix of liberal debate over justificatory strategy thus generates four possible positions: universalist neutrality, particularist neutrality, universalist perfectionism, particularist perfectionism (see Table 1).

Indeed, these four views are not merely logical possibilities but positions actually held and vigorously contested by contemporary liberal theorists. I shall now briefly review these four positions and the interplay among them in order to get a deeper picture of current liberal theory.

LIBERALISM AND VALUE PLURALISM

Table 1 Justificatory theories of liberalism

	Universal	Particular
Neutral	Rawls (early) Dworkin Larmore	Rawls (late)
Perfectionist	Kant Mill Galston	Raz

2.2.1 Universal neutrality

The dominant approach to liberal justification in the contemporary literature is that of 'neutrality', which in its seminal formulation in Rawls's *A Theory of Justice* (1971) is combined with universality. The origins of this view go back to the roots of liberalism in the movement towards religious toleration that developed in the wake of the post-Reformation wars of religion. Locke's *Letter on Toleration* (1991) is perhaps the defining document of this aspect of the liberal project. For Locke, the attempt to use state power to enforce religious orthodoxy is both cruel and futile: cruel because such enforcement will necessarily involve the use of extreme force against dissenters, futile because inner belief cannot be enforced in any case. The state should enforce only those laws to which its members could reasonably consent, leaving controversial matters of faith to be decided freely by the individual's conscience. Here are the beginnings of the classic liberal distinction between public and private realms of society.[5]

Later liberal thinkers in effect extended the principle of toleration, with its concomitant public–private distinction, from religious questions to other controversial questions of how best to live (Galston, 1991: 7). Mill in the essay *On Liberty* (1974), for example, identifies a 'region of human liberty', a sphere of individual freedom with which it is never the business of either the state or public opinion to interfere. Mill's sphere of liberty goes well beyond matters of religious affiliation to include freedom of thought and expression, freedom of association, and freedom of 'tastes and pursuits' or 'framing the plan of our life to suit our own character' (ibid.: 71). The Millian state intervenes only to prevent its citizens harming one another, not to prescribe or enforce any

28

LIBERALISM AND ITS JUSTIFICATION

substantial conception of how they should live. The nature of the good life is for individuals to judge for themselves: 'The only freedom which deserves the name is that of pursuing our own good in our own way, so long as we do not attempt to deprive others of theirs or impede their efforts to obtain it'; 'To give any fair play to the nature of each, it is essential that different persons be allowed to lead different lives' (ibid.: 72, 128).

It is only in the recent literature of liberalism, however, that the term 'neutrality' has come to the fore, associated in particular with the work of Rawls (1971, 1993) and Dworkin (1977, 1985). For these writers and the many who have followed them, what makes liberalism superior to alternative forms of politics is that it is uniquely 'neutral on what might be called the question of the good life' (Dworkin, 1985: 191). This principle can be seen as a further extension of the logic of toleration beyond the position reached by Mill. For neutrality involves not only the notion that the state ought to tolerate all plans of life that do not harm others, but also the further principle that the rules that secure toleration must themselves be impartial among the different life plans. On this view the liberal state can be thought of as providing a *framework* of rules (in particular securing liberties and rights) within which more substantial, and therefore more controversial, conceptions of the good life can coexist peacefully (Rawls, 1971: 31). Reasonable people may disagree about the nature of the good life, but they can be expected to agree on the framework that makes it possible to pursue their own conception of the good unimpeded by others. The framework itself is 'neutral' in the sense that, unlike the substantial conceptions of the good it contains, it is the object of reasoned agreement. The liberal framework can be the object of reasoned agreement because it does not depend on any particular conception of the good to the exclusion of others.

In Rawls's *A Theory of Justice* the ideal of neutrality receives an especially distinctive and influential treatment. There, principles of justice are chosen by the parties to an 'original position' characterized chiefly by a 'veil of ignorance' that prevents them from knowing details about themselves that would tend to bias their judgement in their own favour. Among the items screened off by the veil of ignorance is the parties' conception of the good. The original position thus models a fundamental commitment to impartiality, including impartiality among ways of life, when it comes to thinking about justice. A similar commitment to

LIBERALISM AND VALUE PLURALISM

neutrality is still more explicit in Rawls's famous doctrine that 'the concept of right is prior to that of the good' (ibid.: 31). By 'the right', Rawls means the rules and principles that make up what I have called the liberal framework enclosing and regulating the field of contending conceptions of the good. The right is prior to the good in two senses. First, when the liberal right comes into conflict with the claims of a particular conception of the good, it is the right that takes precedence. Second, the right is itself defined in a way that is not biased in favour of any particular theory of the good in preference to any other.

But is liberalism really neutral? The doctrine of liberal neutrality has been subjected to several powerful lines of objection. First, there is the objection from differential impact. The enforcement of liberal rules and procedures, rights and liberties, does not affect all ways of life equally. Inevitably, those conceptions of the good that do not share the core liberal commitments to equal concern and respect, personal autonomy, toleration and private property will be more restricted, will have less room in which to flourish, than those ways of life that lie closer to the liberal outlook.

Liberals might reply that even if the objection from differential *impact* is correct, liberalism nevertheless remains neutral at a deeper level, namely in the *reasons* it offers for public policy, that is, in its definition of the putatively neutral framework.[6] Although it may be true that liberal policies restrict some ways of life more than others, that is merely the unintended consequence of applying principles that are themselves neutral among conceptions of the good. It is at this level, that of the 'neutrality of reasons', that liberal neutrality is usually defended, as for example by Rawls and Dworkin.

The neutrality of reasons, however, attracts its own line of objection. 'Liberal neutrality' clears a space for individuals and groups to pursue their own conceptions of the good free from persecution by other individuals or groups or the state. In effect this amounts to the promotion of certain values in preference to others: toleration rather than orthodoxy, freedom rather than solidarity, diversity rather than community, debate rather than agreement, experiment rather than tradition. There is no such thing as state neutrality in the literal sense. 'Neutrality' itself, one may say, stands for a bundle of value commitments, a particular ranking of goods.

This point is a staple of the 'communitarian' critique of liberalism that has developed since the 1980s in response to Rawls in particular. Michael Sandel, for example, argues that Rawls's

LIBERALISM AND ITS JUSTIFICATION

supposedly impartial theory of justice in fact presupposes a 'Kantian' notion of the person that impossibly requires us to conceive of ourselves as separable from the ends, identifications and values that make us who we are (Sandel, 1982). Charles Taylor holds that even the most neutral or 'procedural' liberalism in fact rests on a substantial conception of the good life, namely a liberal conception of the good in which persons are seen as radically, and desirably, 'atomistic' (Taylor, 1989a, 1989b). Alasdair MacIntyre, similarly, sees liberalism as constituting a definite, historically contingent (and peculiarly unsatisfactory) 'tradition', based on a privileged set of goods in competition with alternative accounts of the good (MacIntyre, 1985, 1988). Similar points to these have been made not only by critics of liberalism but also by writers who explicitly identify themselves as liberal, yet who have registered dissatisfaction with defences based on neutrality (Nagel, 1973; Barry, 1991).

All of these objections contain highly questionable elements, but these have already been thoroughly debated in the literature and there is no need for me to pursue them here (see e.g. Kymlicka, 1990; Mulhall and Swift, 1996). What is important for my purposes is to accept the force of the general communitarian point that liberalism cannot be wholly neutral, either in impact or reasons, and to indicate two liberal responses that seek to accommodate that point while still affirming some form of the neutrality ideal.

First, liberals can argue that even if liberalism cannot be wholly neutral in the sense either of impact or reasons, it is still *approximately* neutral. That is, a liberal political order is as neutral as possible, and more neutral than the alternatives.[7] The communitarians, it should be conceded, are correct that any political system must rest in the end on some conception of the good. Even liberal 'neutrality' stands for a commitment to a particular set of goods (especially toleration) privileged over alternative sets. Nevertheless, some conceptions of the good are more capacious, or accommodating of different ways of living, than others. Liberals should concede that their principles are not limitlessly accommodating, since those principles necessarily exclude or oppose ways of life that do not value equal respect, personal liberty, private property and toleration. But liberals can still argue that the political framework they offer is more inclusive than that of any rivals. I take this 'approximate' version to be the most defensible form of liberal neutrality in its universal form, and it is in this sense that I later connect neutrality with value pluralism (Chapters 6–7).

2.2.2 Particularist neutrality

For some liberals, however, the 'approximate' qualification to neutrality does not go far enough; liberalism's traditional claim to universality is also a problem. Consequently, a second form of liberal response to the communitarian critique of neutrality is to retain a commitment to a neutrality of reasons but to abandon the claim that such a commitment has universal force. This is the course taken by Rawls. In *A Theory of Justice*, Rawls appeared to be seeking a wholly objective 'Archimedean point' from which to derive principles of justice of universal application (1971: 261). In his articles of the 1980s, however, responding in part to the communitarians, he began to distance himself from claims to universality and to move towards a defence of liberalism that was explicitly 'political, not metaphysical' (1985). Rawls's revised theory of justice does not depend on claims to universal truth or accounts of the essential nature of persons, but rather begins with the contents of an actual political culture. 'It tries to draw solely upon basic intuitive ideas that are embedded in the political institutions of a constitutional democratic regime and the public traditions of their interpretation. Justice as fairness is a political conception that starts from within a certain political tradition' (ibid.: 225). The original position is still presented as modelling a neutralist or anti-perfectionist approach, but this is now explicitly contextualized within the particular political culture of modern constitutional democracies such as the United States of America and Britain.

Rawls's 'political' turn is confirmed in *Political Liberalism* (1993). There he tries to broaden the appeal of justice as fairness to attract people in addition to those who already possess a comprehensively liberal outlook. The argument of *A Theory of Justice* depended on the reader sharing such an outlook, because it began with a set of comprehensively liberal intuitions, including the notion of persons as intrinsically free and equal and the idea of certain goods as, without qualification, 'primary' (or necessary for any good life). Rawls now thinks that such a comprehensively liberal starting point does not take sufficiently seriously the extent of reasonable disagreement about the truth of comprehensive moral doctrines,

LIBERALISM AND ITS JUSTIFICATION

including those supporting liberalism, in modern societies. The 'fact of reasonable pluralism' under modern conditions must be taken as axiomatic. On the other hand the liberal state must remain committed to 'public justification', or the obligation to base public policy only on principles that can be justified to all reasonable citizens. When the demand for public justification is taken together with due attention to the fact of reasonable pluralism, the result is that liberal states must appeal in the public realm only to 'public reasons' – public in the sense that all citizens can share in recognizing them as legitimate. Hence Rawls argues that such reasons must be sought in the public political culture in which all share. It is there, he says, that we can find implicit the ideas (such as that of society as a fair system of co-operation among free and equal citizens) that ground justice as fairness. Because these implict ideas are part of the shared political culture, they are not peculiar to any particular comprehensive doctrine, including those of liberalism, and so are freestanding or neutral with respect to competing conceptions of the good life. On the other hand they can be reached through any reasonable comprehensive moral doctrine. As Rawls puts it, they are the focus of an 'overlapping consensus' of such doctrines. They are neutral without being abstract or universal.

Liberals are divided over the merits of Rawls's particularist turn. While some see the new political liberalism as a salutary moderation of the excessive ambitions and arrogance of the past, others find in the same developments a dispiriting abandonment of liberalism's historical mission and a reduction of the liberal project to what amounts to preaching to the converted. The first view is represented by Rorty, who compliments Rawls on his 'thoroughly historicist and antiuniversalist' approach, which Rorty sees as rightly appreciating that the legitimation of liberalism at a philosophical level is neither possible nor necessary (1991: 180). Samuel Scheffler, on the other hand, observes that Rawls's new argument 'appears to presuppose a society in which liberal values are already well-entrenched'. Consequently,

in renouncing any universalistic ambitions, Rawls may now seem to have gone too far in the other direction and to have produced a version of liberalism that is so historically specific and so dependent on a prior history of liberal institutions as to be of little relevance in those situations where the justification of liberalism matters most: that is, where liberalism is confronted by, and must engage with, societies whose traditions and practices are not liberal. (1994: 20–1)

Moreover, it is not clear that Rawls's retreat from universality has much strengthened his claims to neutrality, since there remain points at which his theory still seems to depend on a comprehensively liberal moral doctrine that would be rejected by many people given their current beliefs. For example, there is Rawls's basic idea that those people who do not endorse liberal principles in their private lives can still accept such principles for strictly political or public purposes. This willingness to separate one's moral commitments into public and private spheres already suggests a liberal outlook. Moreover, Rawls's view requires the political sphere to be accorded priority as a framework for the private, which means that if there is a conflict between liberal principles and one's own beliefs, it is the former that will prevail. As Will Kymlicka points out, 'accepting the value of autonomy for political purposes enables its exercise in private life, an implication that will only be favoured by those who endorse autonomy as a general value' (1995: 162).[8]

Overall, one is left with the question of whether Rawls has gained anything through his political turn that is worth the price he has paid. What he has supposedly gained is the justification of a liberal political settlement to reasonable people beyond those who already possess comprehensively liberal ideals, but there are doubts about how purely political Rawls's principles really are, and therefore doubts about their justificatory reach. The price he has paid is the retreat from universality, such that he can no longer address those who do not happen to have a pre-existing liberal–democratic political culture.

2.2.3 Universal perfectionism

The perceived attenuation of the liberal project in the hands of Rawls and the neutralists, both universal and particularist (or 'political'), has led some recent liberal writers to seek a more full-blooded recasting of the project and its justification. These are the 'perfectionist' liberals, the most prominent of whom are Joseph Raz and William Galston (Raz, 1986; Galston, 1991). Patrick Neal, writing about Raz, captures the character of the perfectionist liberal as follows:

34

one confident in the rationality of his principles, unafraid of squarely endorsing state action in support of them, willing to walk tall, without guilt about the big stick he carries or the reasonability of swinging it (where warranted only, of course). Such a liberalism would have abandoned the implicit desire, overtly manifested in the discourse of neutrality, to be all things to all people, and would instead dare to speak its name. (Neal, 1997: 136)

The term 'perfectionism' comes from Rawls, who uses it as a label for the view that the role of the state is to identify and enforce a particular conception of the good (Rawls, 1971: 25, 325–32). For Rawls, liberalism is necessarily anti-perfectionist because committed to neutrality, but the perfectionist liberals deny that liberalism and perfectionism are mutually exclusive. Their general strategy is to accept the claim of communitarians and others that liberalism depends on a conception of the good, but to transform that claim from a source of criticism to a position of strength. Liberalism does rest on a conception of the good, they argue, but the liberal theory of the good is valid and superior to the alternatives. Some perfectionist liberals claim that the liberal good is superior universally, others that it is appropriate within a particular cultural and historical context.

No less than their neutralist rivals, perfectionist liberals can find precedents for their view in the history of liberal thought. The problem addressed by the neutralists, that of how to accommodate multiple competing conceptions of the good within a single political association, has not been the only concern of liberals historically. Another central theme has been the liberation of the individual and the assertion of a distinctively liberal conception of the good. Locke, the classic source for the accommodationist strand, also hints at a different line of liberal justification when he suggests that God's earth should be inherited not by the meek but by 'the Industrious and Rational' (1988: section 34). But it is in Kant and Mill that the theme of liberation and the liberal good receives its strongest statement. For Kant, the eighteenth-century Enlightenment represents the coming to maturity of humanity, the liberation of human beings from the ignorance, fears and superstitions of the past (Kant, 1991). The freedom of the individual is that of the person who possesses moral autonomy, who is governed by universal moral rules he freely wills for himself and others as a result of consulting his reason, rather than by irrational impulses and appetites (1956). Similarly, Mill in *On Liberty* provides a seminal account of the cumulative liberation of human beings from a succession of tyrannies, first absolute monarchies, later the tyranny of governments supported by democratic majorities, and, throughout, the tyrannies of opinion and custom (1974: Chapter 1).[9]

What Kant and Mill have in common in this connection is an account of human liberation that implies an ideal of the person, in turn suggesting a conception of the good. In both cases the ideal is one of personal autonomy: for Kant the morally autonomous agent who has cast off the yoke of the passions, for Mill the individualist who makes her own plan of life independently of the tyranny of custom. In each case there is a distinct picture of the best sort of person to be. The good life, for liberals, is the autonomous life, whether understood in Kant's moral terms or as Mill's broader individuality. That ideal excludes conceptions of the person that suppose the good life to be heteronomous, governed by unbridled emotions or by uncritically received traditions. From the formulation of a distinctively liberal conception of the good it is then only a short step to the view that the best polity is that which secures that good, the emancipation and flourishing of the individual person conceived as strongly autonomous. On this reading, the liberalism of Kant and Mill is thus 'perfectionist' in Rawls's sense, since it effectively asserts and enforces a particular conception of the good life.

The neutralist objection to this way of justifying liberalism is, of course, that it is too narrow, exclusive and controversial. The Kantian and Millian ideals of moral autonomy and individuality are at odds with alternative conceptions of the person, and thus of the good, that emphasize (as against Kant) the role of the emotions rather than reason and (as against Mill) custom and belonging rather than individuality. Moreover, and crucially, it is not only (so the objection runs) that many people happen not to accept the perfectionist liberal conception of the good – since a perfectionist liberal might reply that they are simply mistaken in this. In addition, the neutralist objection is that disagreement about conceptions of the good is *reasonable*. As Larmore puts it:

> Over the past four centuries [since the Reformation], the nature of the good life in a great many of its aspects has come

to seem a topic on which disagreement among reasonable people is not accidental, but to be expected. Being reasonable – that is, thinking and conversing in good faith and applying, as best one can, the general capacities of reason that belong to every domain of inquiry – has ceased to seem a guarantee of unanimity. On these matters of supreme importance, the more we talk with one another, the more we disagree. (1996: 122)

If this is correct, then the perfectionist defence of liberalism cannot hope to persuade a great many people, namely all those who, reasonably, do not share a comprehensively liberal understanding of the good. The recovery of the liberationist strand of the liberal project will have been bought at the cost of abandoning the accommodationist strand.

To these objections perfectionist liberals have produced two main lines of response. The first is to reassert the universal superiority of the liberal conception of the good life but in a wider, more inclusive version than those of Kant and Mill. Galston, the leading exponent of this approach, argues that liberalism rests on a distinctive conception of the human good, but a conception that does not amount to 'the "perfectionism" of classical antiquity' because it does not 'culminate in a depiction of the *summum bonum* or of the best way of life for all human beings' (1991: 8). The liberal account of the human good does not single out a particular substantial way of life as superior to all others. Rather, the liberal good identifies various generic values as constitutive of the good life for all human beings: life, normal development of basic human capacities, fulfilment of interests and purposes, freedom, rationality, society, subjective satisfaction (ibid.: 173–7). But these generic values are capable of different specifications or interpretations in different cases. Taken together, they rule out certain alternative accounts of the good as the basis for public policy, but leave room for legitimate human diversity.[10]

The problem with Galston's broadening of universal perfectionism is that it treads a fine line, as he recognizes himself, between proposing an account of human good that is too thin to support liberalism and rule out its rivals, and too thick to do justice to the diversity of legitimate ways of life (ibid.: 177). In his recent work Galston has tended to lean in the former direction, arguing for a form of liberalism that accommodates without demur social enclaves that are distinctly illiberal in character (see later: 9.3).

2.2.4 Particularist perfectionism

The second response offered by contemporary perfectionist liberals to their critics is to retain something like the traditional, relatively strong account of the human good inherited from Kant and Mill but to particularize it. That is, the traditional liberal privileging of personal autonomy is valid, so this argument goes, not universally but only for certain kinds of society.

This is the line taken by Raz (1986). Liberalism is justified, on Raz's account, as the political form necessary to sustain a particular conception of well-being based on personal autonomy. For Raz, what counts as well-being is an objective question, not merely a function of belief, either individual or cultural. Some ways of life conduce better than others to well-being and we can know what these are, namely those we have good reason to accept as beneficial. Contrary to Rawlsian neutrality, Raz is robustly explicit that it is the legitimate task of the state to intervene to promote some ways of life and to discourage others, depending on whether or not the way of life in question conduces to well-being. Liberals hold that well-being always requires personal autonomy, so it follows (*pace* Rawlsian neutrality) that the active promotion of autonomy is a legitimate goal of liberal public policy.

Does Raz's perfectionism amount to a paradoxically illiberal enforcement of morality and a failure to respect those with different conceptions of well-being? Raz tries to allay this fear in several ways, including an innovative account of the relation between the value of autonomy and the plurality of values which I shall discuss in detail later (8.3.1). The important point for present purposes is that Raz does not insist that autonomy be regarded as a privileged value for all human societies. 'Not everyone has an interest in personal autonomy. It is a cultural value, i.e. of value to people living in certain societies only' (1986: 189, note 1). That is because what is required for well-being varies across societies, not according to different *beliefs* ('conventionalism' or cultural relativism) but because of differing *conditions*. Personal autonomy, for example, is a social and political value only in modern industrial societies 'with their fast-changing technologies and free movement of labour. They call for an ability to cope with changing technological, economic and social conditions, for an ability to adjust, to acquire new skills, to move from one subculture to another, to come to terms with new scientific and moral views' (ibid.: 369–70).[11] Moreover,

LIBERALISM AND ITS JUSTIFICATION

for those who live in an autonomy-supporting environment there is no choice but to be autonomous: there is no other way to prosper in such a society ... [In such a society] the value of personal autonomy is a fact of life. Since we live in a society whose social forms are to a considerable extent based on individual choice, and since our options are limited by what is available in our society, we can prosper in it only if we can be successfully autonomous. (ibid.: 394)

Some substantial degree of personal autonomy is requisite to the well-being of people in an individualistic, modern industrial society. For that kind of society liberalism, which gives precedence to personal autonomy, is the best political form. The corollary, however, is that no such case for liberalism is available where social conditions are not 'autonomy-supporting'. Raz is explicit that his case for liberalism is not 'conventionalist', that it does not depend on pre-existing pro-liberal beliefs. It is fundamental for Raz that well-being is objective, not merely a function of belief, whether individual or cultural. But his case is particularist or conditional rather than universal, in the sense that it is bounded by variable social conditions.

Consequently Raz's case is open to the same sort of objection as that brought against the later Rawls's, that this is a limited justification of liberalism that amounts to a retreat from the universality of the traditional liberal project. Raz could reply that although his case is bounded by contextual limits, the context in question is a relatively wide one. In effect a liberal politics is recommended not just for those who are liberals already but for all those who live in a modern industrial society. It follows from Raz's view that non-autonomous lives within such a society, including non-autonomous lives sanctioned by minority cultures, are inferior under those conditions to autonomous lives (Mulhall and Swift, 1996: 341, 346).

Problems remain, however. First, one might ask whether the privileging of autonomy is so obviously the only rational response to conditions of social and economic fluidity. Conservatives might argue that these are precisely the conditions under which it is most important to cleave to tradition in order to limit or decelerate potentially damaging change as far as possible.[12] Second, liberals may wonder whether there is still missing from Raz's view something worth retaining from the classic liberal vision, namely

LIBERALISM AND VALUE PLURALISM

the thought that the autonomous life and liberal politics are in some sense desirable goals for all human beings, and not just for those who find themselves living in conditions of social and economic change. Kekes, although no supporter of liberalism, nevertheless captures this liberal thought well when he writes that a relativized defence like Raz's

> would deprive liberalism of one of its most powerful features, namely, the moral vision that is capable of appealing to people living in widely different moral traditions and according to widely different conceptions of a good life. The vision is supposed to capture values that all moral traditions and all conceptions of a good life should aim to protect and foster. But if liberalism is relativized to the present context, it cannot sustain that vision. (1997: 174)

It is questionable whether a Razian position can in the end be entirely satisfying either for liberals or for their opponents.

2.3 Liberal Theory at an Impasse?

The debate over strategies of liberal justification can be summarized as follows. The earlier justifications of liberalism were perfectionist. Kant, Mill, even Locke, avowedly or implicitly appealed to an account of the good for human beings which it is the legitimate business of the state to support. But the universal perfectionism of the classic liberal thinkers, even though it was relatively broad or inclusive compared with non-liberal forms of perfectionist politics, seemed to rest on a conception of the good that reasonable people could reject. It has become increasingly clear since the Reformation that substantial conceptions of the good life attract reasonable disagreement; this applies to comprehensive liberal theories of the good as much as to others. Liberalism, it has been objected, could not be widely acceptable on the basis of universal perfectionism.

To this problem, contemporary liberals have produced two principal responses. The first is the neutrality strategy: controversial questions of 'the good' can be bracketed as subject to permanent disagreement, while agreement can still be reached on a neutral framework of 'the right' within which disagreement over the good can be contained peacefully. The problem with the neutrality response is, first, that the closer liberalism manages to

LIBERALISM AND ITS JUSTIFICATION

approximate to neutrality the more insipid it is likely to be, the more afraid to confront or even argue against illiberal forms of life; second, that even the most neutral form of liberalism implicitly rests on a liberal conception of the good after all. Overall, it must be asked of the neutrality approach whether the price paid in the attenuation of the traditional liberal project of individual liberation is worth the supposed return of greater inclusiveness, especially since the extent to which liberal neutrality can appeal to those who do not share a comprehensively liberal conception of the good remains doubtful.

The alternative liberal response to the objections to universal perfectionism is the particularist strategy. Here it is not necessarily the perfectionism but the universality of traditional liberal arguments that is subjected to revision. Liberalism, whether perfectionist or neutralist, can be recast more modestly as the political form appropriate to a particular kind of society rather than for all human beings. The problem with this approach is that it is liable to amount to no more than preaching to the converted, justifying liberal principles on the basis of beliefs or conditions that apply only to those who are liberals already. The particularist approach is in danger of having nothing to say to those people, namely non-liberals, whom one might have supposed liberals would be most concerned to address.

What, then, is the best justificatory strategy for liberals to pursue? As my summary suggests, I do not believe that the existing literature reveals any of the main contending positions to be clearly superior to its rivals. All have their strengths and weaknesses, and these tend to be complementary. On the question of universalism versus particularism, universalist approaches are strong in their fidelity to the liberal tradition of emancipation, but look vulnerable to accusations of cultural bias. The relative modesty of the particularist response, on the other hand, seems to draw liberalism's critical teeth. When it comes to the issue of perfectionism versus neutrality, perfectionism, like universality, answers to the emancipatory side of the historic liberal project, but appears to be baulked by reasonable disagreement. Neutrality takes reasonable disagreement and cultural diversity seriously, but seemingly at the cost of producing an insipid liberalism that dares not speak its name, and an evasive liberalism that tries to conceal the fact that, like any political view, it depends on a foundational conception of the good.

LIBERALISM AND VALUE PLURALISM

Is there any way out of this apparent impasse of liberal justificatory theory? This will remain a background question as I explore the relation between value pluralism and liberalism in Part II. The question will return to the foreground when, in Part III, I set out my value-pluralist case for liberalism. There I shall argue, among other things, that value pluralism can ground a case for liberalism that is universalist and that combines elements of both neutrality and (predominantly) perfectionism. But I must first examine the meaning of value pluralism itself.

Notes

1. The principal sources that have influenced my account of liberalism include the following: Locke (1988, 1991), Kant (1956, 1991), Mill (1974), Bullock and Shock (1967), Hayek (1960), Rawls (1971, 1993), Nozick (1974), R. Dworkin (1977, 1985), Manning (1976), Gray (1986), Kymlicka (1989, 1990, 1995), Shklar (1989).
2. By 'property' here, Locke means not only material possessions but anything that belongs by nature to persons, including their 'Lives, Liberties and Estates' (1988: section 123). The intimate link between persons and possessions is developed in the famous Chapter 5 of the *Second Treatise*, 'Of Property'.
3. It may be, however, that neither of these thinkers is as complacent as they sometimes appear. Fukuyama (1992) does not rule out the possibility of liberal–democratic decline in the future, and he exerts himself to offer a justification of liberal democracy as meeting the tripartite Platonic demands of reason, material well-being and recognition (see Wintrop, 1993). In the case of Rorty (1989, 1991), the impossibility and redundancy of philosophical justification does not exclude the need for, or efficacy of, other kinds of persuasion such as that of imaginative literature.
4. For non-Western challenges to liberalism see Huntington (1996). Western debates within and around liberalism can be sampled in Sandel (1984), Rosenblum (1989), Douglass, Mara and Richardson (1990), Mulhall and Swift (1996), Yack (1996).
5. The Lockean case for toleration is examined critically by Barry (1991) and Waldron (1991). See my discussion later (9.3).
6. 'Neutrality of reasons' is distinguished from 'neutrality of impact' by Patrick Neal (1997: 5).
7. I take the expression 'approximate neutrality' from Kekes, who describes the idea (although he does not endorse it) as follows: 'What is important, according to this liberal response, is not so much that the state should be

LIBERALISM AND ITS JUSTIFICATION

neutral, but that it should foster a political system in which as many moral traditions and conceptions of the good life as possible could compete with one another for resources and for the allegiance of people' (1997: 175).

8. Similar and related points are made by Sandel (1994) and Jones (1995). For other criticisms of Rawls's political liberalism as still depending on a liberal comprehensive moral doctrine, see e.g. Mulhall and Swift (1996, Chapter 7).

9. The split between a liberalism of liberation and a liberalism of accommodation has been variously described as a contrast between: 'Kantian' and 'modus vivendi' liberalism (Larmore, 1987), 'comprehensive' and 'political' liberalism (Rawls, 1993), 'Enlightenment' and 'Reformation' liberalism (Galston, 1995), and autonomy- and tolerance-based liberalism (Kymlicka, 1995).

10. Galston gives the following as examples of accounts of the good ruled out by the liberal view: 'secular nihilism', 'theological withdrawalism', 'moral monism', 'Nietzchean irrationalism' and 'barabarism' (1991: 177).

11. Raz qualifies this: 'It would be wrong to identify the ideal with the ability to cope with the shifting dunes of modern society. Autonomy is an ideal of self-creation. There were autonomous people in many past periods, whether or not they themselves or others around them thought of this as an ideal way of being' (1986: 370). I read this as meaning that what is uniquely modern is not the incidence of personal autonomy but the valuing of autonomy by society at large. Moreover, personal autonomy only becomes valuable as a social and political ideal under modern conditions which give rise to an 'autonomy-supporting environment' (ibid.: 391).

12. 'Intolerance flourishes most where forms of life are dislocated, roots unsettled, traditions undone. In our day, the totalitarian impulse has sprung less from the convictions of confidently situated selves than from the confusions of atomized, dislocated, frustrated selves, at sea in a world where common meanings have lost their force' (Sandel, 1991: 249). See also Gray's observation that some East Asian societies have successfully modernized by developing forms of capitalism which do not emphasize the value of personal autonomy (Gray, 1995b: 83).

CHAPTER 3

Value Pluralism

In this chapter I develop the account of value pluralism outlined in Chapter 1. The analysis offered is not intended to be comprehensive or to enter deeply into the many controversial and difficult questions that the idea of pluralism raises. My purpose is merely to lay out the basic materials, and to open up some of the fundamental issues, to which I shall refer when I come to the political matters that are my main concern.

My discussion is divided into three sections. First, I look more closely at the meaning of value pluralism by examining the four elements outlined earlier: universal values, plurality, incommensurability and conflict. I shall pay most attention to incommensurability as the most distinctive and complex of these. Second, I consider the ethical implications of value pluralism, asking how we can choose rationally among plural values when they conflict. I shall argue that pluralism implies two kinds of ethical guideline. The first is particularist: at the level of particular cases it is possible to choose rationally among conflicting plural values by reference to the context of the choice, which may include a background conception of the good. The second is universalist: at a more abstract level, the formal features of pluralism itself suggest ethical norms that apply across a generality of cases. Both universal and particularist approaches will contribute to my case for liberalism. Finally, I review some of the arguments for the truth of value pluralism. How persuasive is the claim that values are plural and incommensurable in the sense described? Here I shall argue that although the truth of value pluralism eludes absolute proof, there is good reason to accept the case for pluralism as persuasive on balance.

3.1 The Four Elements of Value Pluralism

I have suggested that value pluralism may be analysed into four chief claims: that there are certain universal values, that values (both universal and local) are plural, that values may be incommensurable with one another, and that they may come into conflict. I shall now consider these claims in more detail.

3.1.1 Universal values

The first component of value pluralism is the claim that there are certain values that are universal and objective. To say that some values are 'universal' is to say that these are valuable for all human beings at all times and in all cultures. This universality has the crucial significance for later arguments that it opens up the distinction between value pluralism and ethical relativism. Ethical relativism, at its strongest, is the view that all values are the products of particular cultures or perspectives, and possess ethical force only relative to that particular point of view: there are no values with universal force. Value pluralism, if it is to count as a view distinct from relativism, implies that at least some values are transhistorical and cross-cultural. However, it must be added that value pluralists insist that the human values are universal only at a high level of generality, and are interpreted and applied in different ways in different contexts, both historical and cultural. Value pluralism, therefore, although it denies strong or extreme relativism, is nevertheless compatible with a moderate form of relativism according to which some values are particular, varying along with cultural practices, while others are universal or generic. Pluralism and moderate relativism overlap on the view that many particular values are local instantiations of the generic universal values (see e.g. Kekes, 1993; Nussbaum, 1986, 1990, 2000b).

In what sense are the universal values to which pluralists are committed 'objective'? Most pluralists present universal values as objective in the sense that they are not merely valued de facto but valuable for human well-being or flourishing independently of what particular persons or cultures may believe. Gray, for example, writes that the value-pluralist outlook can be compared to that of Aristotle or J.S. Mill, in that it 'specifies as the subject-matter of ethics human well-being or flourishing', albeit pursued in a variety of ways (1993b: 295). What Kekes calls the 'primary values are connected with benefits and harms that count as such for all conceptions of a good life . . . [S]ome things will normally benefit all human beings' (1993: 38). Similarly, Nussbaum, also with Aristotle in mind, advances a set of basic values as constituting 'a conception of good human functioning' or account of 'what it is to function humanly' (1990: 205, 208). Having the opportunity or 'capability' of realizing these values is part of any life that can be counted as 'truly human' or 'worthy of a human being' (2000b: 73). For these pluralists, certain things are valuable for human flourishing independently of their actually being valued in some cases.[1]

This is not to say, however, that such values can be identified without any reference to actual patterns of belief and practice. The claim is that there are commonalities among the beliefs and practices of most human societies such that certain values, or at least the capability of realizing those values, must be seen as promoting the flourishing of any human life (Nussbaum, 1990: 217). To summarize in these terms, value pluralists typically hold that we can identify certain basic or generic universal values as universal and objective in the sense that they make any human life better than it would be otherwise. The next question is, what is the content of these universal values?

3.1.2 Plurality

Value pluralists believe that values, including universal values, are *plural*. Several, indeed many things are valuable for human flourishing. This is a plurality both of substantive values and of types of value. As to the latter, Berlin, for example, refers variously to values, ends, goals and purposes, although he makes no clear distinction between these (Lessnoff, 1999: 222–3). More systematically, Thomas Nagel analyses 'the fragmentation of value' into five fundamental types: specific obligations, general rights, 'utility', 'perfectionist' ends or values, and commitment to one's own projects (Nagel, 1991). In perhaps the most comprehensive account, Kekes divides values into categories of 'naturally occurring' and 'humanly

46

VALUE PLURALISM

caused', moral ('humanly caused values in which the benefits and harms primarily affect others') and non-moral, and 'primary' and 'secondary' (1993: 18). Primary values are 'universally human', while secondary values 'vary with persons, societies, traditions, and historical periods' (ibid.).[2]

The substantive values said by value pluralists to be both fundamental and plural are also variously identified. Berlin mentions political equality, efficient organization, social justice and individual liberty among the more specifically political values, and more generally justice, generosity, public and private loyalties, the demands of genius and the claims of society, and the values of paganism and Christianity (1969: 167; 1981: 45). Kekes is again more systematic, identifying the primary or universal values as falling into three main categories, corresponding to three kinds or levels of need set by human nature. First, 'the goods of self' satisfy physical needs, such as needs for food, water, air, motion and rest, and psychological requirements for 'satisfying our needs in whatever ways happen to count as civilized', for learning from the past and planning for the future, for acting on desires and aversions, and for exercising thought, memory, imagination, emotions and self-restraint (1993: 39). Second, 'the goods of intimacy' make it possible for us to establish close relationships with others, including parents or guardians, sexual partners, children and friends. Such goods develop out of experiences of friendship and enmity, competition and co-operation, admiration and contempt, approval and anger. Third, 'the goods of social order' contribute to the maintenance of a society in which we can enjoy the goods of self and intimacy. These goods include 'the establishment of some authority, the emergence of institutions and conventional practices, and the slow development and deliberate formulation of rules' (ibid.: 40). All of the foregoing, Kekes writes, 'are universally good, because it is good for all human beings to have the capacity to satisfy and actually to satisfy' the three areas of need outlined (ibid.: 41). Again, however, he adds that 'these primary values may take different forms in different contexts', moreover that different traditions may produce values quite other than the primary values (ibid.: 41–2). All this adds further to the plurality of values.

Another pluralist account of the substantive content of universal values, in several respects similar to Kekes's, is given by Nussbaum (2000b). To count as 'fully human' or worthwhile, any life must include certain 'central functional capabilities': being able to live to

47

the end of a human life of normal length; to have good health, including reproductive health, adequate nourishment and shelter; to enjoy bodily integrity, including security against assault, and freedom of movement; to use the senses, to imagine, think and reason; to have emotional attachments to things and people outside ourselves; to form a conception of the good and to engage in critical reflection about the planning of one's life; 'to live with and toward others', to engage in social interaction, and to have 'the social bases of self-respect and non-humiliation'; 'to live with concern for and in relation to animals, plants, and the world of nature'; to laugh, play and enjoy recreational activities; to participate effectively in political choices that govern one's life, and to have real opportunity to hold property (ibid.: 78–80). The list, Nussbaum writes in an earlier formulation, amounts to a 'thick vague' conception of the good: 'thick' in that it gives an account of multiple human ends, not just preferences or means to satisfying preferences; 'vague' in the sense that it provides an 'outline sketch' of the good life, the components of which (as in Kekes) 'admit of many concrete specifications' (1990: 217). The list is also, Nussbaum says, 'open-ended', for we must allow for the possibility of changes in the natural circumstances of human beings, and for the need to revise the list in order to reflect what we may yet have to learn from encounters with other human societies (ibid.: 219).

Just as the notion of human universal values distinguishes value pluralism from the stronger forms of relativism, so one might suppose that the notion of human values as plural immediately implies another important distinction, namely that between value pluralism and monism. Is it not true that value plurality necessarily contradicts the notion of ethical monism, the belief that values are in some sense unitary? The answer is, no, not by itself. To believe, as monists do, that some one or a narrow range of values overrides all others is to hold that ultimately there is only one intrinsic value, that is, one thing that is valuable for its own sake. But that is consistent with allowing that there are many other genuine values; it merely commits the monist to holding that those other values must be instrumental or subordinate to the super-value. The idea of plurality *alone* does not distinguish value pluralism from monism. Rather, value pluralism requires the further claim that the plurality is a plurality of intrinsically different values or ends, things valuable for their own sake. At this point we come to the key notion of 'incommensurability'.

VALUE PLURALISM

3.1.3 Incommensurability

Value pluralists characteristically hold that values are not only plural but *radically* so. Value plurality extends to intrinsic as well as instrumental values, each generating its own distinctive considerations. This vital element is stressed by Nussbaum, who is describing what she sees as a value-pluralist tendency in Aristotle:

> The ethical works display a conception of the best human life as a life inclusive of a number of different constituents, each being defined apart from each of the others and valued for its own sake ... [T]here are many things in life that we choose for their own sake ... but to value each of these separate items, each of which has its separate account, for what it itself is, seems to entail recognition of its distinctness and separateness from each of the others'. (1986: 296)[3]

This notion of the radical distinctness of values, including the universal values, is commonly given the label *incommensurability*. But what exactly is meant by incommensurability is often unclear. To clarify the idea for my purposes, I shall distinguish three different ways in which values might be said to be incommensurable. First, they might be *incomparable*; second, *immeasurable*; third, *unrankable*, or at least hard to rank. The first and second of these interpretations make, respectively, the strongest and weakest claims. It is the middling third sense, that of difficulty in ranking, that I shall take as central to my argument.

According to the first of these versions, to say that values are incommensurable is to say that they *cannot be compared*. Kekes writes that 'the basic idea of incommensurability is that there are some things so unalike as to exclude any reasonable comparison among them. Square roots and insults, smells and canasta, migrating birds and X ray seem to exclude any common yardstick by which we could evaluate their respective merits or demerits' (1993: 21).[4] But how far are moral and political values strictly incomparable along these lines? A problem with this very strong interpretation of incommensurability is that if values were wholly incomparable, then we would never have any rational basis for deciding among them where they conflict. If competing options were like square roots and insults, how could we reasonably choose one course rather than the other? Yet we do seem to be able to make such decisions, for good reason, at least in particular cases. Even-handed fairness and personal

49

loyalty are very different values, and there is no good reason to rate one as superior to the other absolutely. But there is good reason to focus on justice and to put personal connections aside for the judge presiding at a trial or the official allocating public money. The 'incomparability' interpretation of incommensurability is too strong. Reasoned choice among plural values may be 'hard' in certain ways, but that is not to say impossible.[5]

The second common interpretation of incommensurability involves a much weaker or narrower claim. This is that plural values, although in some sense comparable for the purpose of decision making, cannot in any very precise manner be weighed or measured against one another, because they cannot be represented in terms of a common denominator of measurement. Supposing that plural values can be compared in order to choose rationally among them, one might still ask how exactly that comparative judgement is possible. One answer, familiar from utilitarian and rational choice theory, is provided by a model of practical reasoning as 'calculation' or 'maximization'. As Henry Richardson explains: 'Things would work out very simply indeed if there were at bottom but one kind of intrinsic value – pleasure, say – in terms of which all value could be measured together, or commensurated. Then rational choice would concern itself with maximizing that "commensurans", as I will call the commensurating value or good' (1997: 15). Similarly, Kekes refers to value pluralism as opposing the notion that values are somehow 'fungible' in terms of a common 'medium' of measurement (1993: 67–74). To say that values are incommensurable in the second, narrower sense is thus to deny that values can be commensurated by a common denominator.

As the quote from Richardson suggests, this view of incommensurability is often directed against utilitarianism.[6] There are many different forms of utilitarianism, but they all involve the notion of a common denominator or medium for weighing values. In the classical utilitarianism of Bentham, the common denominator is 'pleasure'. Pleasure is the only thing that is desired and desirable for its own sake; all other values are desirable only so far as they produce pleasure. Consequently, to decide rationally among competing options is to represent these in terms of the units of pleasure they produce, and to select that option that produces the most pleasure-units. The right action is thus the one that maximizes value. The trouble with this procedure from a value-pluralist point of view is that it fails dismally to appreciate the distinctiveness, the radical

VALUE PLURALISM

plurality of values. First, it is false to suppose that one value, say justice, can be adequately 'represented' in terms of another, say pleasure. Second, pleasure itself is not a single, unitary value; rather, there are many different kinds of pleasure (as J.S. Mill saw), or rather many different pleasures, each with its own character and value: the pleasure of eating ice-cream, the pleasure of listening to Mozart, and so on. If pleasure is not a single value, then there cannot be quantifiable units of pleasure, and pleasure-units cannot commensurate other values.

There have been, of course, more sophisticated versions of utilitarianism than Bentham's, but these fare no better from a value-pluralist point of view. J.S. Mill's emphasis on the 'higher' pleasures scarcely come closer to commensurating all values, which include goods that are closer in kind to the lower pleasures, and other values, such as obligations, that are hard to understand as 'pleasures' at all (Kekes, 1993: 67–9). Nor does contemporary preference-utilitarianism solve the problem. According to this version, the right action is that which maximally satisfies the preferences of all affected. 'The satisfaction of preferences' might seem broad enough, on the face of it, to embrace all values, and so to qualify as a genuinely comprehensive common denominator. But what people happen to prefer is not necessarily the same as what is a genuine value, since what happens to be valued by a particular person or even a whole society may not in fact conduce to human well-being – for example, practices of ethnic and nationalistic aggression. The satisfaction of preferences refers only to people's attitudes to values rather than to any commensurating feature of the values themselves. Preference-utilitarianism is at best a superficial form of commensuration, or commensuration 'after the fact'. As Richardson puts it, 'preference-based utility is not a form of commensurability useful in making choices but rather a way of representing choices, once made' (1997: 102). Preference-utilitarianism summarizes choices already made among plural values rather than guiding those choices by showing what they antecedently have in common.

This second sense of incommensurability as excluding measurement is part of what incommensurability means for value pluralists, but it is not the whole of what they usually understand by that idea. That is because incommensurability as immeasurability is consistent with the possibility of *ranking* values in ways that most pluralists would want to challenge. If values are incommensurable in this second sense, then we cannot choose among them by quantifying

51

LIBERALISM AND VALUE PLURALISM

them in accordance with a common denominator. But that leaves open the possibility of choosing among them by ranking without quantifying them. Incommensurability in the second sense rules out the kind of *cardinal* ranking of values involved in, for example, ranking books according to the most copies sold. Such a ranking is dependent on the availability of a commensurating unit, in this case 'copies sold'. But where there is no such common denominator, it may still be possible to produce an *ordinal* ranking, or order determined by certain qualities rather than quantities – for example, the ranking of books according to literary merit. *Heart of Darkness* might be ranked before *A Christmas Carol*, although not by any assignable number of units.

Value pluralists would typically see not only cardinal but also ordinal rankings of values as problematic. That is because of the basic idea that if values are incommensurable they constitute considerations that are radically distinct from one another. If justice and loyalty, say, are radically distinct criteria for human conduct, then we have no reason to produce a general ranking in which one always or usually comes ahead of the other. This is true in the sense that there is no common denominator which either justice or loyalty could be said, in the abstract, to maximize. But it is also true in the sense that there is no reason always or generally to place justice *qualitatively* ahead of loyalty, or vice versa. There may be a good reason to rank one before the other in a particular case, as where impartiality must come before personal allegiances for a judge in a trial. But there seems to be no such reason for an abstract or general ranking.

There is therefore a third possible interpretation of incommensurability, one that stops short of incomparability but goes further than rejection of measurement. To say that values are incommensurable in this third sense is to question the extent to which we can rank values for good reason in the abstract or in general. The principal critical targets for this sense of incommensurability include notions of a *summum bonum* or super-value that overrides all other goods in all cases, such as Plato's 'Form of the Good' or Bentham's 'happiness' understood as a quantity of pleasure.

Note, however, that I have not said that incommensurability in the third sense rules out all ranking of values. The opposition between incommensurability and ranking is subject to two qualifications. First, what is ruled out by incommensurability in the third sense is ranking *for a decisive reason*. Even if values were

52

VALUE PLURALISM

strictly incomparable we would still be able to rank them in the sense that we could decide simply to plump for one rather than the other without reference to any determinate reason for doing so. But in the field of political philosophy we are concerned with the rational ranking of values and systems of values, and this does seem to be put in question by incommensurability.

The second qualification is more important. The kind of ranking that becomes a problem because of incommensurability is *abstract* ranking, or ranking irrespective of context. If values are incommensurable in the relevant sense, then it seems on the face of things that we shall have no reason to rank them the same way in every case or even in most cases. Impartial justice may be an overriding principle for a trial judge but not for someone with a friend in trouble. Under value incommensurability it looks as though we shall have no good reason to construct hierarchies of values in the abstract — hierarchies abstracted, that is, from particular cases and contexts. To put it another way, reason seems to permit multiple legitimate rankings of plural values depending on the circumstances. The corollary is that although incommensurability in the required sense appears to rule out abstract ranking for good reason, it is consistent with the reasoned ranking of values in particular cases. Value incommensurability seems to imply a particularist approach to ethics, one that requires us to decide value-related questions by attending to the particular circumstances of the case rather than to the guidance of abstract rules.

A preliminary understanding of incommensurability in value pluralism is therefore as follows. The incomparability reading is too strong, and the immeasurability reading, although part of the story, too weak. The sense in which incommensurability is involved in value pluralism falls somewhere in between these two extremes. As a preliminary formulation, we can say that values are incommensurable, on the value-pluralist view, when they raise radically distinct considerations such that there seems, prima facie, to be no reason to rank one ahead of another in all or most cases. This account will require major qualification in due course. In particular I shall argue that the pressure towards particularism is only one aspect of the ethical implications of pluralism. There is also a more abstract side to pluralist ethics that is suggested by the conceptual components of pluralism itself. All four elements of pluralism imply normative principles that together constitute a general framework for particular judgements. But I shall take this matter up in the next section (3.2).

53

LIBERALISM AND VALUE PLURALISM

Before proceeding, I wish to raise one further question concerning incommensurability. Incommensurability, and therefore value pluralism, may be said to apply at different 'levels' (Gray, 1995a: 43–4; Wolf, 1992). Up to this point I have been assuming that incommensurability applies at the level of values, that is, that it is values, in the broad sense and with the variable content described, that are incommensurable. A second level comes into play, however, if we allow that values themselves may be *internally* complex: 'equality', for example, might be analysed into incommensurable notions of equality of opportunity and equality of outcome. Third, and most significantly for later discussion, Gray argues that whole moralities or value systems may be incommensurable with one another. Whether incommensurability applies at this third level, labelled by Gray 'cultural pluralism', is a question I shall postpone for the time being. In Chapter 5, I shall show that cultural pluralism has relativistic, and in Gray's hands conservative, implications, and I shall argue against it.

3.1.4 Conflict

The final constitutive claim of value pluralism is that plural and incommensurable values may, and frequently do, come into *conflict* with each other. The many goals of human beings are, as Berlin puts it, 'in perpetual rivalry with one another' (1969: 171). Values, both universal and local, may in particular cases be incompatible, such that one may be realizable only at the cost of sacrificing or curtailing another. For example, I may have to choose between the benefits of negative and positive liberty or between the principle of impartiality and the ties of friendship. As Nussbaum puts it: 'The "gods" do not always agree – that is, one strand in our common humanness may not be harmoniously related to another, given the circumstances of life' (1990: 226).

Berlin's reference to 'perpetual' rivalry overstates the case, since the ends people pursue are not always at odds. Depending on the circumstances, I could combine trips to both the library and the beach on the same day: values of knowledge and relaxation can coexist within the same sphere of activity, depending on how this is delimited. Such values can even harmonize with one another in some situations. I may learn more while relaxing, reading Rawls while sunbathing on the beach. But value pluralists tend to emphasize the

54

VALUE PLURALISM

centrality to moral and political experience of conflict. As Stuart Hampshire writes: 'Our everyday and raw experience is of a conflict between contrary moral requirements at every stage of almost anyone's life' (1983: 151). Conflicts among values (universal and local, moral and non-moral) run through all spheres of human experience; they are absolutely pervasive. At the level of an individual life, value conflicts are embodied in decisions about careers and personal relationships, for example. Should I pursue the high-salary legal career or the non-material satisfactions of the creative artist, the intimacy of a close family or the freedom of remaining single? At the social and political level, there are familiar conflicts between negative and positive liberty, liberty and equality, individual rights and democracy, justice and utility, community and personal autonomy.

That value conflict is a pervasive feature of familiar experience is a claim that could be accepted by monists as well as pluralists. Where pluralists differ is in holding that such conflicts are, first, inescapable and, second, sometimes hard (although not always impossible) to resolve rationally. I shall come to the second point in the next section. As to the first, some monists tend to believe that the conflicts we experience are matters more of appearance than reality. The 'utopians' I shall discuss in Chapter 4, Marx and the classical anarchists, are cases in point. For these thinkers, it is human ignorance or wickedness, self-interest or class interest, that prevents us from understanding the ultimate unity or coherence of value, which if only we grasped it would show us how to bring our apparent conflicts to a final resolution. Value pluralists, on the other hand, see conflict among values as not merely contingently pervasive but unavoidable in any world recognizable as human.

Here we should take note of two principal sources of value conflict.[7] First, the ability of human beings to pursue or enjoy different values is constrained by empirical circumstances which impose limitations of various kinds and degrees of strength. Given the laws of physics, I cannot be at the library and the beach simultaneously, and given other desires and obligations, and ultimately the finitude of human life, I may not even have time to go to one after the other. Some choices among values are forced on us by circumstances that are, at least at present, unchangeable. Second, some conflicts among values arise from the very nature of the values concerned. Kekes gives the example of a life of independent, unencumbered self-reliance as necessarily excluding a

55

life dedicated to a large family and marital intimacy (1993: 54). Of course, one might compromise between the two, combining a degree of independence with a degree of settled intimacy, but to do so will necessarily involve a corresponding degree of sacrifice in both directions. The pluralist point here is not that such choices must be all-or-nothing, but that such choices are inescapable because they are occasioned by inescapable conflicts.

Having inspected the component parts of value pluralism, we are now in a position to see more clearly how they combine to produce a problem for rational choice or practical reasoning. All the components of value pluralism — universal values, plurality, incommensurability and conflict — play a role in generating the problem. If no values were universal there would be little occasion for reasoning about them (that is, for deciding which combination of values we have reason to promote) because value judgements would be determined either by local cultural conventions or by the subjective preferences of individuals. If values were not plural in any sense there would be no occasion to choose among them. Similarly, values might be plural, even radically plural (incommensurable), but if they did not come into conflict there would still be no problem for rational choice: knowledge and relaxation may be plural and incommensurable, but there may be circumstances in which I can accommodate them both and not have to choose between them. On the other hand, conflict among values is not by itself a serious problem for rational choice, because such conflict might be readily resolved by an absolute or general rule for decision making. Rational choice becomes more difficult when the conflict is among values, including universal values, that are plural and incommensurable, since that radical plurality rules out the possibility of resolving the conflict by applying simple rules like those of the utilitarians.

3.2 Ethical Implications

Can we choose rationally among plural and incommensurable values when they conflict? Such choices must be made without the guidance of simple monist rules that bid us maximize a commensurating medium like preference-satisfaction or rank values in accordance with their relation to a super-value. But does that mean that reasoned choice is impossible? There are three main

VALUE PLURALISM

answers to this question, respectively 'subjectivist', 'particularist' and 'universalist' accounts of choice under pluralism.

First, the *subjectivist* view is that if values are incommensurable then we can choose among them only in some non-rational way: by 'plumping' arbitrarily for one or another, by relying on preference or desire or intuition, or by employing some random decision-procedure like tossing a coin. Berlin, for example, sometimes seems to believe this, when he refers to our being 'faced with choices between ends equally ultimate, and claims equally absolute', and to our 'irrational and disordered lives' (1969: 168–9).[8] Elsewhere, however, he repudiates that view, insisting that we do in fact make rational choices among plural values all the time, at any rate in particular cases (Berlin and Williams, 1994).

Whatever Berlin really believes, the better view is that value pluralism does not exclude reasoned value judgement. There may indeed be cases where a conflict between plural values yields no resolution that is decisively more rational than the alternatives. The truth of value pluralism certainly does not exclude the possibility of genuine moral dilemmas; on the contrary it explains how such dilemmas can occur. But to allow that there may be no right answer in some situations is not to deny the possibility of such an answer in others. The claim that pluralism excludes reasoned value judgement altogether assumes that reasoned value judgement requires commensurability.[9] That assumption is mistaken. Pluralists can account for the possibility of rational choice despite the incommensurability of values.

What account of practical reasoning can pluralists give that does not depend on commensurability of values? They can give two such accounts. The first is a *particularist* account, according to which reasons to choose among plural values are generated by attention to the context of the choice. The second is a *universalist* account, according to which certain ethical or normative principles are implicit in the notion of value pluralism itself.

The particularist account of reasoned choice under pluralism takes as its starting point the observation that although value pluralism appears to make more abstract or general rankings of values problematic, there seems to be less difficulty in choosing rationally among plural values in particular cases or contexts. How does attention to context enable rational choice among plural values? The short answer is that specification of context reveals the values that are most important to us, hence the values that guide

57

choice. Conversely, to get clearer about the values guiding my choice in a particular case involves my specifying the choice situation or context.

This picture of ethical judgement may be at odds with commensurating accounts like those of the utilitarians, but it is supported by a powerful and subtle tradition of moral philosophy, namely that of Aristotle. Aristotle's moral theory provides the leading alternative to the great monistic ethical theories of modernity, utilitarianism and Kantianism. While the latter appeal to abstract rules of universal application that rest upon the commensuration of values, Aristotle insists that the particularity and diversity of ethical experience is such that no general rules can be formulated to apply authoritatively to all cases. Rather, the only criterion of ethically right action is the example of the 'person of practical wisdom' (*phronemos*), who apprehends the best course in any particular case through his experience of ethical questions and responses in the past, experience with which he shapes his conception of the good life. Practical wisdom (*phronesis*) is itself part of the good life for all human beings, along with many other goods the pursuit of which, in varying instantiations in different concrete situations, is the business of the person of practical wisdom.

Nussbaum (1986, 1992b, 1993, 1995) provides an especially useful interpretation of Aristotle for my purposes because she emphasizes the extent to which his account of practical reasoning is conditioned by a notion of value pluralism. According to Nussbaum, Aristotle's starting point is his rejection of the 'scientific' conception of moral knowledge found in Plato. For Plato, the Good is like any other object of knowledge in that it can be understood from a detached, 'god's-eye' standpoint as a single entity with an essence, the implications of which can be formulated as law-like rules of universal application. Aristotle, by contrast, sees ethical thinking as consisting of 'concrete situational judgments of a more informal and intuitive kind' (Nussbaum, 1992b: 66). Against the scientific view, Aristotle sees the good not as a seamless unity but as irreducibly plural. Its component parts each raise distinct considerations among which there is no common denominator – goods are plural and incommensurable. Choices among such goods must therefore be qualitative rather than quantitative: 'Choice among alternatives will involve weighing these distinct natures as distinct items, and choosing the one that gets chosen for the sake of what it itself is' (ibid.: 59).

VALUE PLURALISM

Moreover, such choices will be strongly particularist, informed by a particular situation rather than being merely one application of a general rule. For Aristotle, practical wisdom is concerned with 'ultimate particulars', concrete situations that cannot be subsumed within universal principles 'but must be grasped with insight through experience' (ibid.: 68). This point is connected with incommensurability, since attention to the particularity of goods leads to attention to the particularity of cases. Rules may still play an important role, but only as rules of thumb or convenient summaries of experience, useful for those who lack experience themselves or for situations where there is insufficient time for proper reflection. Rules should not be normative for experience. It follows that the question of how one should choose among conflicting plural values cannot be given a wholly general or rule-based answer. The nearest approach to a general rule on this account is: 'Choose as the person of practical wisdom would choose.'

Nussbaum denies, however, that Aristotle's particularist ethic is empty. The Aristotelian agent cannot rely wholly on antecedently formulated rules, but that does not mean that anything goes. Nussbaum draws an analogy between Aristotelian practical judgement and improvisation in the theatre or in music. The improvisor does not merely follow a prepared script or score, but neither is her performance random or arbitrary: she must attend and respond to the evolving situation and to other performers (ibid.: 94). Attention and responsiveness to the concrete context might thus be advanced as a general guideline, even a rule, on the Aristotelian view. Furthermore, attention to context will include attention to the agent's own background values and concerns. 'The perceiver brings to the new situation a history of general conceptions and commitments, and a host of past obligations and affiliations (some general, some particular), all of which contribute to and help to constitute her evolving conception of good living' (ibid.). It is not that the Aristotelian account leaves us without guidance in choosing among plural values. Rather, guidance is supplied not by abstract rules alone, but by a combination of rules, attention to context, and (as part of context) reflection on one's background values and concerns, in particular one's conception of the good life.

In other words, reasons to choose among plural values in particular cases may be generated not so much by rules as by context. The Aristotelian point can be restated in the following three-step account indebted to the work of Ruth Chang (1997).

59

First, to choose rationally between two valuable options is usually to compare those options. If I choose to go to the library rather than the beach today, the reason is that I judge the library option to be better. But 'better' in what way? The second step is to recognize that to compare values is always to invoke a 'covering value'. That is, to compare items of value is to judge their relative merits in some respect. It makes no sense to say simply that 'X is better than Y' unless this is eliptical for 'X is better than Y in respect of Z'. Z is the covering value. If going to the library is superior to going to the beach, then that superiority must be with respect to some particular covering value. The library may be better than the beach with respect to the gathering of knowledge and the avoidance of ultraviolet light; the beach may be superior with respect to relaxation and getting a tan. What the covering value is in any particular case depends on the circumstances of that case. This is the third step. To specify the covering value requisite to a rational choice among rival options is to specify the circumstances of the choice, that is, the context. Why might it make more sense for me to go to the library rather than the beach? Perhaps because if I go to the library I can complete a piece of writing the deadline of which is fast approaching. Completing the work in order to meet the deadline is the more imperative, because the more urgent, goal in the circumstances in which I find myself than getting relaxation and exercise. In identifying the covering value for my choice, I am necessarily specifying the whole choice situation or context. To summarize, choice involves comparison, comparison invokes a 'covering value', and to specify the relevant covering value is to specify the context for choice.

To choose rationally among plural values is to specify what matters most to the chooser in a particular context. The next question is, what sort of things does 'context' include? That is, what sort of contextual considerations may generate reasons for choice among plural values? Such considerations, I suggest, can be divided into two broad categories: facts and values. Although intimately and perhaps inextricably linked in particular cases, these can be separated for the sake of analysis.

First, the proper understanding of a context of choice will include an understanding of the relevant facts. The facts are significant in setting the limits of what can reasonably be chosen, that is, what is possible and what is impossible in a given situation. In the familiar slogan, 'ought implies can'. Such facts may concern various matters

VALUE PLURALISM

to which correspond various gradations of limitation or impossibility. For example, the laws of physics make it impossible for me to be present at both the library and the beach at the same time. Richardson offers a list of types of impossibility, graded from stronger to weaker, as follows: conceptual, physical, impossibility given human nature, impossibility given the constraints of technology, improbability (1997: 145). Facts concerning the existing character of society or culture may also place limits on rational choice. In Chapter 2, for example, we noted Raz's argument (1986) that personal autonomy cannot be repudiated as an ideal by wishing to live well in a modern industrial society characterized by rapidly changing conditions (2.2.4).

The second major constituent of context is that of the values at stake. Values are important to understanding contexts in various ways, not least in understanding the nature of the options the context presents. But when it comes to choosing rationally among those options, another contextual source of value that figures crucially is the chooser's background *conception of the good life*. As Berlin writes: 'Where ultimate values are irreconcilable, clear-cut solutions cannot, in principle, be found. To decide rationally in such situations is to decide in the light of general ideals, the over-all pattern of life pursued by a man or a group or a society' (1969: 1). Similarly, for Kekes (who also quotes the passage from Berlin): 'The grounds on which such judgments rest are the conceptions of a good life regarded as acceptable in the surrounding tradition. What such judgments express is the respective importance of particular values to some one of the acceptable conceptions of a good life' (1993: 77–8). When we have to decide what matters most to us in a particular situation, a crucial question will be how the rival options and values confronting us relate to our background ideas about who we are and how we ought to live our lives in general. Our background conception of the good will enable us to rank the contending values. This is the way Kekes understands reasonable conflict-resolution among plural values: 'The resolution of such conflicts depends upon shaping our attitudes toward the conflicting values. This is done by ranking the values. Their comparative ranks depend on their importance within the conception of good life of the person who faces the conflict' (ibid.: 79). If I go to the library rather than the beach, that decision may reflect the more general background commitments (e.g. to scholarship) that constitute my conception of the good.

61

To summarize, one way in which pluralists can account for practical reasoning without commensuration is (following the particularist Aristotelian tradition) by drawing attention to the reason-generating potential of context. Attention to the particular context of a decision involves the specification of (1) the relevant facts, which delimit possibilities, and (2) the relevant values, especially those that are part of a background conception of the good, which provide a standard for deciding what matters most to us in the circumstances, that is, for deciding how to rank the values that concern us. This approach contrasts with the monist assumption that value conflicts can only be resolved rationally by commensuration. Pluralists can reply that commensuration is impossible (or superficial) but in any case unnecessary for practical reasoning, since we can look for guidance to the features of the particular context.

Nor does this particularist account exhaust the possibilities for practical reasoning under value pluralism; there is also a universalist view. I noted earlier that Nussbaum does not see Aristotelian contextualism as excluding an important role for general rules where these are recognized as no more than shorthand summaries of concrete experience. This is true, but I would add that value pluralism not only permits but implies another source of general principles, namely reflection on the nature of value pluralism itself. If values are plural and incommensurable then does that very fact not suggest norms capable of guiding rational choice among plural values? I believe it does. There is a second, more abstract dimension to pluralist ethics, one implicit in the concept of pluralism itself. Each of the four constitutive elements of pluralism implies a universal principle capable of guiding ethical and political choice. I shall develop these principles and their implications in detail as my argument proceeds in the chapters to follow, but it may be helpful, briefly, to outline them in advance.

First, the pluralist view that at least some values are universal implies a commitment to universal respect for those values. The life of an individual or a society that neglects or suppresses any of the universal values cannot, to that extent, be desirable (see, especially, Chapter 5).

Second, the incommensurability of values has important practical implications for both attitudes and conduct. If values are incommensurable, then the losses that result from trade-offs cannot be wholly compensated but will inevitably possess an absolute and

VALUE PLURALISM

perhaps tragic quality. To acknowledge the truth of pluralism is thus to recognize the seriousness of personal and public policy decisions that require trade-offs. These are not to be taken lightly: pluralism encourages us to face up to the fact that such decisions have real costs, and not to hide behind comforting notions of 'the greater good' or the end justifying the means. As a consequence, incommensurability implies the necessary futility of political visions that aim at the elimination of real loss and conflict in human life, recommending instead those more realistic views that accept the permanence of conflict and seek to contain it (Chapter 4).

Third, the idea of the plurality of values suggests a commitment to what I shall call an 'ethic of diversity', which has two elements. First, if there are many genuine values then a desirable society will be one that promotes or permits the pursuit of a wide multiplicity of values rather than only a few. Second, multiplicity alone can be self-defeating unless balanced by a degree of coherence among its component parts. The desirable society will thus be one that balances the accommodation of many values with the recognition that these cannot be unlimited but must be bounded by some kind of coherent framework (Chapter 6). Moreover, if a desirable society embraces many legitimate values, it must also respect many different accounts of how to combine or rank those values, that is, many different conceptions of the good life. Again, there will be limits from a pluralist point of view on the range of conceptions that ought to be tolerated or promoted. But within those limits the pluralist outlook will insist that 'reasonable disagreement' about the nature of the good life should be accommodated (Chapter 7).

The final element of value pluralism, the possibility of conflict, has implications that connect with the particularist theme already discussed. We have seen that when plural and incommensurable values conflict in a particular case, one way in which we can reach a decision about what to do is to attend to the particulars of the case, including its constitutive facts and values. Indeed, I shall argue, apart from applying the principles implicit in pluralism itself, which are very general (although sufficient to point to liberalism as the most desirable political *framework* for choice), it is only through this kind of particularism that specifc rational choices are possible under pluralism. It follows that in order to cope adequately with choices under pluralism – that is, to choose for good reasons – we must cultivate the kinds of skill that particularistic practical reasoning requires. In the face of pluralism, the best life at an

63

individual level will exhibit the virtues necessary for choosing wisely under pluralism, and the best political form will encourage those virtues (Chapter 8).

To summarize again, value pluralism is consistent with, indeed implies the possibility of rational choice among conflicting values. It does this in two ways, first through particularist attention to context, second through the application of universal principles implicit in pluralism itself. How do these two approaches relate to one another? Does the particularism of the first not pull apart from the universality of the second? My answer, briefly foreshadowed, will be that the universal principles implied by pluralism itself provide a political or public framework for the private process of particularist choice. It is principally through the normative inferences I derive from the elements of pluralism that I shall construct my case for liberalism. But, as we have just seen, the last of these inferences returns us to particularism, and this will have a crucial influence on the kind of liberalism that pluralism endorses.

3.3 Is Value Pluralism True?

My final concern in this chapter is with the question of why anyone should believe that value pluralism is in fact true.[10] *Are* values plural and incommensurable in the sense, and with the implications, described? In this section I sketch a case for the affirmative. This will be no more than a sketch, since a comprehensive case would itself occupy a substantial book, and I have many other matters to consider. Indeed, it might be possible to sidestep the issue entirely simply by assuming the truth of value pluralism and making the political argument that is my main concern contingent on that assumption. My question would then be: supposing that values are plural and incommensurable, what follows from this for the justification of liberalism? However, I think it is important to offer at least some argument for the truth of pluralism in order to motivate interest in the case to follow. I shall not attempt a conclusive demonstration of pluralism, but I shall argue that the claims of pluralists are not fanciful. There is at least good reason to believe that values are plural in the required sense, hence good reason to take the political issues raised by pluralism seriously.

What is required to show that we should take the idea of value pluralism seriously? First, to argue for the truth of value pluralism is

VALUE PLURALISM

to argue against those conceptions of the nature of value to which it is opposed. One idea with which I earlier contrasted value pluralism, namely the idea of the plurality of belief, is not strictly an opponent, since value pluralism and the plurality of belief are compatible, even complementary notions. The value-pluralist view on this point is merely that the full extent and nature of ethical pluralism is not captured by reference to the fact of plural beliefs alone but involves the additional dimension of value pluralism, which helps to explain why plurality of moral belief is likely to be permanent (see Chapter 7). The principal opponents of value pluralism are two: monism and (strong) relativism. A case for the truth of value pluralism must therefore show that these opponents are mistaken. Such a case must also show that there are positive reasons to believe in pluralism, that is, positive reasons to accept pluralism's four main constitutive claims. Of these four claims, two are relatively uncontroversial. That values are plural and that they may come into conflict are claims that, as noted earlier, could be accepted by relativists and monists as well as pluralists. The pluralist claims that generate controversy are, first, that there are universal values, a claim that is rejected by strong relativists, and second, that there are values that are not just plural but radically plural or incommensurable, a claim rejected by monists. I shall concentrate on these two controversial issues.

As to the first, I shall not attempt to rehearse the entire contest between universalist and relativist theories of value, which is as old and as complex as Western philosophy. What is important for my purposes is to note that the kind of universalism that is required for the value-pluralist outlook is comparatively moderate and philosophically respectable. Recall the pluralist claim that, while many values are particular or local, some values are universal. These are 'universal' in the sense that they are valuable for any form of good life for human beings. The values that are universal in this sense can be identified only at a high level of generality, as in Nussbaum's 'thick vague' conception of the good. According to this conception they are best seen as generic values which are interpreted and instantiated in different ways in different cultural and historical contexts. This kind of universality, it is recalled, is compatible with moderate versions of ethical relativism according to which ethical diversity is in part framed by universal patterns. It excludes or opposes only those extreme forms of relativism which deny any universal values and assert that culture is the only source of ethics. Such a moderate form of universalism is well supported by argument and evidence in philosophy and the social sciences. The claim that some things are valuable for any good life for human beings is controversial but has a respectable philosophical pedigree that includes Aristotle, Hume and the whole natural law tradition. It is backed by a good deal of empirical evidence from social anthropology that there are at least some things that are in fact valued across all human cultures (Murdock, 1945; Kluckhohn, 1965; Bock, 1974; Turnbull, 1984). The step from the empirical claim to the evaluative, although distinct, is short. That all human beings in all times and places have valued certain generic goods does not demonstrate the objective value of those goods by logical implication – all could logically have been mistaken. But it is at least reasonable to suppose that these goods have been universally valued because they are in fact valuable for beings trying to live well within the potentialities and constraints of a common humanity.

Much of the resistance to the notion of universal values in contemporary moral and political philosophy comes from the liberal search for social consensus. The concern felt by Rawls and others is that any substantial conception of the human good is bound to be sectarian and divisive because grounded in 'metaphysical' claims about the ultimate nature of human beings, that is, claims that are dependent on some particular, often religious perspective that could reasonably be rejected by those who do not happen to share it. But as Nussbaum points out, her 'thick vague' theory of the good life for human beings

> is not, in the sense that worries liberals, a metaphysical theory. That is, it is not a theory that is arrived at in detachment from the actual self-understandings and evaluations of human beings in society; nor is it a theory peculiar to a single metaphysical or religious tradition. Indeed, it is ... both internal to human history and strongly evaluative. (1990: 217)

The theory begins not with abstract speculation but the conceptions of humanity contained in actual 'myths and stories from many times and places, stories explaining to both friends and strangers what it is to be human rather than something else' (ibid.). And when we examine and compare these stories, we find that there is a consistency among them, in their basic patterns and concerns, that suggests more than coincidence:

> The great convergence across cultures in such storytelling, and

VALUE PLURALISM

its singling out of certain areas of experience as constitutive of humanness, gives us reason for optimism that if we proceed in this way, using our imaginations, we will have, in the end, a theory that is not only the parochial theory of our own traditions, but also a basis for cross-cultural attunement. (ibid.: 218)

Universal convergence of evaluation does not imply objectively universal values as a matter of logical inference but surely points in that direction. The objectivity of (some) values is the best explanation for the fact of (limited) universal convergence.

On the other hand, the extreme kind of ethical relativism that is excluded by the value-pluralist account of universality is deeply unattractive, unsupported by the evidence, and perhaps incoherent. First, if there are no universal values at all, only the value-systems of particular cultures, then those cultures become wholly authoritative for their members, and impervious to rational criticism from any vantage point other than their own. It follows that the consistent relativist, in this strong version, is obliged to endorse any practice that counts as authorized by the culture, regardless of its content and consequences for human well-being. On this view, there are no grounds to reject the culture and practices of Nazi Germany or the Stalinist Soviet Union. Second, the main item of evidence usually adduced in support of extreme relativism, namely the observation that different cultures have different value systems, falls well short of an adequate justification of that position. Some philosophers might argue that this observation has no relevance at all to the nature of value, since the mere fact of disagreement does not show there is no truth of the matter. I cannot go so far, since I have accepted Nussbaum's argument that the fact of convergent beliefs, if not a logically sufficient ground for the universality of some values, is at least a relevant and important piece of evidence in favour of universality. If convergent beliefs count as evidence for universality, then divergent beliefs must count as evidence for relativism. However, value pluralists do not have to reject relativism entirely; they only have to reject the extreme view that all values are relative. On this point, pluralists need only question the *reach* of the 'difference' argument. Just because we observe some, perhaps even many, differences among the value systems of different cultures, does it follow that these value systems are different in every respect, that there are no commonalities at all? Here again, the more

67

plausible view is surely that there is evidence of both difference and commonality, hence evidence of a combination of universal and relative elements in human morality. Third, the very coherence of extreme relativism is questionable, since it involves a contradiction: the claim that all values are relative is itself commonly asserted as a non-relative truth. If the thesis of extreme ethical relativism were itself relativized, then relativists would be obliged to re-admit ethical universalism as a valid view, albeit in paradoxical parity with relativism.

There is also a distinctively pluralist reason for rejecting extreme relativism, namely that the latter does not do justice to the universal experience, both individual and social, of moral conflict in the form of genuine dilemmas. As Bernard Williams observes: 'That there is nothing that one decently, honourably, adequately, *can* do in a certain situation seems a kind of truth as firmly independent of the will or inclination as any truth of morality seems' (1979: 224). Relativist views tend less to account for such conflict than to '*explain it away* by proposing a structure in which apparently conflicting claims are each acceptable in their own place' (Lukes, 1991: 4; also Bellamy, 2000: 191). By redescribing moral conflict in terms of the divergent prescriptions of different cultures or moral systems, strong relativism dissolves the sense of conflict or disagreement that it was supposed to explain in the first place. In the process, relativists tend to assume that different moralities, and the cultures in which they arise, are homogeneous entities, internally whole and sharply distinguishable from external influences. In reality, cultures and moralities are typically divided, contested and shaped by contact with other cultures and moralities. The internally complex, conflictual character of all human moralities is better captured by the value-pluralist notion of the incommensurability of human values. It is this idea that enables pluralists to appreciate genuine ethical dilemmas as permanent possibilities both within and across all cultures.

I conclude that the kind and degree of universality that is required for value pluralism is moderate and plausible, and at odds only with ethical relativism of an extreme kind that ought to be rejected for the reasons given. Extreme relativists would no doubt reply to these objections, but I leave readers to pursue that debate elsewhere. My argument on this point is far from comprehensive, but what is important for my purposes is to establish the claims of value pluralism to be plausible and worth taking seriously. On the score of universality the pluralist case seems to me to be distinctly superior to that of its relativist rivals.

My second concern in assessing the truth of pluralism is with its incommensurability component. Why should we believe that there are incommensurable values? To claim that values are 'incommensurable', again, is to claim that they are not merely plural but radically so, irreducibly different, each generating separate and distinct considerations. Incommensurability opposes monism, the view that all values can be commensurated either by a common medium of measurement such as preference-satisfaction or by subordination to a super-value or some other scheme of ranking independent of context. I shall briefly review four principal arguments, logically separable but mutually supportive, for upholding incommensurability against monism.

First, pluralists typically argue that incommensurability is borne out by our everyday, pervasive and persistent experience of conflict among values (Berlin, 1969: 168). This is the most common argument for pluralism, and it possesses a good deal of raw intuitive force. By itself, however, it is not conclusive. The fact of value conflict can be admitted by monists, too, who merely add that such conflicts can be resolved rationally by applying some favoured monist standard. Pluralists might respond that it is not just the experience of moral conflict that suggests incommensurability, but the evidently deep, sometimes intractable nature of much of that conflict. In many cases opposing courses of action seem equally compelling, and it seems plausible to explain such cases as arising from the demands of incommensurable goods. Yet here, too, monists could still reply that such dilemmas are more a matter of appearance than reality. We could reach a rational resolution in such cases if we possessed a clear understanding of the monist structure of morality, but this still eludes us.

At this point, pluralists might supplement the argument from experience with a second argument, drawing attention to the weaknesses of the monist alternative. Even after centuries of Western moral philosophy no monist standard has yet proved convincing, a point that strongly suggests, if it does not demonstrate, that no such standard is likely to be found. Thus Kekes refers to 'the historical failures of the numerous attempts to establish the compatibility and commensurability of values' as telling against the possibility of success in this endeavour (1993: 58). Of course, monists could reply that the mere fact of failure in the past does not guarantee failure in the future, but this is a rather hollow response, reminiscent of persistent hopes for the Marxist and other millennia. Moreover, there is good reason to suppose that the historical failures of monism result from a deep conceptual flaw in the monist project itself. We saw earlier the difficulties specific to the two main versions of monism. Preference-based commensuration merely summarizes choices already made rather than identifying a feature common to the values themselves that could be used to guide choices among them. Value-based monism does purport to commensurate values prior to choice, but only by implausibly supposing that just one or a few values can override all others in every context. Behind these specific difficulties there is a general problem. Is it really possible to embrace the immense diversity of human values within a single end or formula? It is hard to avoid the conclusion that in this ambition monists are trying to square the circle: to reduce the entire field of values to a single dimension while at the same time claiming that nothing has been lost or distorted. The past failures of monism are unlikely to be accidental. They are more likely to flow from the fact that no single commensurating medium or super-value or general ranking can 'do justice to all the different types of values there are', or adequately 'represent all of the considerations pertaining to some choice in terms of some single dimension' (Kekes, 1993: 58; Richardson, 1997: 104).

A third argument makes a further contribution to the pluralist case for incommensurability. Nussbaum (1986) argues that an appreciation of the incommensurability of values is required for a proper understanding of the human good. To understand what it is to function well or flourish as a human being is to appreciate the diversity of values that make up a complete human life. Nussbaum thus attributes to Aristotle 'a conception of the best human life as a life inclusive of a number of different constituents, each being defined apart from each of the others and valued for its own sake' (ibid.: 296). To value such a life is to value its constituent elements, which is in turn to value these separately, each on its own terms. To try to commensurate these values is to fail to appreciate them for what they are, consequently to fail to appreciate the nature of the good as a (plural) whole:

> A world in which wealth, courage, size, birth, justice are all put into the same scale and weighed together, made in their nature functions of the same thing, will turn out to be a world

VALUE PLURALISM

without any of these items, as now understood. And this, in turn, looks likely to be an impoverished world: for we value these items enough in their separateness not to want to trade them in. (*Ibid.*)

This argument, like the first, is by itself inconclusive, since it presupposes rather than demonstrates incommensurability. It is because the good life is composed of incommensurable values that a proper appreciation of the good life requires seeing its component values as incommensurable. But again, Nussbaum's argument answers to some powerful intuitions about what it is to lead a fulfilling life, intuitions that add to those mobilized by the argument from experience of moral conflict.

Finally, pluralists may argue that incommensurability is implied by our experience of choices involving rational regret for the loss of 'lesser goods', including tragic choices (see Kekes, 1993, Richardson, 1997). Our intuition is that some choices may reasonably be regretted even when we believe they are correct, and that in some of these cases the choice has a tragic quality. We are confronted with an inescapable choice among conflicting values such that gains in one value will result in losses in the other. Moreover, and crucially, the losses that result are in a sense absolute: they are not compensated by the gains, even when we are sure we have made the best choice possible under the circumstances.

Such choices range from the banal to the tragic. At the level of the banal, I may choose to go to the library as the better choice today all things considered, but still reasonably regret not being at the beach. Even though I am sure the benefits of the former have superior claims in the circumstances, so that the beach represents the 'lesser good' in this sense, the benefits of the library do not wholly compensate for the benefits of the beach. One would not, however, say that the loss involved in this case was 'tragic'. The case is genuinely tragic when the losses involved are extraordinary or severe. A classic example is that of the *Antigone* of Sophocles, for Hegel 'that supreme and absolute example of tragedy' (1962: 325). Antigone chooses to fulfil her duties to her family, and thus to defy the city's laws, by giving decent burial to the body of her brother, who has been killed while taking part in a rebellion. King Creon must decide between upholding the laws of the state in his political role, which will oblige him to execute Antigone, and honouring the claims of family relationship in his role as Antigone's uncle and

71

LIBERALISM AND VALUE PLURALISM

prospective father-in-law. His decision in favour of the state's laws does not blind him, at least at the end, to the absolute nature of the price for that decision. As A.C. Bradley puts it, endorsing Hegel's reading:

> The family and the state, the bond of father and son, the bond of mother and son, the bond of citizenship, these are each and all, one as much as another, powers rightfully claiming human allegiance. It is tragic that observance of one should involve the violation of another. (ibid.: 372)

The pluralist argument is that we can account for the strong intuition that such cases are possible only if we accept the notion of value incommensurability; it cannot be accounted for by monist theories. If monism were correct, and I choose in accordance with an approved monist standard, then whatever loss of value I incur must be compensated according to the standard. The lesser good will always be compensated by the greater, and no rational choice can be tragic or regrettable. For example, if values can be commensurated as units of pleasure, and I choose the library over the beach because that option maximizes pleasure, then the rejected option cannot be rationally regretted because it would have produced measurably less value than the approved option. In choosing the option that produces more pleasure, I have lost no value overall, so there can be nothing to regret. It is only when values are conceived as intrinsically distinct from each other, as on the pluralist view, that the notion of rational regret for a forgone lesser good makes sense. If in choosing the library over the beach I am opting for knowledge as distinct from pleasure, I may have made the better choice in the circumstances but I may still reasonably regret the pleasure I forgo. The pleasure forgone is the lesser good, but it has a value quite distinct in kind from that of the knowledge I gain. On this view I have lost something even though I have made the right choice. The idea of incommensurability is needed to capture the distinctness of values that explains rational regret of this kind.[11]

I do not claim that the forgoing arguments for incommensurability are decisive either individually or even in combination. Monist thinkers are not without resources to reply to all these points. The case for incommensurability, and for value pluralism more generally, is not logically watertight, but few if any interesting claims about the nature of morality are wholly impregnable in that sense. My claim is merely that the arguments

VALUE PLURALISM

reviewed amount, when taken together, to a persuasive case for incommensurability, and so for value pluralism, on balance. Our pervasive experience of value conflicts presenting hard choices, the persistent absence of a convincing monist solution to such problems, our sense of the irreducible complexity of human flourishing, and the possibility of rational regret even in situations where we have made the best choice – none of these is conclusive in itself, but their combined force gives us more reason to accept incommensurability than to reject it. Together with the points made earlier on behalf of pluralist universality, these arguments show, at the very least, that there is good reason to take value pluralism seriously, and consequently good reason to take seriously the arguments to follow.[12]

The argument of this chapter may be summarized as follows. The idea of value pluralism involves four main elements: the universality of certain values, plurality, incommensurability and conflict. From the conjunction of these elements flow certain consequences for practical reasoning. On one hand, rational choice among plural values is hard in the sense that we must choose without the guidance of simple monist rules, and in the sense that such choices may involve losses that cannot be wholly compensated. On the other hand, pluralism does not completely exclude reasoned choice among conflicting values. On the contrary, reasons to choose in such cases can emerge not only from attention to the context for choice but from attention to the formal components of value pluralism itself. That is, the possibility of practical reasoning is both compatible with value pluralism and implied by it. As to what conclusions that reasoning will yield, especially in the political field, that is the question to which I now turn. If rational choices among plural values are possible, what should those choices be in the political sphere? More specifically, should they privilege the values characteristic of liberalism?

Notes

1. Nussbaum's formulation of the objectivity required for value pluralism is probably too strong, since a life that lacked certain of the capabilities she lists may still, surely, count as recognizably 'human', and even a good life to some degree. All that is necessary from a pluralist point of view is that

LIBERALISM AND VALUE PLURALISM

there are certain goods that *contribute* to human well-being universally and independently of particular beliefs, that is, that such goods make human lives go better than they would otherwise. On the other hand, Berlin's version of value objectivity is probably too weak for pluralist purposes. Berlin sees universal values as those goods that all human beings in fact value: 'There are universal values. This is an empirical fact about mankind, what Leibniz called *vérités du fait*, not *vérités de la raison*. These are values that a great many human beings in the vast majority of places and situations, at almost all times, do in fact hold in common, whether consciously and explicitly or as expressed in their behaviour, gestures, actions' (Berlin and Jahanbegloo, 1991: 37). Berlin's account yields a version of value objectivity in its requirement that a genuine universal value must be something normally valued by all human beings, which is a question of fact independent of belief. This is similar to Hume's view that much of what is morally desirable is what people happen to approve of, but that certain ends and virtues are in fact approved of by all or most human beings (Hume, 1978). Berlin's account is therefore sufficient to exclude relativism, at least in the extreme form that pluralists must oppose. However, this comes at the price of letting in a species of monism. If 'value' is defined simply as what people in fact value, then all values will be strongly commensurable as functions of the act of valuing, and will not possess the separateness and distinctiveness – the 'incommensurability' – claimed for them by pluralists. The field will then be open to views such as preference-utilitarianism, which holds that all values can be reduced to terms of preference-satisfaction, which then becomes the sole end to be maximized. I shall say more about this when I come to the subject of incommensurability, but for the present conclude that Berlin's partly subjectivist understanding of universal values is not adequate to the purposes of value pluralism. For similar concerns about the ambivalence of Berlin's 'realist' meta-ethics, and especially the possibility that some of his formulations are in danger of collapsing pluralism into relativism, see MacKenzie (1999: 333).

2. Even this may not be comprehensive enough for some, since Kekes defines a value as something that benefits human beings, leaving out some religious and ecological conceptions of value as including things and actions that benefit only God or the natural ecosystem. This point was put to me by Henry Hardy. But see Nussbaum for a defence of moral thinking as necessarily 'anthropocentric' (1986, 1990).

3. Whether Aristotle should be counted as a value pluralist is controversial, since many scholars would interpret him as a monist. Nussbaum's reading is explicitly contested by Charles Larmore (1996). But even if it were mistaken as a reading of Aristotle, it could still provide a persuasive account of rational choice among incommensurable values.

4. See similar formulations in Raz, 1986: Chapter 13; Gray, 1995a: 1, 47.

74

VALUE PLURALISM

5. This seems to be Kekes's more considered view, despite his preliminary definition of incommensurability; see 1993: 56. But compare ibid.: 76.
6. See Stocker (1990), Nussbaum (1990), Kekes (1993), Richardson (1997).
7. For a more detailed typology of kinds and degrees of value conflict or impossibility, see Richardson (1997: Chapter 7).
8. Certainly this is how Berlin is interpreted by Kekes (1993: 60, note 5). See also Gray: 'When incommensurable values and counter-values must be reconciled in practice, it is human commitment and authenticity rather than reflective deliberation, or reason, that are called upon – these are themes that are common to the Romantic critics of the Enlightenment and to Berlin' (1995a: 135). Gray himself appears to endorse this view when he defines incommensurable to mean 'not comparable by any rational measure', when he rejects 'less radical' understandings of value pluralism 'which accept that the goods of human life are many ... but which deny their rational incomparability', and when he writes that incommensurability 'marks a limit to rational choice, and an occasion for radical choice – for the kind of choice that is not, and cannot be, reason-based, but consists in making a decision or a commitment that is groundless' (1995a: 1, 41, 47; 1995b: 70).
9. See Richardson: 'It appears to be widely assumed that to respond rationally to cases of value conflict is in effect to weigh or balance the importance of the values involved, and that weighing or balancing cannot be rational unless there is a common measure of value according to which it proceeds' (1997: 89).
10. For recent discussions of this question see Newey (1998), MacKenzie (1999).
11. This claim is disputed by Thomas Hurka (1996), who argues that although goods must be intrinsically distinct if we are to account for rational regret for forgone lesser goods, that distinctness can be accommodated by monists.
12. I shall later discuss two further arguments for the truth of value pluralism, in particular of incommensurability: an argument based on 'reasonable disagreement' (7.2), and Raz's argument from the value of personal autonomy (8.3.1).

PART II

Pluralist Arguments: Liberal and Anti-Liberal

CHAPTER 4

From Pluralism to Anti-Utopianism: Berlin's Case

I now embark on the question of pluralism's political implications, in particular its implications for liberalism. In Chapter 1, I considered and rejected two attempts to argue from value pluralism to liberalism. In this chapter I examine the original and best-known pluralist case for liberalism, that of Isaiah Berlin.[1] Berlin's classic 'Two concepts of liberty' contains two main lines of argument from pluralism to liberalism. First, his more explicit argument is that pluralism gives us a reason to value choice, hence the freedom of choice emphasized by liberals. I argue that this claim, as Berlin states it, is unsuccessful. A second argument, implicit in Berlin's project as a whole, is more convincing. This is that the pluralist outlook, especially in its emphasis on value conflict and incommensurability, requires an 'anti-utopian' approach to politics. For pluralists, political schemes that aim at the harmonious realization of all human goods must be repudiated. Consequently, pluralist anti-utopianism involves the rejection of certain traditional rivals to liberalism, namely classical Marxism and anarchism. Pluralists are committed to a form of politics that accepts conflict and hard choices as permanent features of human experience that must be coped with rather than transcended. Liberalism answers to this requirement. But so, too, on the face of things do conservatism and pragmatism. Berlin takes us from pluralism to anti-utopianism, but this is not yet a complete case for liberalism.

I begin by reviewing Berlin's argument for the value of choice before turning to the central theme of his pluralist anti-utopianism.

FROM PLURALISM TO ANTI-UTOPIANISM

The latter argument is developed in relation to Berlin's attack on monism and on positive liberty. In the final section I evaluate Berlin's case and identify its limits.

4.1 Pluralism and Choice

For Berlin, if values are plural and incommensurable then we must make hard choices among them when they conflict, and if that is so then we must place especial value on the freedom to make such choices:

> The world that we encounter in ordinary experience is one in which we are faced with choices between ends equally ultimate, and claims equally absolute, the realization of which must inevitably involve the sacrifice of others. Indeed, it is because this is their situation that men place such immense value upon the freedom to choose; for if they had assurance that in some perfect state, realizable by men on earth, no ends pursued by them would ever be in conflict, the necessity and agony of choice would disappear, and with it the central importance of the freedom to choose. (1969: 168)

This looks like an argument from pluralism to liberalism. Although Berlin does not say so explicitly, the suggestion is that the political ideology that answers best to the pluralist outlook will be a liberal one, since it is liberalism that places the greatest emphasis on freedom of choice.[2]

This argument may seem attractive at first sight, but one does not have to reflect on it for very long to see its problems. The initial problem is to get clear about exactly what Berlin is saying. The crucial move is from the fact of value pluralism to the valuing of freedom of choice, but why exactly does pluralism make freedom of choice valuable? Consider three different possibilities: indeterminacy, necessity and human dignity.

4.1.1 Indeterminacy

Michael Sandel (1984) interprets Berlin's point as essentially an appeal to indeterminacy: if basic human values are 'equally ultimate', then many different configurations of values are equally valid, and individuals should be given the freedom to choose among these for themselves. But if values are equally ultimate, Sandel argues, then no particular value (or set of values) has any 'morally privileged status', and that applies as much to freedom of choice as anything else. He draws attention to Berlin's approving quotation of Joseph Schumpeter: '"To realise the relative validity of one's convictions, and yet stand for them unflinchingly, is what distinguishes a civilised man from a barbarian."'

> But then, asks Sandel, if one's convictions are only relatively valid, why stand for them unflinchingly? In a tragically-configured moral universe, such as Berlin assumes, is the ideal of freedom any *less* subject than competing ideals to the ultimate incommensurability of values? If so, in what can its privileged status consist? And if freedom has no morally privileged status, if it is just one value among many, then what can be said for liberalism? (ibid.: 8)[3]

It is unclear whether Berlin intends the kind of argument that Sandel attributes to him, but if he does, the objection is well-taken. The argument is essentially the simple 'argument from indeterminacy', the failings of which were noted earlier (1.1). As Sandel points out, liberals cannot allow unrestricted indeterminacy or relativism when it comes to liberalism's own values. Berlin is not an unrestricted relativist because he insists that legitimate moral claims are framed by a set of universal goods. The variety of human ends 'cannot be unlimited, for the nature of men, however various and subject to change, must possess some generic character if it is to be called human at all' (1992a: 80). But this kind of universality is too thin to help Berlin against Sandel. Within the common horizon of ends determined by human nature, an emphasis on the particular values characteristic of liberalism, like freedom of choice, remains only one possibility among many others. The argument so far is much too wide to support a determinate case for liberalism in the face of value pluralism.[4] Further principles are required, of the kind I shall argue for later. Berlin hints at some of these, as we shall see, but his explicit comments provide no defence so far as he is taken to be arguing from indeterminacy.

FROM PLURALISM TO ANTI-UTOPIANISM

4.1.2 Necessity

Is there a more favourable way of interpreting Berlin's argument from pluralism to liberal freedom of choice? A second way of making this connection might be by way of necessity. Perhaps Berlin is saying that it is because pluralism implies that we *must* choose among conflicting values that choice is so valuable. Why should that be so? Berlin's reasoning on this point is rather oblique. What he actually says is that if people were assured that 'no ends pursued by them would ever be in conflict, the necessity and agony of choice would disappear, and with it the central importance of the freedom to choose'. In other words, if values did not come into conflict we would not have to choose among them, and therefore would not value the freedom to do so. To put this in the affirmative, it is because values conflict that we have to choose among them, and therefore that we value the freedom with which to choose.

As soon as we clarify Berlin's claim in this way, its weakness as an argument from pluralism to liberalism becomes obvious. The valuing of freedom of choice does assume that values can conflict, since valuable choice must be choice among valuable options. But conflict among values does not necessarily presuppose value pluralism in Berlin's sense. We have already seen that monists can allow that there are several values and that these can conflict; they merely add that such conflicts can in principle be resolved by some monistic decision-procedure. Value pluralism does not uniquely determine conflict among values, and consequently the need to choose; monists can allow this too. But although Berlin appears mistaken on this point, this mistake is not a great setback for his argument overall, because he does not have to show that value pluralism is the *only* reason to acknowledge a need to choose, merely that it is *one* reason to acknowledge that need. And this latter claim is unexceptionable. If it is plausible to say that one must choose among conflicting values even under monism, then under pluralism the same need must arise a fortiori.

The more serious problem with Berlin's argument arises at its next step, from the necessity of choice to the value of freedom of choice (Crowder, 1994: 297–9). If freedom of choice is valuable, choice itself must be valuable. Berlin must show that value pluralism gives us a reason to value choice. Granted that pluralism shows that we *need* to choose among conflicting values, how does it follow that we must *value* that act of choosing? The fact that

81

something is necessary or unavoidable does not make it valuable. Just because we must choose among plural values does not mean that our having to make that choice is desirable. Berlin himself refers to 'the agony' of choices among incommensurables, but if such choices are painful, as they often are, why should we value having to make them? If we have to choose between liberty and community, for example, either way losing something of great value, that painful choice is not obviously a cause for celebration — recall that the possibility of tragic choices is one of the major pieces of evidence for the truth of value pluralism. And if we have no reason to value such choices, why should we value the freedom with which to make them? Would it not make more sense to reduce the need to make hard choices to the minimum necessary rather than expand the scope for them and therefore the frequency with which we have to deal with the problem? The basic problem with Berlin's argument from necessity is that it commits a version of the naturalistic fallacy: it tries to derive a value from a fact — the value of choice and the freedom to choose from the fact of having to choose.

4.1.3 Human dignity

Someone might try to salvage Berlin's argument as follows. Value pluralism implies the necessity not of just any sort of choice but of a special kind of choice, namely choice among incommensurables, 'hard' choices in the senses defined earlier. Perhaps this special kind of choice is valuable not just because it is necessary or unavoidable, but because it is *symbolic*. Certain choices have value because they symbolize something else to which we attach value (Scanlon, 1988). For example, I may value my vote, even though I never use it, because it symbolizes my status as a citizen. Perhaps, then, Berlin's argument is that my freedom of choice is valuable, independently of the use I make of it, because it symbolizes my moral status as a human being. To acknowledge value pluralism, and consequently the need to make hard choices among incommensurables, is to sharpen our sense of human beings as essentially and distinctively choice-making beings: 'The necessity of choosing between absolute claims is then an inescapable characteristic of the human condition' (Berlin, 1969: 169). As a distinctive mark of humanity, our choice making focuses the respect owed to humanity. Human dignity thus understood is most fully respected in a regime that makes freedom

FROM PLURALISM TO ANTI-UTOPIANISM

of choice a priority, that is, a liberal regime.

If this is Berlin's point, it broadens the basis of his argument beyond choice itself to the wider notion of 'human dignity' that choice is said to symbolize or focus. But this new argument raises a fresh set of problems. First, it might be objected that this is not a distinctively pluralist argument, because all the work is being done by the notion of human dignity rather than value pluralism. What is crucial here is the particular conception of human dignity involved, and this can be invoked without reference to pluralism. This is not a strong objection because it can be replied, as before, that Berlin does not have to claim that pluralism is the only route to this view, merely that it is one possible route. There could be other ways of alerting us to the picture of human beings as choosers, but value pluralism (it could be argued) is one way, and an especially vivid one.

A deeper problem with this extended version of Berlin's argument is that choice is not the only thing that makes us human. Choice is no more than a part of our distinctively human make-up, and therefore of whatever unique dignity attaches to that distinctive humanity. Moreover, this is a truth highlighted by value pluralism itself, which teaches that the good life for human beings is complex, containing many distinct features and dimensions. The capacity to make rational choices among incommensurables is just one of many distinctive human functions. And not all of those functions lead as unequivocally in the direction of liberalism as does choice; indeed, some may arguably be more readily developed or satisfied in a non-liberal environment. For example, the capacity of human beings to develop a conscious sense of belonging to a particular cultural group with its own unique identity may be, although to some degree compatible with liberalism, also in tension with the liberal tendency to universality implied by the principle of equality of moral worth (Taylor, 1994). Therefore, what seems to be Berlin's deeper point about the significance of pluralist choice, namely that it implies a conception of human dignity as essentially the dignity of choosers, is too selective and one-dimensional. That is indeed the implication of value pluralism itself. If Berlin is arguing from pluralism to human-dignity-as-choice to liberalism, the argument fails at both steps. If values are radically plural, then there is more to human dignity than choice, and if that is so then 'human dignity' is probably compatible with a wider range of political regimes than just liberalism.

So far, Berlin's case is unconvincing. His general claim is that there is a link between value pluralism and freedom of choice, but he does not persuasively establish what this is. The first possibility, the argument from indeterminacy, fails because the radical indeterminacy Berlin appears to accept is a poor foundation for liberal values, and because indeterminacy of this strength does not follow from pluralism in any case (1.1; also 9.2 below). Second, the argument from necessity fails because the mere fact of our having to choose among plural values does not show that having to make such choices is desirable, hence something that ought to be unrestricted. Third, so far as Berlin is making the deeper point that value pluralism implies a conception of human dignity focused on the capacity for choice, his understanding of the implications of pluralism for human dignity is too narrow. Later (8.3) I shall attempt an improved form of Berlin's argument from choice as part of my 'perfectionist' or virtues-based link between pluralism and liberalism. I shall argue that autonomous choice is an especially significant value given the kind of practical reasoning required by value pluralism. That argument must appear in its proper place, however. Now let us see what else Berlin has to offer.

4.2 Anti-Utopianism

A second line of argument from pluralism to liberalism that can be extracted from Berlin is more immediately compelling. In brief, the argument is that value pluralism points to the permanence of imperfection and conflict in the political arrangements of human beings, thus ruling out certain political positions as utopian and implying a case for liberalism as a realistic and reasonable response.

To understand this argument, we need to set it within a broader picture than I have given so far of Berlin's political thought as a whole. In particular, I shall relate what Berlin says about pluralism and monism to his famous critique of positive liberty in contrast with negative. These two themes – the pluralism–monism contrast on one hand and the negative–positive liberty distinction on the other – have generally been treated in isolation from one another by the critics, and are not clearly integrated even by Berlin himself. Yet it is only through their interconnection that we grasp Berlin's pluralist case for liberalism. In this section and the next I shall argue that Berlin's broader pluralist case for liberalism emerges out of the

FROM PLURALISM TO ANTI-UTOPIANISM

connection he makes between ethical monism and political authoritarianism. That connection, in turn, can be understood on the same pattern as the link between authoritarianism and positive liberty.

Berlin's political thought emerges from his confrontation with twentieth-century totalitarianism. His project is essentially that of combating totalitarianism by unmasking its deepest assumptions, identifying the point at which our thinking has gone astray. According to Berlin, totalitarianism rests on utopianism, typically expressed in the language of 'total liberation' through the realization of 'real' or 'positive' liberty. At the root of the utopian outlook lies moral monism. Against the utopian conceptions of positive liberty and moral monism, Berlin urges us to prefer the 'truer and more humane' ideals of negative liberty and value pluralism, hence the institutions of liberal democracy within which those ideals flourish best (1969: 171). Berlin's broader case can thus be divided into two main phases, the first tracing the roots of totalitarianism to monism by way of utopianism, including his critique of positive liberty; the second his positive account of the link between value pluralism, anti-utopianism and liberalism.

First let us trace Berlin's archaeology of totalitarianism. The distinguishing mark of the totalitarian thinker or leader, Berlin believes, is ruthless single-mindedness. A totalitarian system is one in which all values, desires and interests, and ultimately all persons, are subordinated to a single overriding goal: the fulfilment of a nation's destiny, the emancipation of a class, and so on. 'The pursuit of the ideal' demands sacrifice, but if the ideal is lofty enough no sacrifice is too great. The loftiest of all goals is the creation of the perfect society, the genuinely free society that has achieved a total integration of all human interests and values. 'Any method of bringing this final state nearer would then seem fully justified, no matter how much freedom were sacrificed to forward its advance' (1969: 168). Social and political perfection is, by definition, worth any price.[5]

The utopianism that sustains totalitarian programmes rests ultimately on monism:

> One belief, more than any other, is responsible for the slaughter of individuals on the altars of the great historical ideals — justice or progress or the happiness of future generations, or the sacred mission or emancipation of a nation

PLURALIST ARGUMENTS: LIBERAL AND ANTI-LIBERAL

or race or class, or even liberty itself, which demands the sacrifice of individuals for the freedom of society. (ibid.: 167)

That belief is 'the conviction that all the positive values in which men have believed must, in the end, be compatible, and perhaps even entail one another' (ibid.) – that is, monism. Common to all monist views is the idea that there is, in Berlin's words, a 'final solution' waiting to be discovered and applicable to all cases of ostensible conflict. The belief in the possibility of a final moral solution translates readily into the belief in a final political solution, the notion, dreamed of by Plato, Rousseau, Hegel and Marx, 'of total human fulfilment ... of a final harmony in which all riddles are solved, all contradictions reconciled' (ibid.: 168). Monism, that is, leads to utopianism. And since utopianism will necessarily be thwarted by, among other things, the recalcitrance of people with values at variance with those privileged by the utopian blueprint, the determined utopian will have to pursue his ideal by force. He will become an authoritarian, ultimately a totalitarian.

A further feature of totalitarian regimes is that they redefine the oppression they preside over as 'liberation'. The imposition of monist ethical and political schemes has often been defended as an expansion of 'real' or 'positive' freedom, as opposed to an inferior, merely 'formal' or 'negative' liberty. Berlin lays out the negative–positive distinction as follows. I am free in the negative sense when I am not 'prevented by others from doing what I could otherwise do' (ibid.: 122). Negative liberty is the absence of deliberate human interference with what I might want to do. The starting point for positive liberty, on the other hand, is the thought that my wants may not be truly 'my own'. They may, for example, be the result of my ignorance or irrationality or of social conditioning over which I have no control. 'The "positive" sense of the word "liberty" derives from the wish on the part of the individual to be his own master' (ibid.: 131). Positive liberty, then, is the idea that I am free only when I am governed by what is 'authentic' to me.

What is original to Berlin is not the negative-positive distinction itself but his critique of the positive idea, the famous 'inversion' thesis. The positive idea has often, more often than the negative, been distorted into the very opposite of genuine liberty. Berlin distinguishes a series of steps by which this occurs (ibid.: 132–3). The starting point is the idea of the divided self, the notion that the human personality contains distinguishable and competing ele-

FROM PLURALISM TO ANTI-UTOPIANISM

ments, traditionally reason and the passions. A second step is taken when one element of the self is identified as the higher or authentic element. True freedom will then be rule by the true self: reason, for example, rather than the passions. The third step is to go on to associate the true self with a collective self: who 'I' truly am is a vehicle or instrument of the will or spirit of the tribe, the nation, the Party. True freedom is conformity with that will. The way is then open to a fourth and final step, where I recognize that what the will or the nation or Party demands is something that the leaders know better than I. True freedom is obedience to the leaders.

Berlin's thesis is not merely historical, it is conceptual as well. Historically, Berlin claims, it is simply a matter of fact that positive liberty has often been twisted into the opposite of any conception of liberty that accords with common sense. This has happened much less frequently to the negative idea (ibid.: xlv). But there is in addition something about the positive *concept*, by contrast with its negative counterpart, that renders it distinctively vulnerable to the process of distortion Berlin describes. For Berlin, that 'something' is present in the very first step of the positive liberty sequence: a willingness to second-guess people's actual desires and wishes as authentic expressions of their will. The negative idea takes people's desires for granted in the sense that no question is raised as to whether my desires are 'my own'. But the very first steps in the positive concept place that identification in question and so, according to Berlin, open the way to the later, overtly totalitarian steps where what people happen to want is overridden by what their leaders know they 'really' want.

Berlin goes too far in his blanket suspicion of all forms of positive liberty in contrast with negative. He himself allows that the later steps in the sequence he describes do not *follow* from the earlier. It would be possible to stop at any one of them and give reasons for proceeding no further. Positive liberty, that is, can be conceived in non-authoritarian terms. In particular, the claim is not authoritarian that a person's desires may fail to be in any substantial sense 'her own' because they are the result of conditioning or uncritical acceptance of convention. Consequently, it is far from authoritarian to claim that there is a valid and important kind of freedom that involves subjecting one's options, and one's desires, to an authenticating process of critical reflection (Crowder, 1988, 1991). Indeed, such a thought is surely an essential part of liberalism. When Mill (1974) champions the cause of personal

PLURALIST ARGUMENTS: LIBERAL AND ANTI-LIBERAL

autonomy against 'the despotism of custom', this is the kind of freedom he has in mind. Liberals typically want people to be able to make their own lives, and that entails the thought that some lives people might lead are not truly 'their own'. The kind of positive liberty involved here, namely personal autonomy, surely has a legitimate and important, indeed central, role to play in liberalism (Christman, 1991). Moreover, I shall argue later that the value of positive liberty understood as autonomy receives powerful support from value pluralism (8.3.3).

Berlin's better point is directed not against all positive liberty, but only against those versions of it that are genuinely authoritarian. Although he is not explicit about this, his implication is that the more authoritarian versions of the positive idea presuppose monism. First, such versions of the positive idea entail the notion that freedom is enforceable, that in Rousseau's phrase one can be 'forced to be free'. That notion depends on the view that the authentic will may be something other than the individual's actual will, and moreover that those in authority may know better than the individual what that authentic will commands. Such ideas do not fit easily with the pluralist idea that there may be several equally reasonable ways to rank competing human goods, depending on the circumstances. The authoritarian view becomes more compelling on the assumption that moral considerations form a monist unity, such that a single end or principle resolves value conflicts in every case regardless of the circumstances. Such an assumption lends weight to belief in the possibility of formulating uniform rules or decrees or slogans that can be readily promulgated and enforced by the state or some other coercive apparatus. Moreover, monist views of morality aid and abet monist views of the self (the 'true self') that is the subject of freedom. If there is only one moral end or principle, then there is only one sort of person to be, hence only one way to be free. Add to this the thought that certain classes of political leaders can generally be relied upon to know better than others what morality, true selfhood and consequently freedom require, and we have the final ingredient of the authoritarian recipe outlined by Berlin.

A second way in which authoritarian positive liberty presupposes monism is through its all-inclusiveness. Once freedom is understood to require obedience to the fully rational and moral will, 'freedom' becomes equated with 'morality': to be free, to be rational, to act morally – all these are identical. Freedom, that is, comes to encompass all moral goods; to be forced to 'act rightly' is to be

88

FROM PLURALISM TO ANTI-UTOPIANISM

forced to be free. Again, this sequence of reasoning makes better sense on monist than pluralist premises. If values are plural, then 'freedom' will be merely one incommensurable value among others, and indeed there may be different, incommensurable kinds of freedom of which the negative and positive senses are just two (Berlin, 1969: 130). We must then acknowledge

> the claims of other, no less ultimate, values: justice, happiness, love, the realization of capacities to create new things and experiences and ideas, the discovery of truth. Nothing is gained by identifying freedom proper, in either of its senses, with these values, or with the conditions of freedom, or by confounding types of freedom with one another. (ibid.: lvi)

It is only on the monist understanding that all genuine goods dovetail with one another that we can conceive of freedom as encompassing morality and of morality as necessarily entailing freedom. Authoritarian versions of positive liberty are thus intimately linked with monist conceptions of morality.

Monism is thus, for Berlin, a dangerous idea, underwriting utopianism in general and the more dubious forms of positive liberty in particular. It is also false. In truth, moral values, including fundamental political values such as liberty, equality, justice and community, are not monistic in structure but plural: irreducibly multiple and incommensurable. There is no final or absolute ranking of moral and political values, no single value or limited range of values that always override or commensurate others. At the most fundamental level our moral life is inescapably a life of difficult choices among conflicting goods. It follows that this too must be the character of our social and political life:

> If, as I believe, the ends of men are many, and not all of them in principle compatible with each other, then the possibility of conflict – and of tragedy – can never wholly be eliminated from human life, either personal or social. The necessity of choosing between absolute claims is then an inescapable characteristic of the human condition. This gives its value to freedom as Acton had conceived of it – as an end in itself, and not as a temporary need, arising out of our confused notions and irrational and disordered lives, a predicament which a panacea could one day put right. (ibid.: 169)

If values are plural and incommensurable, hard choices must

always be made and there can be no political panacea. The dreams of the completely fulfilled, integrated and liberated society, the kind of society upheld as a goal by Plato, Rousseau, Hegel, Marx and the anarchists, will be purely utopian. A humanly realistic politics must acknowledge and cope with conflict, disagreement, division and imperfection as permanent features of social and political life. Thus a humanly realistic politics will have individual freedom at its centre, permitting people, within agreed limits, to go their own way in deciding matters for which there is no absolute blueprint. This is the liberal solution.

4.3 Issues

Berlin's argument raises many questions of which two are salient. First, does monism have the intimate connection with utopian and authoritarian thinking that Berlin alleges? Second, does value pluralism conversely imply a case for liberalism by way of the rejection of utopia?

4.3.1 Monism, utopianism and totalitarianism

As to the first question, an immediate objection is that by no means all monist thinkers have been utopian and authoritarian as well. The classical anarchist thinkers of the nineteenth century, the tradition that runs from Godwin and Proudhon to Bakunin and Kropotkin, are paradigmatically monistic and utopian, but they are avowedly anti-authoritarian. Indeed their utopianism consists precisely in their rejection of all political authority, even in the restricted form advocated by liberals, as not only undesirable but unnecessary. Government is unnecessary because there is a single, coherent moral law of nature which all human beings are capable of recognizing and following without having to be forced to do so. The anarchist utopia is thus underwritten by a monism based on natural law − thus far Berlin's thesis is borne out. But the anarchist utopia will be, in principle, a non-authoritarian society in which that law will be self-imposed by every individual rather than enforced by an agency claiming authority. The super-value for the anarchists is 'moral self-direction', a species of positive liberty in which the authentic self is identified with willing obedience to the moral law (Crowder, 1991).

FROM PLURALISM TO ANTI-UTOPIANISM

The anarchists, then, appear to fit Berlin's pattern only in part. Their monism underpins their utopian picture of the desirable society but does not seem to involve authoritarianism, indeed quite the reverse.

Other monists are neither authoritarians nor utopians. Indeed, among these are some of the great names of liberalism: Locke, Bentham, J.S. Mill and Kant. Locke, like the classical anarchists, is a monist from the natural law school. Like the anarchists, he places a high value on personal liberty – he is not an authoritarian. Unlike the anarchists, however, Locke does not rely on the private judgement of individuals to identify and secure compliance with the moral law. The state of nature contains serious 'inconveniences', permanent sources of conflict and injustice, which can only be remedied by the institution of government – Locke is not a utopian. In the case of Bentham and Mill the monist premise is that of utilitarianism: liberal freedoms and restraints on the authority of government are said to maximize utility. Kant would seem to count as a monist on the ground of his summation of morality as a single categorical imperative, yet Kant was a dedicated supporter of the rights of man. In recent times Ronald Dworkin (1977, 1985) bases his liberalism on the paramount value of 'equality of concern and respect'. Nor are these associations of monist ethics with liberal politics purely coincidental. The super-value of a monist system could well be a liberal goal such as negative liberty or toleration or personal autonomy (or the anarchist goal of moral self-direction). Although focusing on such a goal to the exclusion or downgrading of everything else may not be a recipe for the best kind of society, it would be another thing to claim that it must lead to authoritarianism or utopianism. If there is a link between monism and authoritarianism, it is not one of logical implication; authoritarianism does not follow necessarily from monism.

If there is no *logical* link between monism and authoritarianism, could there be a less formal connection nevertheless? Such a connection can be understood on the same pattern as that between authoritarianism and positive liberty. First, although monism is not necessarily authoritarian, it has in fact been frequently turned in that direction historically. Berlin's examples are apposite: Plato's encompassing conception of the Form of the Good, which can be apprehended only by the philosopher–ruler; Rousseau's General Will, according to which citizens can be 'forced to be free'; and the different pictures presented by Hegel and Marx of the 'end of history', a goal which places entire classes and civilizations at its service.

Second, and more importantly, monist and authoritarian ways of thinking are linked, as in the case of positive liberty, by more than mere historical accident. Rather, monism is especially vulnerable to the authoritarian turn, more so than pluralism. Again, the link is by way of utopianism. If there is one overriding value or set of values or formula, then there will be one in-principle solution to all conflicts of values and interests: 'Do whatever will realize or maximize the super-value'. As in morality so in politics there will be, in Berlin's phrase, a 'final solution'. Through the determined, universal application of the formula we can expect to resolve all significant conflicts. In order to achieve this end, any means is justified. This is true as a matter of necessity, since by definition the value of the end overrides or encompasses all other considerations. Once a single value or relatively narrow range of values is held up as overriding or commensurating all other concerns, the way is open to the marginalization, downgrading and suppression of much that is in fact important to people:

> Once I take this view, I am in a position to ignore the actual wishes of men or societies, to bully, oppress, torture them in the name, and on the behalf, of their 'real' selves, in the secure knowledge that whatever is the true goal of man (happiness, performance of duty, wisdom, a just society, self-fulfilment) must be identical with his freedom. (Berlin, 1969: 133)

This passage is part of Berlin's discussion of positive liberty, but it would fit just as well in his account of the implications of monism. Just as positive liberty need not lead to authoritarian politics but is especially vulnerable to that kind of development, so monism, while not necessarily authoritarian in its political implications, is structurally prone to such abuse. If the final solution can be achieved only through the massive use of force or coercion, then so be it. And the use of force will indeed seem to monists the only route to the promised land since (if pluralism is correct) that goal will always recede before us. Both the prospect of utopia and its inevitable frustration will combine to lead ambitious monists towards authoritarianism and even totalitarianism.

Berlin's main critical target in this regard is Marxism. He refers to Marx's 'rigid belief in the necessity of a complete break with the past, in the need for a wholly new social system as alone capable of

FROM PLURALISM TO ANTI-UTOPIANISM

saving the individual' (1963: 19). This belief places Marx 'among the great authoritarian founders of new faiths, ruthless subverters and innovators who interpret the world in terms of a single, clear, passionately held principle, denouncing and destroying all that conflicts with it' (ibid.). It is because Marx's vision of the ideal community 'was of that boundless, absolute kind which puts an end to all questions and dissolves all difficulties', that is, because of its strongly monist character, that Marx was happy to subordinate all other considerations to its realization (ibid.: 19–20). Marx and his followers are for Berlin classic examples of thinkers whose ultimate authoritarianism stems from utopian aspirations that rest on value monism.

How far is Berlin's pluralist attack on Marxism convincing? Those sympathetic to Marx will no doubt resist the accusations of 'utopianism' and 'authoritarianism'. Moreover, it might be objected that even if Marx's thought is both utopian and authoritarian, that is not because he is an ethical monist. First, it may be said, Marx avoids making ethical judgements at all, since he regards these as merely 'ideological', the expressions of class interest. This view of Marx, although widespread in the past, is too simple. It is true that Marx regards certain kinds or levels of morality as merely class-based or relative to particular stages of historical development, for example the preoccupation with justice and individual rights that he sees as characteristic of bourgeois capitalism. But commentators such as Steven Lukes have argued persuasively that underlying this relativist level in Marx there is a deeper 'morality of emancipation' (1985: 29). Marx's discussion of alienation, for example, reveals a conception of humanity's 'species-being' or distinctive nature, which is primarily that of a free and creative producer. Human history is essentially the story of the progressive liberation of this capacity. Marx's vision of its full development amounts to a tacit conception of the good life for human beings.

A second, and stronger, objection to Berlin's treatment might be that although ethical values do enter into Marx's thought, these reveal him to be, if anything, a value pluralist. Consider this famous passage from *The German Ideology*:

> In communist society, where nobody [has] one exclusive sphere of activity but each can become accomplished in any branch he wishes, society regulates the general production and thus makes it possible for me to do one thing today and

93

another tomorrow, to hunt in the morning, fish in the afternoon, rear cattle in the evening, criticize after dinner, just as I have a mind, without ever becoming hunter, fisherman, cowherd, or critic. (Marx, 1977: 169)

Here and elsewhere, it might be argued, Marx acknowledges the legitimacy of a multiplicity of activities, each of which possesses its own value, and each of which is part of a fully realized good life for human beings. All of these fall within the umbrella of free creativity, the realization of species-being, but all are distinct dimensions of it. Is such a view not on all fours with the value-pluralist outlook?[6]

The passage quoted is indeed instructive, because it shows both what Marx has in common with pluralists and where he differs from them. His view shares with that of the pluralists an acknowledgement of a multiplicity of human goods. But what is missing in it from a pluralist point of view is any strong sense that those goods may come into conflict with one another, and that when they do we are faced with hard choices among them because they are incommensurable. Marx seems cheerfully to assume that all the desirable activities he mentions, and therefore the goods associated with them, can be seamlessly combined not only within the same society but even within the same individual life. There is no hint that to choose one of these goods, or one combination of them, is necessarily to exclude other options, still less that such choices are problematic in the relevant senses. In short, while Marx accepts two of the components of value pluralism, namely universality and plurality, he shows no appreciation of the remaining two, conflict and incommensurability. Marx is not a value pluralist.

On the contrary, Marx is, as Berlin claims, a value monist, since monistic assumptions are the necessary underpinnings of his utopian aspirations. Marx's utopianism (judged by pluralist standards) is most directly on view in his various remarks about the fate of rights, justice and the state in the society of the future. Under 'full communism' there will simply be no need for these. Thus in the essay 'On the Jewish question' Marx dismisses 'the rights of man' proclaimed by the American and French Revolutions as 'nothing but the rights of the member of civil society, i.e. egoistic man, man separated from other men and the community' (ibid.: 52). Individual rights are seen as a mere expression of bourgeois self-interest. At best, rights are a necessary corrective to the tendency of

FROM PLURALISM TO ANTI-UTOPIANISM

capitalism to commodify and dehumanize people. As such they will no longer be needed when the conditions giving rise to them disappear in the future epoch of post-capitalism. Similarly, 'justice, on this view, is a remedial virtue, a response to some flaw in social life. Justice seeks to mediate conflicts between individuals, whereas communism overcomes those conflicts, and hence overcomes the need for justice' (Kymlicka, 1990: 161). In the same way, Marx anticipates the eventual abolition of the state, or at least its radical mutation into an agency for 'simple administrative functions' (cited by Evans, 1975: 161). The state as we know it has its *raison d'être* in the ostensible need to restrain interpersonal and social conflict. In the society of the future, there will apparently be no such need. The common theme in all these cases is the transcending of current values and institutions through the transcending of significant social conflict. The notion of the end of conflict in turn assumes the possibility of a human society in which all genuine interests and values will harmonize naturally, a characteristically monist view. Marx's vision of the political harmony depends on the monist idea of the possibility of ethical harmony.

The example of Marxism thus confirms Berlin's link between monism and authoritarianism. The monist outlook, according to which values and interests can be harmonized or embraced in a single formula, may not lead necessarily to utopianism, but it makes utopianism thinkable – at any rate the kind of utopia suggested by Marx's vision of the transcending of social conflict, and therefore of rights, justice and the state. From there it is a further step, but a relatively short one, to the view that in order to reach the promised land no sacrifice is too great. Indeed, any such 'sacrifice' must necessarily be compensated by the overriding value of the ultimate goal. Marx cannot be held wholly responsible for the excesses of some of his followers, but Berlin is right in claiming that the seeds of their later ruthlessness were planted by the master.

The claim that monism is especially vulnerable to the authoritarian turn is true even if the monist super-value is freedom, however 'freedom' is defined. Marx's goal, for example, may be defined as one of liberation, the realization of a 'realm of freedom' in which the productive powers of humanity will be freed from constraint and allowed to develop fully. But broad though this goal undoubtedly is, it does not embrace all human values, even all conceptions of freedom (negative liberty being one notable omission), and its pursuit to the exclusion of other goods can

95

PLURALIST ARGUMENTS: LIBERAL AND ANTI-LIBERAL

become oppressive. Nor is it only positive conceptions of freedom that have been elevated into super-values with oppressive consequences. Berlin notes explicitly that negative liberty too can be abused in this way, as demonstrated by 'the bloodstained story of economic individualism and unrestrained capitalist competition' (Berlin, 1969: xlv). Indeed, the excessive worship of negative liberty above all else, in regimes of libertarianism or 'unrestricted laissez-faire', has ironically led to gross violations of that same value in the lives of the poor and the powerless: 'Freedom for the wolves has often meant death to the sheep' (ibid.).[7]

Another example of how even the idea of freedom can become oppressive in the hands of monists is provided by the anarchists. I earlier invoked the classical anarchists as an apparent counter-example to Berlin's thesis, since they appear to be monists and utopians but not authoritarians. One could argue, however, that the official libertarianism of anarchism is belied in the case of those anarchists like Bakunin who are prepared to sanction the use of terrorism and violent revolution. On the face of it, such methods seem at odds with the anarchist condemnation of the state because of its characteristic reliance on coercion. According to the logic of their own deepest commitments, the anarchists should rely solely on education and enlightenment to persuade people of the merits of the stateless society. But the revolutionary anarchists are impatient with waiting for the spontaneous convergence promised by their monist assumptions. Moreover, violence may be more easily justified if one is willing to separate means from ends. The familiar thought pattern re-emerges: given a sufficiently valuable end, any means are legitimate. The anarchist goal is necessarily of overriding value, therefore violence is justified if that is the best or quickest means to its realization. Berlin's linking of monism, utopianism and authoritarianism is borne out once more.[8]

Pluralism, on the other hand, is not so vulnerable to the authoritarian turn. Where goods are recognized as incommensurable, it follows that each has, in a rough sense, an equal claim on our attention. Only in particular circumstances does it seem possible to rank plural values for good reason, and in such cases our reasons for ranking must attend to the particulars of the case in hand rather than rely on an abstract or utopian super-value or formula. Pluralism teaches us that positive conceptions of liberty must be counter-balanced by negative, since negative liberty is also a significant human value. Indeed, there are many distinct values, all of which

FROM PLURALISM TO ANTI-UTOPIANISM

have a legitimate claim on our attention, none of which should be merely ignored or denied, even when we have to choose against them. It is not possible to combine all of them within a single life or a single society – there can be no wholly perfected, frictionless political society. A politics that takes account of value pluralism cannot be 'the pursuit of the ideal'. From the pluralist perspective, in short, it is harder to blind ourselves to the claims of different competing wants, interests and values, and therefore harder to justify the single-minded and ruthless pursuit of narrowly conceived political goals that characterizes authoritarian politics.

Monism, then, if it does not logically imply authoritarian politics, leaves open a door to it in a way that pluralism does not. First, monism underwrites the more authoritarian versions of positive liberty. Second, monist notions of morality make it easier to blind ourselves to goods other than the favoured super-value or commensurating unit. Consequently it becomes easier to ignore or devalue the actual wishes of people so far as these are for merely subordinate goods or for things that do not count as goods according to the favoured scheme. Third, monism encourages utopianism through its message that a single formula will solve all problems and resolve all conflicts, reconciling all goods and interests. Utopian schemes, going against the grain of the human condition, can be persisted in only through the use of repressive force. Monism encourages an expectation of the possibility of a total convergence of the values and interests of human beings that is unrealistic and has consequences that are ultimately inhumane. This warning is the central theme of Berlin's thought, and it is well-founded.

4.3.2 Pluralism, anti-utopianism and liberalism

We come now to the second major issue raised by Berlin's anti-utopian case: how far does that case imply a positive argument for liberalism? Berlin teaches that monism opens the door to utopianism, and in turn to authoritarianism or even totalitarianism when utopianism is inevitably disappointed. But does it follow that a pluralist politics must be liberal? The acceptance of pluralism helps to undermine any temptation to utopianism and its consequences. But there remains a considerable gap between the dismissal of utopian politics and the endorsement of liberalism. How far does Berlin's case take us towards bridging that gap?

PLURALIST ARGUMENTS: LIBERAL AND ANTI-LIBERAL

What Berlin shows is, first of all, that a pluralist politics must be non-utopian. In effect, Berlin emphasizes two elements of the pluralist idea, namely the incommensurability of plural values and their potential to come into conflict. This emphasis yields the second of the five general principles identified earlier (3.2). The first was that of respect for universal values. Berlin's anti-utopianism points to a further imperative: that all social and political systems ought to acknowledge the fact of value incommensurability and its implications. The chief implication is that hard choices in the pluralist sense have to be accepted as an ineradicable feature of the human condition, and therefore of politics. Political experience is indefeasibly characterized by trade-offs involving losses that cannot be fully compensated by what is thereby gained. Moreover, there can be no easy answer to the question of which trade-offs we should endorse; guidance on such matters cannot be summarized in a single blueprint that will solve all social and political ills. The pluralist outlook insists that our politics acknowledge these truths. We must recognize that no political arrangement is capable of delivering a complete and harmonious realization of all genuine human goods.[9]

It follows that pluralism rules out certain political views that have been advanced as alternatives to liberalism in the past. These include, most notably, classical Marxism and classical anarchism. Both of these are utopian doctrines in the relevant sense, namely views that look forward to the reconciliation and harmonization of all goods in a perfected society of the future. If pluralism is true, then value incommensurability and conflict render that hope vain. Berlin therefore takes a further step towards making a pluralist case for liberalism by eliminating two of liberalism's historical rivals.[10]

If pluralism points to a non-utopian politics, what political form best fits the bill? Liberalism is surely a strong candidate. For the pluralist view that moral and political dispute is a permanent part of the human condition and cannot be transcended is also the liberal view. For liberals, the rational and humane response to this fact is not to try to transcend it, but rather to accept, accommodate and contain it within non-destructive bounds. As Charles Larmore (1997/8) writes: 'If we recognize that knowledge, virtue, and happiness may diverge, we will then see that the just society aims not at perfection, but at striking a balance among the different, conflicting goods which human beings espouse'. Here again is a description of the broad project of liberalism: to accept religious, cultural and ethical divergence as inevitable, and to try to prevent

FROM PLURALISM TO ANTI-UTOPIANISM

the resulting disputes and conflicts from becoming violent and damaging by containing them within a framework of principles that all or most can accept. As Chandran Kukathas puts it: 'Division, conflict, and competition will always be features of human society; the task of political institutions, according to liberal theory, is to palliate this condition, rather than to attempt a cure' (1997: 134). Liberals differ with one another over the kind and extent of realistic and desirable palliative action, or on the precise balance to be struck among competing goods. But they are agreed that disagreement (within reasonable limits) must be accommodated rather than transcended. Liberalism, then, with its attempt to accommodate conflict through an emphasis on personal freedom within agreed bounds, is a strong contender for the non-utopian politics indicated by value pluralism.

However, the pluralist case for liberalism is not yet complete. Indeed it has barely started. That is because liberalism is not the only contender along these lines. It might be argued that the non-utopian qualification implied by pluralism is met not only by liberalism but also by conservatism and pragmatism. First, conservatives can agree with both pluralists and liberals that a humanly realistic politics must accept conflict and disagreement among human beings, and among members of the same group, as a permanent possibility that can never be resolved by a single formula. However, they disagree with liberals over the best response to that state of affairs. In contrast with the liberal solution of maximal personal freedom within agreed limits, conservatives argue that human conflicts are best resolved by reference to *tradition*. It is by building up and staying close to a particular local tradition that people are best able to contain and resolve personal and group conflicts, and, behind these, conflicts among plural and incommensurable values. Similarly, a broadly 'pragmatic' view of politics is, apparently, compatible with pluralist anti-utopianism. Pragmatists, too, take the inevitability of moral conflict as their starting point. Where they differ from both liberals and conservatives is in arguing that conflict cannot be managed by applying any substantial set of moral principles, whether universal or local, since these too will be disputed. Rather, conflict can be contained only by the pursuit of modus vivendi, or strongly context-specific compromise.

I shall examine these conservative and pragmatist claims more fully in the next chapter. For the present, however, enough has been said

PLURALIST ARGUMENTS: LIBERAL AND ANTI-LIBERAL

to conclude that the pluralist case for liberalism will take us beyond Berlin. We have seen that although his more explicit arguments from pluralism to liberalism are sketchy and unconvincing, a more holistic view of his thought enables us to infer an underlying 'anti-utopian' argument that is much more compelling. Even that argument, however, does not uniquely identify liberalism as the appropriate politics of pluralism. While it tells against a number of rivals, notably classical Marxism and anarchism, it does not, as so far stated, exclude conservatism or pragmatism as a proper response to the deep plurality of values. To complete the pluralist case for liberalism it therefore remains to show that liberalism is superior to conservatism and pragmatism, and to other alternatives, from a pluralist point of view. I begin that task in the next chapter, but it will only be completed when I have set out the arguments of Part III. These moves take us well beyond Berlin. Nevertheless, Berlin's case already contains the seeds of the arguments to come. Two aspects are especially important, corresponding to two of the three principal lines of argument I shall pursue in Part III. First, Berlin's emphasis on the need to accept value conflict and incommensurability as deep and inescapable anticipates the argument from reasonable disagreement, according to which pluralism brings about a permanent divergence of conceptions of the good life which is best contained by liberal principles and institutions (Chapter 7). Second, Berlin's singling out of choice as a link between pluralism and liberalism suggests a 'perfectionist' or virtues-based argument, in which the hard choices imposed by pluralism imply the need for virtues of practical reasoning that include, especially, liberal autonomy (Chapter 8). But these arguments will be considered in due course. I must first examine the claims of the anti-liberal pluralists.

Notes

1. The most comprehensive bibliographies of work by and about Berlin are to be found on the website maintained by his editor, Henry Hardy (2001). Other bibliographies, also assembled by Hardy, are contained in Ryan (1979) and Berlin (1997). Among the considerable and rapidly expanding body of commentary on Berlin there are, to date, three book-length studies: Kocis (1989), Galipeau (1994), Gray (1995a). There is also an excellent biography: Ignatieff (1998). Collections of articles discussing

FROM PLURALISM TO ANTI-UTOPIANISM

Berlin's work include Ryan (1979), Margalit (1991) and Mack (1994). Two recent articles surveying Berlin's general contribution to political philosophy are those by Harris (1996) and Kenny (2000).

2. It is not entirely clear whether or in what way Berlin intends to be making a case for liberalism on the ground of value pluralism. Compare the passage quoted with these remarks in an interview: 'I believe in both liberalism and pluralism, but they are not logically associated' (Berlin and Jahanbegloo, 1991: 44). Yet he immediately goes on to say: 'Pluralism entails that, since it is possible that no final answers can be given to moral and political questions, or indeed any questions about value, and more than that, that some answers that people give, and are entitled to give, are not compatible with each other, room must be made for a life in which some values may turn out to be incompatible, so that if destructive conflict is to be avoided compromises have to be effected, and a minimum degree of toleration, however reluctant, becomes indispensable' (ibid.). Retaining the beginning and end of this sentence, and omitting the intervening Byzantine subclauses, one arrives at a statement to this effect: 'Pluralism entails ... [a case for] toleration.' Moreover, in 'Two concepts of liberty' Berlin refers to 'pluralism, with the measure of "negative" liberty that it entails' (1969: 171), and in 'My intellectual path' he writes that 'If pluralism is a valid view ... then toleration and liberal consequences follow ...' (1998: 53). It is hard to believe that Berlin does not intend to support some kind of argument from pluralism to liberalism.

3. Another commentator who criticizes Berlin along these lines, i.e. as a relativist, is Leo Strauss (1989).

4. On this point I disagree with Jonathan Riley (2000), who argues that Berlin can link value pluralism and liberalism through his notion of the 'common moral horizon' alone. According to Riley, the common horizon is sufficient to indicate a 'minimal liberalism'. But the examples he gives of the minimally liberal values said to be part of the common horizon, including rights not to be enslaved and to be free from arbitrary killing and starvation (ibid.: 140–1), are too general to count as distinctively liberal. They could be accepted by regimes which nevertheless rejected threshold liberal commitments to freedom of speech and religion. Although acknowledgement of a set of values that all human beings have in common is a step in the right direction, I agree with Gray (2000b: 109) that such generic values are so far consistent with non-liberal forms of politics.

5. The dangers of the belief that the end justifies the means is a theme that runs throughout Berlin's writing. See *The First and the Last*, in which Henry Hardy juxtaposes 'the first known piece and the last essay' (Berlin, 1998). The first piece, 'The purpose justifies the ways', was written when Berlin was a schoolboy of eleven, and draws on his childhood experience of the Russian Revolution. As Hardy explains, 'Berlin always ascribed his

PLURALIST ARGUMENTS: LIBERAL AND ANTI-LIBERAL

lifelong horror of violence, especially when ideologically inspired, to an episode he witnessed at the age of seven during the February Revolution in Petrograd in 1917: while out walking he watched a policeman loyal to the tsar, white-faced with terror, being dragged off to his death by a lynch-mob. This story surely vividly reflects the power of this early experience' (ibid.). The phrase 'the pursuit of the ideal' occurs in Berlin's last essay, 'My intellectual path', and is also the title of the leading essay in the collection, *The Crooked Timber of Humanity* (Berlin, 1992a).

6. For another passage in which Marx seems to take a value-pluralist view, see his ironic attack in the *Economic and Philosophical Manuscripts* (1843) on money as a false commensurator of distinct goods and aspects of human well-being: 'I who can get with money everything that the human heart longs for, do I not possess all human capacities?' (Marx, 1977: 109) And see 9.2 below.

7. See 9.2 below for a more fully developed pluralist case against laissez-faire (but compare the discussion in 6.2, which links pluralism to private property *as a starting point* when it comes to economic distribution).

8. On the role of violence and terrorism in anarchist thought, see Miller (1984: Chapter 8) and Crowder (1991: Chapter 4).

9. Compare Ryszard Legutko, who argues that 'value pluralism is not itself immune from ... utopian inclinations'. According to Legutko, pluralism leaves open the possibility of 'Robert Nozick's "utopia of utopias" or "meta-utopia", as he calls it, an order that potentially consists of infinitely many communities, each serving different values or combinations of values. The dilemmas of incommensurability are thus retained, though at the same time rendered powerless, because in an order of segmented pluralism all divergent ethical systems may very well coexist and all forms of life may be represented, while individuals have a chance to go at will from one to another' (1994: 9). But there is nothing in pluralism to lead us to expect that such segmentation is a realistic possibility, which surely it is not. In any case, as long as 'the dilemmas of incommensurability are retained', none of the communities will be *internally* harmonious.

10. Note that this argument against classical Marxism and anarchism does not affect all forms of socialism, since not all are utopian in this sense. Indeed, moderate forms such as social democracy are virtually indistinguishable from the social or egalitarian form of liberalism that I shall ultimately defend (9.2). But stronger forms of (non-utopian) socialism should be rejected on other pluralist grounds: see 6.2.

CHAPTER 5

Pluralism against Liberalism? Conservatism and Pragmatism

In Chapter 4 I endorsed Berlin's claim that value pluralism implies anti-utopianism, but conceded that anti-utopianism alone is consistent with non-liberal forms of politics, namely conservative and pragmatic positions. I shall now argue that conservatism and pragmatism should be eliminated from a pluralist point of view. I show this by examining the arguments of two writers who purport to take value-pluralist premises to conservative or pragmatic conclusions: Kekes and Gray. The 'anti-liberal pluralists', as I call them, emphasize the extent to which rational choice among competing plural values is possible only in context. It follows, they say, that the standard universalist justifications of liberalism should be rejected. Liberalism should be either dismissed altogether or at least recognized as no more than one legitimate option among others. Rather, pluralist particularism suggests that basic values can be ranked only by taking local tradition as authoritative or by reaching a pragmatic modus vivendi among rival ways of life. Pluralism, that is, implies not liberalism but conservatism or pragmatism.

I argue that pluralist anti-liberalism should be rejected. In the first section I show that Kekes's conservative view rests on the assumption that pluralist particularism requires deference to local tradition.[1] Even if this were true, pluralism would support liberalism in cases where the local tradition happened to be liberal. But in any case, Kekes's traditionalism is an unduly narrow interpretation of 'context'. A wider notion of context lets in a wider

103

defence of liberalism. In the second section I trace the development of Gray's interpretation of pluralism through a series of phases, culminating in his advocacy of modus vivendi in opposition to liberal universalism. Despite its accommodating appearance, I argue that this too is closer to a monist than a pluralist position. In the final section I challenge the assumption, common to both Kekes and Gray, that choice under pluralism must be wholly contextual. As we have seen already, the formal features of pluralism imply a set of critical principles which are universal in scope. The first of these, respect for universal values, confirms the incoherence of pluralist conservatism and pragmatism, and hints at the possibility, to be pursued in Part III, of a universalist case for liberalism.

5.1 Kekes's Conservatism

Kekes's commitment to value pluralism will already be evident from Chapter 3, where he is one of the main sources for my own account. Inspired in particular by Berlin and Oakeshott, his *Morality of Pluralism* (1993) is a trailblazing investigation of the nature of pluralism and its moral and political implications. For Kekes, human values are both plural and 'conditional' (ibid.: 17–21). Radically different sorts of things benefit or harm human beings and so contribute to or detract from the possibility of a good life. Values are 'conditional' in the sense that no single value or limited set of values is 'overriding', or always more important than others. A good life requires the coherent ordering of these plural and conditional values, but such an ordering is made problematic by conflict and incommensurability. Conflicts among values arise because of incompatibilities among them either in a particular situation or in their very nature. One then has to choose among them. Choosing among conflicting values, however, is often complicated by the fact that some are so radically different as to be hard to compare and so to weigh up – they are incommensurable.

Nevertheless, Kekes believes, conflicts among plural and incommensurable values can be resolved reasonably. This cannot be done by applying absolute principles such as utilitarianism in any of its forms, since these depend on accepting one or a few values as overriding, an assumption denied by value pluralism. Rather, 'rankings are reasonable only in particular situations because they depend on the variable and individual conceptions of a good life

FROM PLURALISM TO ANTI-UTOPIANISM

held by the participating agents' (ibid.: 22–3). There is no good reason to rank one value above another in the abstract, but such rankings may be reasonable in a concrete context. 'Pluralists think that there is one right ranking in each context, but what that is varies with contexts; and they think that what makes the ranking right is not determined by subjective preferences, but by objective, albeit local, not universal, considerations' (Kekes, 1998: 61). Chief among these local, context-dependent considerations is the guidance of the individual agent's conception of the good, or the way he or she tends to order competing values in general.

So far there is little in Kekes with which liberal pluralists would disagree. But in the last chapter of *The Morality of Pluralism*, and later in *Against Liberalism* (1997), he seeks to derive from the pluralist outlook political conclusions which are explicitly anti-liberal. Kekes's basic claim is that while pluralism rules out the absolute privileging of some values above others, liberalism advocates just such an absolute privileging of the values it favours. Liberalism and value pluralism are therefore incompatible, and if value pluralists are correct, liberals must be mistaken. Value pluralists cannot be liberals. As Kekes puts it:

> Pluralism is committed to the view that there is no conception of a good life and no particular value that, in conflicts with other conceptions and values, always takes justifiable precedence over them. But if liberalism is to avoid the charge of vacuity, it must be committed to holding that in cases of conflict the particular conceptions of a good life and values that liberals favor do take justifiable precedence over nonliberal ones. (1997: 159)

Liberals differ as to the precise content of the values to be accorded priority. The chief candidates listed by Kekes are: justice (Rawls), rights (Berlin, Nozick), equality of concern and respect (Ronald Dworkin), and freedom or autonomy (Raz) (1993: 201–2; 1997: 171). Liberals nevertheless agree that *some* such value, or combination of values, is overriding – that is, that one of these values, or some combination of them, has priority over all others in all cases. Thus 'their language is permeated with talk about absolutes, inviolability, trumps, ultimate justification, fundamental prohibitions, first virtues, uncompromising claims that cannot be overridden, and so forth' (1997: 171). Such absolutism or universality is precisely what value pluralism denies.

105

Having rejected liberalism, Kekes then sets out his case for conservatism. Conservatism is distinguished from other views above all by respect for tradition (Harbour, 1982: 6). It is because of the primacy of tradition that Burke, for example, urges 'infinite caution' on those thinking of 'pulling down an edifice which has answered in any tolerable degree for ages the common purposes of society' (Burke, 1968: 152). Typically, conservatives have justified the central place they attribute to tradition by reference to the frailty of human nature, in particular of the individual's powers of reason. To these familiar arguments Kekes adds a new twist, namely his grounding of traditionalism in value pluralism. The reasoned ranking of plural values is possible within a particular, local context by reference to the individual agent's conception of the good life. This in turn will be guided by the background conception of the good approved by his or her society. 'The grounds on which such judgments rest are the conceptions of a good life regarded as acceptable in the surrounding tradition' (1993: 77). Local tradition is thus the chief source for the reasonable resolution of conflict among plural and incommensurable values.

This view is confirmed and developed in Kekes's most explicit defence of traditionalism, *A Case for Conservatism* (1998). Conservatism, he argues there, is the form of politics that best fits the value-pluralist outlook. Pluralism requires that values be ranked only in context, and to rank in context is to rank in accordance with a particular tradition. People can rationally resolve conflicts among plural values only by 'following the historical practices of the traditions in which they participate' (ibid.: 66–7; see also 1993: 22–4, 77–9; 1998: 62–3). Traditions 'represent a local way of organizing and responding to some aspect of life', one that endures through time and becomes customary (1998: 63). In this way, 'each tradition provides a way of ranking the comparative importance of the values in its domain' (ibid.). Traditions, that is, provide people with a model they can follow in negotiating the ethical conflicts and choices with which they are confronted throughout life. Where those conflicts involve incommensurable values, as they often do, traditions are especially valuable, since, as we have seen, methods of decision making by calculation or the application of abstract rules are not adequate to the task. Consequently, the good society, a society that enables its citizens to live good lives, will be one that attends actively to the maintenance of its guiding traditions. The citizens of such a society make choices and judgements, 'but they do so in the frameworks of various traditions which authoritatively provide them with the relevant choices, with the matters that are left to their judgments, and with standards that within a tradition determine what choices are good or bad, reasonable or unreasonable' (ibid.: 39). Traditions, on this view, are encompassing and authoritative. For Kekes, then, the proper resolution of conflicts among plural values implies an explicitly conservative politics, a politics of 'traditionalism' (ibid.: 38–9).

To summarize, Kekes's pluralist case for conservatism consists of three main claims. First, practical reasoning under pluralism must be particularist. A fundamental implication of value pluralism is that absolute rankings of values are ruled out and even general rankings are questionable. However, there may be good reason to rank plural values in a particular way in a particular context. Second, pluralism implies a critique of liberal arguments that support an absolute ranking of values regardless of context. While pluralism rules out the absolute privileging of some values above others, liberalism, at least in its traditional universalist forms, advocates just such an absolute privileging of the values it favours. It follows for Kekes that pluralists cannot be liberals. Third, pluralism is said to generate a positive case for conservatism. To appeal to 'context' in order to rank values is above all to appeal to one's background conception of the good, which in turn is shaped primarily by social tradition. Tradition is best protected not by liberalism, which tends towards a universalism that questions and erodes inherited practices, but by conservatism.

Can liberals reply to Kekes's conservative case and still do justice to value pluralism? Two main lines of liberal response are possible, corresponding to the contextual and universalist approaches to pluralist choice introduced earlier (3.2). I shall deal with the contextual response in this section; the universalist response will be introduced in section 5.3 and pursued in Part III. My question in this section is, then, assuming a commitment to particularism, what response might liberal pluralists make to the other two main components of the conservative case, the critique of liberalism and the affirmative case for conservatism? I shall argue that even within the constraints of strict particularism, liberals can reply strongly to the conservative pluralist case. First, particularism does not rule out a case for liberalism because such a case may be contextual. Even assuming the narrowest interpretation of 'context' as equivalent to pre-existing tradition, a case for liberalism is possible where the relevant tradition is liberal. Moreover, there is no reason why the context for pluralist choice should be interpreted so narrowly. A wider interpretation is indeed *required* by the pluralist outlook, making possible a wider case for liberalism. Second, this latter argument also undermines the affirmative case for conservatism, which depends on linking the pluralist outlook with an emphasis on tradition. The link is broken if tradition turns out to be no more than one contextual consideration among others. Taken together, these points amount to a refutation of most of the conservative pluralist case. But I shall also suggest that liberals should not be wholly satisfied with the particularist response, and should look beyond context both to confirm the rejection of conservatism and to justify liberalism.

Before entering into the question of context, however, it is worth noting two other replies that liberals might make to Kekes, but which are less than satisfactory. Recall that the conservative pluralist critique of liberalism is that while pluralism implies that plural values may only be ranked within context, liberal justifications characteristically give priority to liberal goods absolutely or universally. One response might be to argue that the defence of liberalism does not rest on the ranking of values at all, since liberalism is neutral among conceptions of the good. To say that the liberal state is neutral is to say that it avoids ranking any particular goods or ways of life ahead of others. Individuals and groups may arrive at their own ranking, but the neutral state neither helps nor hinders them in this.

Liberalism cannot be defended by the claim that it does not rank values at all. We saw in Chapter 2 that liberal neutrality can be at best 'approximate' (2.2.1). Liberalism, like any other comparable political view, involves a commitment to some conception of the good and the rejection of others. The idea of neutrality itself has affinities with the good of toleration, the pursuit of which involves down-playing the value of orthodoxy or unity. The liberal good is arguably more capacious than the alternatives, more accommodating to different interpretations or instantiations – I shall be arguing along these lines in the next chapter. But that does not make liberalism wholly neutral.

Moreover, pluralism provides a distinctive reason why this is so. An often-repeated lesson of pluralism is that the range and diversity of human ends is such that not all of these can be accommodated within a single life, certainly the life of an individual person, but even the life of a whole society. As Rawls writes: 'Any system of institutions has, as it were, a limited social space' (1993: 57). A society may, for example, promote religious toleration or religious orthodoxy, but hardly both in any great strength simultaneously. In such cases a choice must be made, or at any rate the society must tend in one direction or the other. That is, it is an implication of pluralism that social and political systems cannot be wholly neutral. The choice of one good constrains or marginalizes another, whatever we do.

But if the ranking of values is unavoidable under any social system, that suggests a second liberal response to the conservative critique, namely that conservative societies must rank values too. Conservatives might object that to rank goods within the context of a particular society is one thing, but to claim that a particular ranking is valid universally or generally, as liberals typically do, is quite another. But here, too, liberals reply that conservatives are guilty of the same offence. The only difference is in the content of the privileged values. While liberals accord a general priority to freedom, equality of concern and respect, justice and rights, the conservative outlook attribute a corresponding status to tradition in particular, and to other goods such as law-abidingness, civility and security (Kekes, 1997: 173).[2]

This second liberal response, as so far stated, amounts at best to a Pyrrhic victory. It succeeds merely in tarring conservatives with the same brush that they apply to liberals, and does nothing to show that liberalism does not deserve the tarring in the first place. For a more complete reply along these lines liberals need to develop the theme, foreshadowed above, of the extent to which the liberal good is relatively accommodating or 'approximately' neutral in comparison with alternatives such as conservatism. Liberals need to argue that even if they do rank certain goods ahead of others in all or a generality of cases, that ranking amounts to a conception of the good that permits the flourishing of a greater range or diversity of values and ways of life than alternative rankings, including the conservative. This is indeed a key argument in my pluralist defence of liberalism, but I shall postpone its fuller development until the next chapter.

I come now to the main theme of this section, the liberal reply to the Kekes's conservative case by way of particularism. This allows that liberalism does involve ranking values, but denies that this is a ranking independent of context. Liberals can argue, consistently with pluralism, that there is good reason to choose liberal values ahead of others within some particular context. The question is, what contexts give rise to a case for liberalism? 'Context' is capable of a range of interpretations, some wider, some narrower.

On the widest understanding of 'context', it might be argued that *all* justifications of liberalism are contextual. On this view, pluralism does not rule out any of the standard arguments for liberalism, since they all, even the most traditional, presuppose *some* context. Natural rights arguments, for example, presuppose the context of 'human nature' or 'human experience'. The experience of humanity is said to reveal a certain list of values as good for human beings, from which is deduced a set of rights. The same can be said of utilitarianism, in which case the list of basic human values is reduced to a single super-value, utility.

The trouble with these arguments from a pluralist point of view is that the context of 'human nature or experience' is so very wide that it provides no criterion for choosing among incommensurable goods when they conflict. The traditional list of goods recognized by natural law thinkers may serve as a rough guide to the identity of the basic human goods (3.1.2). But the pluralist emphasis on the incommensurability of the basic goods points to the impossibility of ordering them in an absolute or even general hierarchy, and consequently to the impossibility of choosing rationally among them, except within particular contexts. Of such particular contexts the idea of natural law itself gives no account: it points to the need for appeal to a particular context in order to narrow down the range of choice among incommensurables, but does not provide such a context itself. Natural law poses the problem of ranking goods but does not answer it, or at any rate it provides little specific guidance, and certainly nothing that approaches a case for liberalism.[3] On the other hand, utilitarianism (a dubious foundation for liberalism in any case) answers the problem of ranking by stipulating that utility be the super-value. But to pluralists this will seem arbitrary. Why must utility be privileged above other goods in every context? The more convincing utilitarian answers to that question will tend to appeal to a more complex notion of utility, which will in turn be vulnerable to the possibility of internal conflict among incommensurable elements.

In short, Kekes is correct in arguing that pluralist particularism rules out some arguments for liberalism, namely the traditional rights-based and utilitarian arguments. These appeal to contexts

110

FROM PLURALISM TO ANTI-UTOPIANISM

('human nature', 'human experience') that are too wide to determine the choice of the goods characteristic of liberalism in preference to rival packages of goods. The context of 'human experience', which is common to both natural law and utilitarian thinking, is consistent with many rational rankings of goods. Depending on which of these rankings is endorsed, which in turn will depend on some more detailed specification of context, natural law (and therefore natural rights) may legitimate non-liberal politics as often as liberal. Utilitarianism asserts the legitimacy of a single ranking, but one which is neither a reliable foundation for liberalism nor defensible from a pluralist point of view.

The lesson to be drawn here might seem to be that rational choice among incommensurables is possible only within contexts that are as narrowly circumscribed as possible. Something like this seems to be Kekes's view as evidenced by his emphasis on existing tradition. To this, two responses are available to liberals. First, even if context is identified narrowly with tradition, there is still a case for liberalism, at least in certain circumstances. Second, the idea of context, even if it should not be extended to include the whole of 'human experience', should nevertheless be read more widely than 'tradition'.

First, suppose that pluralist particularism requires that in choosing among plural values we should be guided by local tradition. That view is still compatible with a case for liberalism, indeed it endorses such a case, if the tradition in question is a liberal one. Walzer makes this point in the course of showing that the methodology of the American communitarians, that is, their appeal to the de facto beliefs and values of a particular community as an ethical standard, does not necessarily yield a wholesale critique of liberalism. He gives the example of the dominant political culture of the United States as evidenced by the moral and political language employed during the civil rights struggle of the 1960s: 'Martin Luther King's speeches evoked a palpable tradition, a set of common values such that public disagreement could focus only on how (or how quickly) they might best be realized' (1990: 14). To appeal to 'tradition' in American politics is not to invoke 'some pre-liberal or anti-liberal community waiting somehow just beneath the surface or just beyond the horizon', because no such community is 'waiting' (ibid.: 15). Rather, it is to endorse liberalism.

Nor is liberal tradition confined to the United States. As we saw in Chapter 2, Rawls's later work takes as its starting point 'a certain political tradition' which he identifies as 'modern constitutional democracy' and finds instantiated in the political systems of not only the United States but also the United Kingdom and Western Europe (2.2.2). The contents of that tradition are complex and contested, since it contains different streams that are liable to come into conflict. The 'liberties of the moderns' represented by Lockean rights of thought and conscience, person, property and the rule of law sometimes clash with the Rousseauian 'liberties of the ancients', which emphasize 'the equal political liberties and the values of public life' (Rawls, 1985: 227). Nevertheless, the public political culture of constitutional democracy does reveal a 'shared fund of implicitly recognized basic ideas and principles' that can serve as a basis for agreement. These include 'such settled convictions as the belief in religious toleration and the rejection of slavery' (ibid.: 228). The most basic values of constitutional democracies, those intuitions that are most widely and deeply accepted and least questioned, are among the classic values of the liberal tradition. Once again, the appeal to local tradition can be an endorsement of liberalism.

Note that this contextual argument raises the possibility not merely of a case for liberalism that is *compatible with* value pluralism, but of a case for liberalism that is *based on* pluralism. Liberalism could be justified within a context without explicit reliance on value pluralism, as it is by Walzer and Rawls. But pluralism can play a role in motivating the necessary attention to context. This is so to the extent that pluralism requires the reasoned ranking of values to be contextual. Context may provide the case for liberalism, but pluralism provides a case for attending to context. This amounts to an indirect passage from pluralism to liberalism (Crowder, 1999: 6–7).[4]

We have also seen, however, the limits of this particularist kind of argument for liberalism (2.2.2). If liberal institutions and practices are justifiable only where liberal traditions already exist, then liberal advocacy can amount to nothing more than preaching to the converted. Those who argue for liberalism on this basis can have nothing to say to people with no such traditions; yet these are the very people whom liberals might most want to persuade of the merits of liberalism.

At this point liberals might argue that even if liberalism can be justified only in context, 'context' can be interpreted more widely than the limits of existing local tradition. A justification of liberalism within a wider context will give liberal principles a wider

FROM PLURALISM TO ANTI-UTOPIANISM

application and critical reach. Recall the suggestion in Chapter 3 that the idea of a context for pluralist choice includes two main elements, namely values and facts (3.2). Prominent among the background values that enable us to choose rationally among rival options are those that form our conception of the good, if we have one. Kekes is correct when he says that among the sources of a person's conception of the good, the traditions of the society they belong to are important. Nevertheless, local social tradition cannot be the only source of a person's conception of the good. That is demonstrated by the fact that people are capable of revising their notions of the good in ways that diverge from, and even conflict with, local traditions. Tradition may provide a starting point, but people commonly revise their understanding of the good as a result of personal experience and reflection. Even within the 'values' aspect of context alone, therefore, tradition is only one component. Particularist argument is wider in scope than argument from tradition.

The scope of particularist argument becomes wider still when one adds to the idea of 'context' the element of facts. Considerations of fact or circumstance, I suggested in Chapter 3, have an important role to play in pluralist practical reasoning, especially in determining which choices are possible and which impossible. How might factual considerations help to generate a case for liberalism that does not depend on the pre-existence of a liberal tradition? One example is provided by Benjamin Constant (1988). Constant argues that the conditions of a modern, commercial culture in which the central concern of people's lives is their private fortune in the marketplace, the collective, republican 'liberty of the ancients' is no longer a possibility, and the liberal 'liberty of the moderns' is the only realistic prospect. The context to which Constant appeals, both grounding and limiting his case for liberalism, is neither the hopelessly wide horizon of human nature nor the excessively narrow fait accompli of existing liberal tradition. Rather, it is the circumstances of the modern age of commercialism and the culture and values to which it gives rise. Liberalism is the appropriate political form neither for humanity as such nor just for societies that are liberal already, but for a particular kind of civilization.

Another example of this kind of particularist case for liberalism, neither universal nor narrowly tradition-based, is that of Raz (1986). As we have seen (2.2.4), Raz argues that the privileging of personal autonomy (and thus liberalism) is not appropriate for all human societies. Nor, however, is it requisite only for those people who are liberals already. Rather, autonomy is unavoidably an ideal under certain modern 'conditions', namely conditions of technological, economic and social change (ibid.: 369–70). Such conditions produce an 'autonomy-supporting environment', within which being autonomous is the only way to prosper (ibid.: 394). Again this is an argument with a wider reach than one based narrowly on existing liberal tradition. For Raz, even those without such a tradition must embrace the ideal of autonomy if they are to flourish in the kind of modern society he describes.

The possibility of this broader liberal particularism is sufficient to refute Kekes's conservative pluralist case. First, it refutes the claim that liberalism is necessarily opposed to pluralism because absolutist rather than contextual. We now have an argument for liberalism which is both contextual and broad enough to capture something of the critical purchase that is part of the liberal project. The kind of argument found in Constant and Raz is contextual or particularist rather than universal, and so answers to the demand for particularism that appears to follow from pluralism. On the other hand this is a broader particularism than that which appeals narrowly to tradition, and so does more than merely preach to the converted.

Second, the Razian argument undermines Kekes's positive case for conservatism, because it severs the claimed link between pluralism and tradition. The distinctive conservative claim is that in practical reasoning the force of tradition is authoritative or primary. For pluralism to support a case for conservatism it must point to the maintenance of tradition as at least the primary criterion in ranking values under pluralism. But pluralism does not have this implication. It suggests at most that tradition is one important consideration among others, perhaps a necessary starting point. So far as rational choice under pluralism requires attention to context, we have seen that 'context' should not be identified solely or even primarily with tradition but interpreted more widely to include other considerations. Tradition is an important constituent of people's background conception of the good, and later I shall argue that this is an important point when we come to consider what kind of liberalism it is that pluralism implies (9.3). But tradition is only part of the picture; it does not necessarily determine people's conception of the good. Furthermore, appeal to context may include

114

FROM PLURALISM TO ANTI-UTOPIANISM

recognition of circumstances that take us beyond (or that qualify) conceptions of the good. Pluralist attention to context is broader than the conservative focus on tradition emphasized by Kekes. From a pluralist point of view, tradition is not ethically primary but only one consideration among others. In short, pluralism does not generate the case for conservatism proposed by Kekes; it refutes that case.

Might liberals go further, and argue that pluralism gives rise to a case for liberalism that is not merely particularist, even on the wider reading of context, but universal? To answer this question I shall need to appeal to considerations beyond the limits of particularism, and I shall come to these in section 5.3. I now turn to the anti-liberalism of Gray.

5.2 Gray's Pragmatism

Berlin's value pluralism is the starting point for Gray as it is for Kekes.[5] 'This is the idea ... that ultimate human values are objective but irreducibly diverse, that they are conflicting and often uncombinable, and that sometimes when they come into conflict with one another they are incommensurable; that is, they are not comparable by any rational measure' (Gray, 1995a: 1). If values are plural and incommensurable, Gray believes, then so too are the cultures or 'forms of life' within which values are instantiated. Within 'the limits of human nature', there is 'a variety of incommensurable human flourishings' (1993b: 291, 298).

Like Kekes, Gray makes this last observation the basis for a critique of liberalism. The logic of Berlin's view, he argues, is far more subversive than Berlin himself realizes or acknowledges (1995a: 1–2).[6] If pluralism is true, then values cannot be ranked for good reason universally. This fact strikes 'a death blow' to the entire 'Enlightenment project' by which a universal, impartial reason will point out the ideal social and political arrangements for all human beings – that is, a universal ranking of values. This point seems to be accepted by Berlin as the basis for his rejection of views such as Marxism and anarchism. Such utopian positions are characterized in part by their monist commitment to an overriding value. Gray pushes Berlin's reasoning a stage further. Liberalism itself is a version of the Enlightenment project; the fall of that project is therefore the fall of liberalism too. From a value-pluralist point of

115

PLURALIST ARGUMENTS: LIBERAL AND ANTI-LIBERAL

view, the traditional liberal arguments based on natural rights, social contract, utilitarianism and perfectionism all share the same basic defect: they seek to show that a universal and impartial reason can be invoked to privilege one relatively narrow set of human goods over others. In effect, Gray sees Enlightenment liberalism as another utopian ideal rendered incoherent by the hard truth of value pluralism. If values are incommensurable, then we have no good reason to accord a universal privilege to any such value, or set of values, over any others. Consequently, we have no good reason to privilege universally the goods characteristic of liberalism: tolerance, autonomy, impartial justice. 'Where liberal values come into conflict with others which depend for their existence on non-liberal social or political structures and forms of life, and where these values are truly incommensurables, there can – if pluralism is true – be no argument according universal priority to liberal values' (ibid.: 155).

But if pluralism rules out liberal universalism, then what kind of political principles does it allow? Gray gives at least three different answers to this question, corresponding to three different phases in his thinking about the nature of choice under pluralism, respectively 'subjectivist', 'particularist' (conservative) and 'pragmatic'.

In his earlier work on pluralism Gray tends towards a strongly subjectivist view of pluralist choice according to which choices among incommensurables must be non-rational: 'In many of such conflicts there is no overarching standard whereby their claims are rationally arbitrable' (1993b: 291; also 1995a: 1, 41, 47; 1995b: 69). Faced with such choices, we can only decide by reference to our own arbitrary preferences or by some procedure selected at random. Logically, the kind of politics this implies can only be some form of ungrounded existentialist or Nietzschean commitment on the part of the individual. Gray stops short of this conclusion, although he does (at this point) see politics as a matter of ungrounded *collective* commitment. On this early view of Gray's, all that is left to the defender of liberalism, for example, is 'the historic inheritance of liberal civil society ... The task of the post-liberal theorist is to illuminate the forms of civil association which are the most profound elements of our historical inheritance' (1989: 262). The theorist in general is to 'displace from their current dominance the ruling abstractions of the age', and seek instead 'to uncover the genealogy or archaeology of our present forms of life and to understand them as historical creations' (ibid.: 263). The task of the liberal theorist is thus simply to elaborate the contents and history

116

of existing liberal cultures rather than to engage in the justification or advocacy of liberal norms.[7]

The problems with the subjectivist account of pluralist choice were discussed in Chapter 3 (3.2). Most importantly, the subjectivist view does not account for our apparent ability to find decisive reasons to choose among plural values in many particular cases. Gray now agrees: 'Value pluralism does not imply that there are not in particular circumstances good reasons for favouring one value, or constellation of values, over others' (1995a: 154; also 1993a: 115). With this realization, his pluralism enters a second, 'particularist' phase. In this phase he holds, like Kekes, that incommensurability makes the reasoned ranking of competing values problematic in the abstract, but not impossible in a particular situation where decisive reasons for ranking may be generated by context.

What are the political implications of Gray's particularist phase? First, it leads him to introduce a qualification to his rejection of liberalism. While Kekes appears to invoke pluralism as a ground for rejecting all forms of liberalism, Gray's critique is expressly directed at certain kinds of liberal argument rather than others. The old Enlightenment justifications of liberalism are ruled out because pluralism excludes the reasoned ranking of basic values across all or most cases. 'What does follow from the truth of pluralism is that liberal institutions can have no universal authority' (1995a: 155). But this leaves open the possibility of a particularist form of liberalism. Gray allows what he calls an 'agonistic liberalism', that is, a view that explicitly accepts liberalism as in competition, on an equal moral footing, with alternative social and political forms. The agonistic view sees the commitment to liberal goods as amounting to 'one form of life among many, with no foundation in human nature or the history of the species as a whole' (ibid.: 146). Liberalism 'neither possesses nor requires "foundations". It is instead best understood as a particular form of life, practised by people who have a certain self-conception, in which the activity of unfettered choice is central' (ibid.: 161).[8]

But although Gray-the-particularist allows that a reasoned defence of liberalism is compatible with pluralism, this will be very limited. Rational argument for liberalism is not only limited by context, but can be determinate only within the narrowest of contexts, namely where liberal traditions and institutions already exist and are accepted. Gray's view in his second, narrowly

117

contextualist phase is thus fundamentally conservative in the broad sense that it emphasizes the moral authority of existing cultural traditions. It denies the possibility of a rationally defensible universalism which could provide critical criteria for judging and improving traditional practices. Instead, it accepts those practices as an ethical bottom line, unassailable because incommensurable with alternative standards.

Gray derives broadly conservative conclusions from pluralist premises in much the same way as Kekes. People faced with a choice among conflicting incommensurable values have no reason to choose one rather than another unless they have the guidance of the patterns already laid down by an existing culture or 'form of life'. When it comes to settling conflicts among incommensurable values, 'what makes a settlement of their conflicts better or worse is a local affair. There are no universal principles that rank or weigh generically human goods. Judgements of the relative importance of such goods appeal to their role in a specific way of life' (Gray, 1998: 31). He takes the neoliberal New Right to task because, neglecting history, it 'reposes its trust in legalist and constitutionalist devices, when our only support is in the vitality of our cultural traditions' (1993a: xiv). Again, 'for most people, the meaning of their lives is a local affair, and the examined life may turn out to be hardly worth living' (ibid.: 52). Nor is the market an adequate organizer of incommensurables, because 'the market is only as strong as the culture that underpins it – a culture of responsibility and choice-making' (ibid.: 64). The basic point is that people need a model or pattern to follow in order to navigate their way through a life of otherwise bewildering clashes among incommensurable goods, and that model is provided by local tradition. And again the best political form will be that which best protects traditions, namely conservatism.

Gray's conservative traditionalism is open to the same objection as that brought against Kekes, namely its narrowness. To the extent that pluralism requires choice to be contextual, why must context be identified solely or primarily with existing tradition? Something like this point seems now to have been accepted by Gray, who in his most recent work explicitly turns his back on conservatism. He still maintains that pluralism rules out the possibility of substantial universal moral and political principles, and that reasons for ranking values must be strongly contextual. But he now rejects the narrow equation of context with existing tradition. The reason he gives is that local traditionalism will not settle conflicts among incommen-

FROM PLURALISM TO ANTI-UTOPIANISM

surable values when the relevant traditions are themselves in conflict. 'I have argued that a balance can sometimes be struck among conflicting incommensurables by invoking the mix of values characteristic of a particular way of life. But how are conflicts among incommensurate ways of life to be resolved?' (1998: 32).

Gray's answer to this question, marking the third and most recent phase of his developing view, is that where traditions or ways of life collide, such conflicts should be 'settled by achieving a modus vivendi between them' (ibid.). To achieve a modus vivendi between ways of life is to 'find interests and values which they have in common and reach compromises regarding those in which they diverge' (ibid.). Gray thus broadens the notion of a context for pluralist choice beyond the claims of existing traditions to include interests and values which competing traditions might have in common. His position is no longer conservative in any straightforward sense.

Nor, however, is Gray's a liberal position. On the one hand, he presents the search for modus vivendi as historically one of the 'two faces of liberalism' (2000b). He urges liberals to return to this pragmatic side of their historical inheritance in preference to what he regards as the currently dominant quest for 'moral consensus', which he associates not only with perfectionists like Raz but also with Rawls and the neutralists. Moral consensus, Gray argues, is rendered impossible by value pluralism, but modus vivendi remains possible and is part of the liberal panoply. On the other hand, he makes it clear that what form a modus vivendi takes will depend on the circumstances. In any particular case it may be satisfied by liberal institutions or it may not: 'Liberal institutions are merely one variety of modus vivendi, not always the most legitimate' (1998: 34; also 2000a: 332). The only limits to legitimate modus vivendi required by Gray consist in a thin conception of universal values, explicitly consistent with non-liberal solutions. 'There are minimal standards of decency and legitimacy that apply to all contemporary regimes, but they are not liberal values writ large' (2000b: 109). It is a strange form of liberalism that endorses arrangements opposed to liberal values.

Gray's advocacy of modus vivendi is perhaps best described as a form of loose political 'pragmatism', in which conflicts are settled by agreement among the parties according to what they are willing to accept in the circumstances. This might seem at first sight to be the perfect political expression of the pluralist point of view, since it

119

seems to rest on the widest possible interpretation of context, and to rely on no substantial moral principles that could themselves be seen as controversial constraints. Ironically, though, it is the very shapelessness of Gray's picture, its paucity of guiding principles, that make it objectionable on pluralist grounds. If the traditionalist version of pluralist particularism is too narrow, Gray's modus vivendi is, in a sense, too wide.

To see this, we should begin by asking the obvious question, how will such settlements be reached and what will be their terms? Gray is vague on this score, identifying modus vivendi with 'accommodation' and 'compromise' but saying little about what these mean. First, it is unclear just how and when the notion of modus vivendi is applicable. Its most obvious application is to relations between states or ways of life. But what about decision making at the level of the individual or questions concerning conflicts among goods rather than cultures? Does pluralism require that when goods conflict we should *always* compromise among them? If so, on what basis or in what way? Where compromise is necessary, is modus vivendi meant to *replace* appeals to tradition or only to operate when appeal to tradition breaks down? To none of these questions does Gray's work so far provide clear answers.

More significantly still, Gray's notion of modus vivendi is crucially ambiguous between two kinds of settlement: interest-based and moral. First, a modus vivendi is typically a compromise reached on the basis of a balance of interests or power between the parties. A major problem with this kind of agreement is identified by Rawls (1993) in the course of explaining why he seeks an overlapping consensus among rival conceptions of the good rather than an interest-based modus vivendi. The latter, he argues, is an inherently unstable basis for agreement (compared with agreements based on shared moral conviction), because the balance of interests on which it depends is (again to a greater extent than moral conviction) so easily changeable (ibid.: 146–9). Moreover, modus vivendi in its interest-based form should be rejected for distinctively pluralist reasons. First, by reducing the values in play to terms solely of self-interest, it denies value incommensurability. This is essentially the same objection as that which pluralists, including Gray himself, direct against preference-utilitarianism. Second, it is in the nature of interest-based modus vivendi that the kind of compromise reached will predominantly reflect the interests and values of the party that happens, for the present, to be the stronger.

FROM PLURALISM TO ANTI-UTOPIANISM

This kind of settlement is unlikely to do justice to the pluralist criteria of 'promotion of diversity', 'accommodation of reasonable disagreement', and practice of the 'pluralist virtues' which I develop in Chapters 6 to 8.

If, however, modus vivendi is to be conceived as an agreement on moral principle, like Rawls's overlapping consensus, then that will generate its own set of problems. What would serve as the settlement's moral basis or point of overlap? The values Gray recognizes as universal are intended merely to set wide limits to accommodation rather than to focus agreement, and are consequently far too thin to be of help here. Another possibility is implicit in the notion of modus vivendi itself, namely that the whole idea of pursuing accommodation rather than alternative responses to conflict presupposes a commitment to peace or stability. But that raises the question of whether peace or stability then becomes the kind of super-value which pluralists like Gray are supposed to reject. Gray sees this objection, and replies that the achievement of mutual accommodation is a common interest of all human beings – in effect part of the common horizon of universal values (2000b: 20, 25, 135–6). But that will clearly not do, since from a pluralist point of view human beings have many interests and values in common and some of these are incommensurable. Peace or stability is only one of these, and must be weighed against others, like justice and community, in cases of conflict. In some cases a pragmatic settlement for the sake of stability may indeed be appropriate, but in other cases other values are properly given priority, as in demands for independence by occupied or colonized peoples. Peaceful coexistence is an important human good, but the pluralist will deny that it must be bought at any price. When Gray advances modus vivendi as a universal goal, subject to no constraints except the thinnest of universal values, he effectively elevates peaceful coexistence to the status of a monist super-value.

Gray's recent anti-liberal pragmatism is no more in keeping with the pluralist outlook than his initial irrationalism or subsequent conservatism. His advocacy of modus vivendi, whether interpreted as a balance of interests or a moral goal, amounts precisely to the kind of universal privileging of a particular notion of the good that he attributes to liberal universalists. That in itself is not the problem. The promotion of some conception of the good is unavoidable in any political view – as pluralists know, some choice or ranking among values is inevitable. The problem is that Gray's

121

underlying conception of the good, despite his talk of 'accommodation' and 'compromise', is, ironically, narrow to the point of monism. That is because his modus vivendi is informed by no guiding principle except either self-interest or peace: one or the other consequently becomes the sole overriding consideration – an instance of monism. By contrast, the liberal good, as I shall argue in Part III, is both principled and capacious, accommodating moral and cultural diversity and reasonable disagreement about the good, and encouraging the kind of virtues necessary for any good life under pluralism.[9]

The notion of the good implicit in Gray's modus vivendi amounts either to an unstable and reductionist reliance on self-interest on one hand, or a narrow and unqualified appeal to peace or stability. Perhaps, though, the most fundamental problem with Gray's view, in all of its various phases, is his overestimation of the extent to which value pluralism implies moral disagreement. While it is true that the pluralist outlook requires us to acknowledge the reasonableness of disagreement about many things, that same outlook also generates reasons to agree about other things. In particular, pluralism gives us reason to agree on the principles implicit in its conceptual elements. Together these will ground a case for liberalism which goes beyond the particularist case constructed so far.

5.3 Beyond Particularism

I hope to have shown two things in this chapter so far. First, value pluralism does not support, indeed it refutes, the conservatism and pragmatism of Kekes and Gray. Second, pluralism does support a case for liberalism, at least within certain contexts. These arguments have been made within the framework of particularism. That is, they have assumed the truth of the claim, made by both Kekes and Gray, that the only reasons to choose among plural values are relative to particular contexts. The time has come to enter a strong qualification to that assumption, as foreshadowed in section 5.1, namely that pluralism also permits, indeed generates, considerations that apply across all contexts, or universally. These are the five principles identified earlier as implicit in the concept of pluralism itself (3.2). The second of these, namely recognition of value incommensurability, played a central role in the previous chapter, ruling out Marxism and anarchism as unrealistic or utopian doctrines (4.3.1). We have just seen that incommensurability has a similar effect on Gray's pragmatism. I now return to the first of these pluralist principles, namely respect for universal values. My argument in this section is that the requirement of respect for universal values strengthens the liberal reply to the anti-liberal pluralists in two ways. First, it confirms the pluralist opposition to conservatism and pragmatism. Second, it points towards a pluralist case for liberalism that is not merely particularist but universal in scope, the case to be pursued in Part III.

How does the principle of respect for universal values reveal the incoherence of Kekes's conservative pluralism (and that of Gray in his middle phase)? The answer is that it reminds us that pluralism must be distinguished from relativism, a distinction elided by the conservative emphasis on the authority of tradition. On the one hand, Kekes argues that local tradition is authoritative for reasoned choice among conflicting plural values, a position which is in effect strongly relativist. On the other hand he subscribes to value pluralism, which involves the rejection of strong relativism (1.1; 3.1.1; 3.3). While strong cultural relativism holds that culture or tradition is the sole source and arbiter of value, pluralists argue that there are universal values that, although incommensurable with one another and potentially conflicting, apply across cultural or traditional boundaries. Cultural relativism rules out the possibility of criticizing the practices of a culture on any grounds but its own. It follows from value pluralism, however, that cultures or traditions can be judged according to standards of universal scope. While cultural relativism is indeed a fundamentally conservative position, pluralism is not. Conservative pluralism is in effect caught between its conservative and pluralist elements, which tend to pull apart.

This contradiction between pluralist universalism and conservative relativism is clearly to be seen in Kekes. We saw earlier that he seems in several places to see local tradition as a final court of appeal in ethics (1993: 24–5, 77). This emphasis on the authority of tradition is most pronounced in his more recent work, where he makes explicit his political conservatism. 'The question pluralists must answer, therefore, is what kind of basis for ranking the comparative importance of conflicting values could there be ...? Pluralists answer that question by appealing to traditions' (1998: 63). 'Conflicts of values are conflicts for people with their particular character and circumstances. How they resolve the conflicts depends

PLURALIST ARGUMENTS: LIBERAL AND ANTI-LIBERAL

on following the historical practices of the traditions in which they participate' (ibid.: 66–7). Again, it is hard to avoid the conclusion that this is a strongly relativist position, since if traditions are the ultimate source of guidance in ethics, then different traditions will count as separate and indefeasible authorities.

Elsewhere, however, Kekes qualifies the claims of tradition and repudiates relativism. In *The Morality of Pluralism*, for example, he concedes that pluralism itself provides grounds for the reasoned criticism of traditions, of which one ground is especially important – 'how they compare with respect to the realization of primary values' (1993: 78). Recall that for Kekes 'primary values' are universal values (3.1.2). A tradition may thus be defective, from a pluralist point of view, to the extent that it fails adequately to protect or promote one of the basic universal values. Thus Kekes speaks of 'healthy' traditions in which the universal values are 'strongly held' in relation to the merely 'secondary' or local values peculiar to the particular tradition. Conversely, 'traditions can go wrong' when excessive weight is placed on local customs with the result that 'some minimum requirements of good lives are insufficiently protected' (ibid.: 84). Moreover, even if a tradition reaches a threshold of adequacy in its protection of a given universal value, it might still be open to criticism, in that area, by comparison with another tradition that promotes that value more fully (ibid.: 82).[10]

Even in *A Case for Conservatism*, where Kekes's traditionalist politics come to the fore, he makes the same concession to the fallibility of traditions, and on the same pluralist ground. 'Traditions may be vicious, destructive, stultifying, nay-saying, and thus not conducive to good lives. . . . Traditions that violate the minimum requirements of human nature are [under desirable political arrangements] prohibited' (1998: 40). Traditional practices may legitimately be judged according to 'the external standard established by the minimum requirements of all good lives and formulated on the universal level of morality' (ibid.: 194). This pluralist view is expressly contrasted with the view of relativists, for whom 'there are no external standards to which moral evaluation across different societies could appeal' (ibid.: 193).

The question now arises, if Kekes allows that traditions can be criticized on the basis of external, universal standards, and so are not morally authoritative, then what remains of his conservative 'traditionalism'? How is his position to be distinguished from that

124

of liberals, for example, who are willing to accept local traditions as a starting point, but who will then subject those traditions to critical scrutiny on the ground of universal principles such as human rights?

By way of reply, Kekes could point to what he identifies as a second universal standard implied by or consistent with pluralism. This is that 'no good society can do without some system of secondary values [i.e. local traditions] and variable conventions, even if the constituents of the system vary from society to society' (ibid.: 196). People can live good lives only in societies which maintain a rich and healthy set of local values and conventions. That is because these constitute an 'evaluative background' within which people can find the 'moral identity' that frames their conception of the good life. 'What is universal and objective is the necessity of *having* a moral identity' (ibid.: 197). It follows, says Kekes, that 'a society that protects its moral identity is morally preferable to one that does not'. Moreover, 'a society that offers more protection, extending to more areas of life, is morally preferable to one that offers less protection and of fewer areas' (ibid.). The moral identity of a society may be justifiably criticized and changed where there are 'good reasons' for criticism and change. But there is 'always a presumption' that attacks on the moral identity of a society will not be reasonable, since most such attacks are not reasoned objections but mere unreasonable violations (ibid.: 198). In short, existing social traditions may be criticized legitimately on the basis of universal standards, but the onus of proof should fall on the critic, who must overcome a presumption in favour of the current practice.

This does seem a reasonable view, but it amounts to no more than a very weak version of 'traditionalism'. Liberals too could allow a presumption in favour of existing traditions that can be defeated by 'good reasons' for change. Even those liberals most hostile to the claims of tradition, like Mill, could hold this view. The rub is obviously in what counts as a 'good reason'. Once Kekes concedes that traditions may be questioned for reasons that do not themselves depend on particular traditions but are universal in scope, he severely limits the force of 'traditionalism'. Yet he is obliged to make that concession because of his pluralist starting point. The commitment to pluralism not only fails to support conservative politics, it positively runs counter to that end. If values are plural in the sense Kekes accepts, then tradition cannot have the ethical authority he needs to claim for it in order to reject liberalism and endorse conservatism.

The same tension between pluralism and traditionalism is on view in Gray's work during his conservative period. In this period he sometimes emphasizes his conservative traditionalism, at other times his pluralist universalism, without ever considering that the one might undercut the other. The traditionalist and relativist side is apparent, for example, in his insistence on the incommensurability of 'forms of life' (cultures or traditions). This follows, he believes, from the incommensurability of values that is the central feature of value pluralism. The irreducible diversity of human goods becomes, Gray writes, 'an irreducible diversity of worthwhile forms of life whose goodness is not commensurable by any universal standard' (1995a: 143). The indeterminacy of choice among such forms of life 'can be closed off, provisionally at any rate, only by a groundless commitment to one among the forms of life with which we are acquainted' (ibid.: 142). From this Gray concludes that liberalism is just one form of life among others, one that some people happen to be committed to while others are not. Those who are not so committed cannot be shown to be mistaken. If cultures are wholly incommensurable, then, like incommensurable goods, they cannot be evaluated except on their own terms. This amounts to saying that different cultures represent different measures or sources of value, a position indistinguishable from a strong form of relativism: 'It is forms of life or activity that are ultimately and intrinsically valuable' (1993b: 309).

Elsewhere, however, Gray endorses Berlin's view that value pluralism refers to a plurality of values that include universal values. 'The diversity of ultimate values, great as it is, is not infinite; it is bounded by the limits of human nature. "Incompatible these ends may be; but their variety cannot be unlimited, for the nature of men, however various and subject to change, must possess some generic character if it is to be called human at all" ' (ibid.: 291). In this passage Gray is quoting from an essay in which Berlin explicitly distinguishes pluralism from relativism. Different cultures, Berlin argues in the passage from which the quote is taken, express different combinations (and interpretations) of the fundamental human ends. Cultural variety, consequently, 'does not entail relativism of values, only the notion of a plurality of values not structured hierarchically' (Berlin, 1992a: 80). Gray does not disagree. 'As to generic human goods, it may be that there are virtues or excellences that, however various their expressions in different forms of life, are not culture-specific' (1993b: 292).

FROM PLURALISM TO ANTI-UTOPIANISM

But if particular forms of life are instantiations of generic human values, then they cannot be, as Gray supposes them to be for the purposes of his anti-liberal traditionalism, wholly incommensurable and therefore impervious to criticism from outside. For they are partly commensurated by the generic values that are common to all forms of human flourishing. If forms of life are not wholly incommensurable then they are not immune to comparison and rational critique. It can then be asked whether and to what extent a given form of life expresses any of the common ends of humanity. We can ask how far a given culture is successful in absolute terms, and also how it compares to the performance of other cultures. One culture may do better than another because it acknowledges a universal value that the other neglects completely, or because it expresses that value more fully. Perhaps both pursue the same basic goods but one has achieved a more satisfactory balance where those goods conflict. It may be, again, that one culture can learn from another's unfamiliar interpretation of an otherwise shared good, an interpretation which suggests a deeper understanding of the good. Tradition or culture cannot, on this view, provide unassailable moral authority. The conclusions of Gray's conservative phase are at odds with his pluralist premise.[11]

The same general point undercuts Gray's pragmatism too. When he advocates modus vivendi as the only legitimate solution to the conflict of plural values, he seems to conceive this principally as a settlement among rival ways of life. Liberal ways of life, on this view, must compromise with non-liberal. What this ignores is the possibility that not all ways of life have equal claims, on a pluralist view, to accommodation. If it is values that must be accommodated rather than ways of life, then some ways of life may have better title than others to be accepted as desirable because they are themselves more accommodating of a diversity of values. In the next two chapters I shall argue that this is indeed true of liberal political regimes: they have superior claims to be seen as accommodating a diversity of values and conceptions of the good. The principle of respect for universal values takes us one step towards that conclusion by opening up the possibility that from a pluralist point of view not all ways of life are on a moral par. As the other pluralist principles come into play, the case is increasingly strengthened.

Pluralism rules out Kekes's conservatism and Gray's pragmatism along with the utopian doctrines discussed in Chapter 4. I now turn to the second issue announced at the start of this section, the

127

possibility of a pluralist case for liberalism that goes beyond the contextual line of justification developed earlier. Even the broader, Razian form of contextual argument is not wholly satisfactory from either the point of view of the critics of liberalism or that of liberals themselves. Critics can reasonably ask how it is that liberalism is uniquely justified by the conditions described. They can argue that Constant and Raz appeal to contexts that are, once again, too wide to single out liberal values as the only ones appropriate. This is an objection raised by Gray. Within the circumstances of modern technology and commerce, Gray argues, liberal societies are not the only ones capable of flourishing. 'The East Asian countries', such as Singapore, China and even Japan, provide examples of social and political systems that have proved highly successful in contemporary conditions, yet which 'remain deeply resistant to Western values' (1995b: 83). Gray thus allows that a contextualist argument for the superiority of liberalism is compatible with pluralism and therefore possible in principle, but then immediately disallows such an argument in practice. Or more precisely, he denies that any existing context can give rise to a case for liberalism, except the context of actually existing liberal traditions.

Moreover, Razian contextualism will not be completely satisfactory to many liberals either, since it still falls short of the traditional liberal aspiration to universality. This is not just a matter of nostalgia for a lost campaign or abandoned mission. It is a deep, indeed defining point of principle for liberals that the moral claims of the human individual should not depend on accidents of social and economic circumstances. Such a commitment is reflected in the concern of social liberals like Rawls to compensate people for economic and social disadvantage resulting from accidents of natural endowment or social circumstances, factors 'that seem arbitrary from a moral point of view' (Rawls, 1971: 15). The same basic concern is present in the liberal tradition more generally in the form of the classical liberal defence of human rights irrespective of cultural or political context. Raz's argument, although broader in scope than other particularist approaches, still allows the most fundamental claims of individual persons to be conditional on social and economic contingencies. It is true of course that under pre-modern conditions the privileging of personal autonomy was unheard of and impracticable. But Raz's view implies that it would have been unjustified as well, since not supported by the appropriate conditions. Yet the liberal belief is surely that the promotion of

128

FROM PLURALISM TO ANTI-UTOPIANISM

autonomy is always justified in principle, even if not always possible in practice, because of the respect due to the capacities of the human individual. Raz's defence of autonomy is not strong enough to permit this thought. Even his relatively capacious contextualism is too restrictive of the liberal ideal.

There are thus limits to the extent to which liberals can adequately respond to the anti-liberal critique by way of a particularist approach. How, then, can they construct a more universal case? Again, the answer is, by working out the implications of the general principles implicit in value pluralism itself. We have begun this task. In this chapter and the previous one, I have invoked the principles of respect for universal values and for the incommensurability of values to rule out a series of anti-liberal views: Marxism, anarchism, conservatism and pragmatism. The next step is to begin constructing a positive justification for liberalism itself. For this purpose I shall have to bring into play the other general principles implied by pluralism. This is my goal in Part III.

Notes

1. 'Deference to local tradition' suggests an affinity between Kekes's position and that of 'strong' communitarians, such as Alasdair MacIntyre (1985, 1988) and Michael Sandel (1982, 1996), who similarly see local tradition as morally authoritative. My conclusions in Kekes's case are intended to apply to these views too.
2. This is implicitly conceded by Kekes in his original examination of value pluralism, where he allows that the liberal commitment to overriding values 'is not peculiar to liberalism. All political ideologies must regard *some* values as overriding, otherwise they would cease to be ideologies, and it is this very fact that makes them incompatible with pluralism' (1993: 211). Kekes makes the same point in his later critique of liberalism, this time explicitly listing conservatism among the ideologies that pluralism rules out (1997: 179). When it comes to his positive case for conservatism, however, the point is quietly dropped, with no explanation of why it ceases to apply (1998). In the absence of such an explanation it is hard to avoid concluding that so far as liberalism is incompatible with pluralism on the ground of its promoting an absolute or general ranking of values independent of context, precisely the same criticism may be made of conservatism.
3. For a natural law treatment of the problem of ranking incommensurables,

PLURALIST ARGUMENTS: LIBERAL AND ANTI-LIBERAL

see John Finnis (1980). Finnis lists seven 'basic values' or goods for human beings: life, knowledge, play, aesthetic experience, sociability (friendship), practical reasonableness, religion (ibid.: 86–9). (Compare this list with those given by Kekes and Nussbaum: 3.1.2 above.) Of the relations among these goods he writes: 'Each is fundamental. None is more fundamental than any of the others, for each can reasonably be focused upon, and each, when focused upon, claims a priority of value. Hence there is no objective priority of value amongst them' (ibid.: 93). This is a good description of values as incommensurable, demonstrating a considerable overlap between natural law and value pluralism. But how can we choose rationally among these values? Finnis answers: 'Of course, each one of us can reasonably *choose* to treat one or some of the values as of more importance in *his* life . . . Each of us has a subjective order of priority amongst the basic values . . . But one's reasons for choosing the particular ranking that one does are reasons that properly relate to one's temperament, upbringing, capacities, and opportunities, not to differences of rank of intrinsic value between the basic values' (ibid.: 93–4). For Finnis (in this passage at any rate), the only reasons we have to choose among conflicting incommensurables are subjective or personal. Another account of natural law which explicitly presents human goods as incommensurable can be found in Grisez (1970: Chapter 6).

4. For the distinction between a case for liberalism that is compatible with value pluralism and a case for liberalism that is based on value pluralism, see Crowder (1996), a rejoinder to Berlin and Williams (1994). I explain the background to this exchange in the Preface to this book.

5. For critical discussion of Gray, see Blokland (1999), Colls (1998), Crowder (1998, 1999), Katznelson (1994), Legutko (1994), Lukes (1994), Weinstock (1998).

6. Gray has been criticized for distorting or failing adequately to render Berlin's own intentions (Walzer, 1995). But these criticisms are beside the point, since Gray makes it clear that his main interest in Berlin's ideas is to follow out their logical conclusions, as he sees them, rather than faithfully to reproduce Berlin's 'own voice' (Gray, 1995a: 150–1).

7. According to one commentator, the role of the political philosopher is limited even more severely in those of Gray's books (1995b and 1997) where he rejects the universalist rationality of 'the Enlightenment project'. 'What remains is not so much our thinking and reasoning – difficult to do outside our own enlightened minds – as a sort of opening of our holistic pores to what is around us, a state of mind expressed for Gray in Heidegger's idea of "releasement" – *Gelassenheit*' (Colls, 1998: 64).

8. In this respect Gray's position bears a close resemblance to that of Rorty (1989, 1991). Gray agrees with what he sees as 'the inexorable implication of Rorty's work', namely 'that liberal cultures are only one sort of human culture among many, and can claim no privileged rational authority for

130

FROM PLURALISM TO ANTI-UTOPIANISM

themselves'. But he goes on to criticize Rorty for inconsistently trying to combine such a view with a defence of human rights. 'Rorty cannot take a full-bloodedly particularist and historicist view of liberal culture and at the same time make the standard liberal–imperialist claim that Western "cultures of rights" are superior to all others' (1995c: 5).

9. My rejection of Gray's modus vivendi position is not meant to deny an important role for compromise under value pluralism. But this will be compromise within more defined limits, ironically more accommodating of plural values, than those allowed by Gray; see 9.4 below.

10. In *The Morality of Pluralism*, Kekes points to several other pluralist grounds for criticising traditions from the outside, in addition to the appeal to universal values (1993: 88–9).

11. Gray now seems to accept this point himself, although not the political implications I draw from it: 'That some values are incommensurable does not mean that all ways of life have the same value. The bottom line for value pluralism is the diversity of goods and evils, not of ways of life. Different ways of life can be more or less successful in achieving universal goods, mitigating universal evils and in resolving conflicts among them' (2000b: 8–9). Also, it is not only on the ground of universal values that Gray's pluralism undermines his conservatism. Pluralism also involves, as we have seen, the recognition of value incommensurability and its implications (Chapter 4). From a pluralist point of view, therefore, different cultures may be critically compared as to their capacity for this kind of recognition. One may have a livelier or deeper appreciation of the incommensurability of values than another, a stronger sense of loss and regret where plural values conflict and force hard choices. The same possibility of inter-cultural critical comparison is raised, as we shall see, by the other general principles implied by pluralism: promotion of diversity, accommodation of reasonable disagreement about the good, and practice of the pluralist virtues, including personal autonomy. In all these ways it is part of a genuine and deep appreciation of the pluralist point of view that local traditions are not ultimate moral authorities but are subject to reasoned criticism. Once again, the local chauvinism defended by Gray is not compatible with the pluralist outlook.

PART III

From Pluralism to Liberalism

CHAPTER 6

From Pluralism to Liberalism I: Diversity

The encounter with anti-liberal pluralism has shown not only that a case for liberalism is compatible with value pluralism, but also that pluralism itself can provide a foundation for liberalism. So far as pluralism directs our attention to context, the context in question may be one that favours a distinctively liberal ranking of goods. We have also seen, however, the limitations of this particularist way of arguing for liberalism. The question then arises, might pluralism generate a case for liberalism that is not merely particularist but universal? I have already indicated the possibility of such a case: pluralism itself implies a set of normative criteria for rational choice among competing values. So far I have noted two of these: respect for universal values, and recognition of the imperfectibility of human life implied by value incommensurability. These two principles, I have argued, together rule out from a pluralist perspective certain rivals to liberalism, namely utopian, conservative and pragmatic forms of politics. But they do not yet amount to a positive justification of liberalism.

The construction of such a universal justification of liberalism on the basis of value pluralism is the task I now commence. In this chapter I set out the first of my three principal arguments from pluralism to liberalism, namely an argument based on the value of 'diversity'. I argue that the list of general principles implied by pluralism includes an ethic of diversity, corresponding in particular to the pluralist conception of the plurality of goods. Roughly speaking, pluralist diversity commits us to promoting as wide a

135

range of values as possible. That ethic is in turn best achieved under liberalism. Pluralism thus gives us a reason to justify liberalism along approximately neutralist lines as amounting less to a substantive conception of the good than to a specifically political settlement accommodating the peaceful coexistence of as wide a range of goods as possible.[1]

I begin by outlining the basic argument before dividing it into two main steps: the first from value pluralism to the promotion of diversity, the second from diversity to liberalism. In the first step I argue that the diversity commended by pluralism is not simply a matter of maximizing quantities of value, but also involves seeking coherence among values. Diversity thus involves a balance between 'multiplicity' and 'coherence' in the promotion of plural goods. In so doing, it rules out political forms based on narrow accounts of the good (e.g. conservative traditionalism) on one hand, and excessively open-ended approaches (e.g. postmodernism) on the other. In the second step I argue that the pluralist balance between multiplicity and coherence is best achieved by the liberal combination of freedom and order. I shall develop these claims by testing them against a series of objections.

6.1 Pluralism, Diversity and Liberal Neutrality

The basic argument from pluralism to liberalism by way of state neutrality is hinted at in a brief passage by Bernard Williams, who is supporting Berlin's claim that there is a link between pluralism and liberalism: 'If there are many and competing values, then the greater the extent to which a society tends to be single-valued, the more genuine values it neglects or suppresses. More, to this extent, must mean better' (1980: xvii). To recognize the truth of pluralism is to recognize, and endorse, the great multiplicity and diversity of human values. A social system will be desirable to the extent that it honours that multiplicity and diversity, likewise a political system. The political form that best accommodates the diversity of human values, it may then be argued, is liberalism. This is not quite the way that Berlin himself argues (as we saw in Chapter 4), but it is consistent with the spirit of his position. Does this argument provide a stronger support for that position than Berlin's own case? I think it does.

Williams leaves his hint undeveloped, but it suggests an

DIVERSITY

argument in two steps: first from pluralism to what may be called an 'ethic of diversity', second from diversity to liberalism. The first step goes as follows. To accept value pluralism is to accept that there are universal goods and that these are many and incommensurable. To accept that there are plural and incommensurable goods is not merely to allow that there are such goods but to endorse them, and to endorse them on an equal basis with one another. That is because, from the pluralist point of view, the universal goods are not merely values that, a matter of fact, some people happen to hold. Rather, the pluralist sees them as goods that contribute to human flourishing objectively (3.1.1). Since pluralists are committed to human flourishing, they must be committed to promoting the various goods that contribute to that flourishing. Furthermore, the pluralist must endorse all such goods equally, in the sense that they have an equal claim on us until we are presented with a particular context in which we must choose among them. The plural goods are incommensurable, and so cannot be said to be equal according to any measure, but they are, as Berlin puts it, 'equally ultimate' (1969: 168). It follows that the pluralist outlook commits us to valuing the full range of human goods. To acknowledge the truth of value pluralism is to acknowledge a multiplicity of genuine goods, of diverse natures, not merely ethical mistakes with which it is nevertheless best not to interfere. It is to acknowledge a duty to promote those goods so far as possible: a duty to promote diversity.

The second step in the argument is from diversity to liberalism: the promotion of diversity is best accommodated by a liberal political order. At this point the pluralist case for liberalism takes a neutralist form. We saw in Chapter 2 that one of the historic goals of liberalism was to provide a political framework for the peaceful pursuit of diverse goods, orginally a diversity of religious faiths, now a diversity of values and ways of life more generally. In recent times this line of liberal justification has taken the form of liberal neutrality. On this view a liberal political order is no more than the minimal framework of principles necessary to permit or enable individuals and groups to pursue divergent ways of life without coming into violent collision. In performing this function liberalism aspires to neutrality in two senses. First, the liberal state tries to be even-handed in its impact on different ways of life, avoiding promoting any particular conception of the good, enforcing only the minimal or 'procedural' framework necessary to maintain order among diverse ways of life. Second, the liberal framework itself is in

137

principle defined without reference to any particular conception of the good. Liberal policy should thus be justified by neutral reasons. We saw that it is doubtful whether any form of liberalism can be wholly neutral, either in impact or reasons. However, we also saw that even if that is true, it may still be argued that liberalism is at least 'approximately' neutral, that is, more neutral or accommodating than the alternative political forms (2.2.1).

In pluralist terms liberal neutrality, even if only approximate, provides the best political framework because it leaves more space for the flourishing of multiple and diverse goods than any known or realistically imagined alternative. That is true even though a liberal order involves a certain ranking of goods, a ranking that necessarily excludes alternative rankings, thus placing limits on the sheer multiplicity of values that can be accommodated within a liberal society. Any political order involves some prioritization of goods, since the range and diversity of human values is such that not all genuine goods can be realized within the same social space. The pluralist ethic of diversity can realistically require no more than that the political ranking endorsed by a given society be as accommodating to diversity as possible in the circumstances and more accommodating than the alternatives. Liberals should concede that liberalism is not unlimited in its capacity to accommodate diversity, but they can plausibly argue that the diversity ethic is more fully satisfied by liberal principles and institutions than by any other.

6.2 From Pluralism to Diversity

Having set out the basic lines of the neutrality argument, I shall now develop it by testing it against a number of possible and actual objections. I start with an objection that might be directed against the first of the two steps in the argument. I have argued that value pluralism implies an 'ethic of diversity' such that a political system is desirable to the extent that it permits or enables the promotion, to the greatest extent possible in the circumstances, of the full range of human values. Does this not amount to a *maximization* ethic of the kind that is incompatible with the value-pluralist approach to practical reasoning? As we saw in Chapter 3, the pluralist emphasis on the incommensurability of values militates against maximization accounts of practical reasoning, such as classical utilitarianism, since

138

DIVERSITY

the latter rely on the possibility of identifying a common denominator which then becomes the unit of maximization (3.1.3). The pluralist objection to this procedure is, we saw, that no such unit can be found that genuinely commensurates all distinct values. An ethic that consisted merely in maximizing the number of values to be pursued would be hard to distinguish from other maximization ethics. The only difference would be its distinctive account of the common denominator as the notion of a value or good rather than, say, utility. Such an ethic would be in conflict with the fundamental pluralist injunction to attend to the distinctiveness of values.

This would be a serious problem if the ethic of diversity I am proposing amounted merely to an injunction to promote 'more rather than fewer' values or 'as many as possible'. But this kind of quantitative consideration – how many values? – is only one aspect of what I have in mind. The maximizing dimension of the ethic of diversity must be supplemented by a second kind of consideration, that of balance or coherence among the values to be promoted. Sheer multiplication of different goods must be tempered by attention to the content of those goods and to the relations among them, since some may impede others. The diversity implied by pluralism is therefore best understood as involving both a quantitative and a qualitative element, both a requirement of a generous range of values and a requirement that the values within that range should be tolerably coherent with one another. The ethic of diversity embraces both 'multiplicity' and 'coherence'.

To explain this more fully, let me start with the notions of sheer multiplicity and maximization. Williams's remark was that 'more is better' to the extent that the more single-valued a society is, the more genuine values it must neglect or suppress. Prima facie, the pluralist point of view implies that societies are less desirable the more narrowly they confine the range of goods that their people can pursue, and conversely that societies are more desirable to the extent that they expand that range. This point is endorsed by Kekes, who argues that good lives are possible only within traditions that 'make available a sufficiently rich supply of possibilities from which we may select some as choiceworthy' (1993: 28). Kekes goes on:

> If the range is too narrow, it fails to satisfy normal human aspirations. Good lives should have some scope for the appreciation of beauty, playfulness, and nonutilitarian rela-

139

> tionships, as well as for tackling difficult projects that require hard work, discipline, and self-control. Lives involving single-minded concentration on a very narrow range of values will be impoverished. (ibid.: 97)

From the point of view of value pluralism, which by definition involves a genuine appreciation of the fact that a wide range of values contributes to the good life for human beings, a society or way of life that focuses on only one or a few of those values to the exclusion of others cannot be a satisfactory society or way of life.[2]

If a prima facie requirement for the good society is that the society accommodate more rather than fewer goods, then that provides us with another critical standard for judging the adequacy of forms of politics. We have already seen that regimes can be open to criticism from a pluralist point of view if they fail to respect the universal goods or to give due recognition to value incommensurability. In the principle that, prima facie, societies are more desirable in proportion to the range of goods they promote, we have a further benchmark with which to separate acceptable political positions from unacceptable. Thus, we can rule out, from a pluralist point of view, those political forms that place such great weight on one or a few values that all others are systematically sacrificed or downgraded. There are, of course, several candidates for this kind of judgement, both from the left and the right wings of political ideology. I have already argued against Kekes's traditionalism and Gray's pragmatism along these lines. This is also Berlin's fundamental point when he inveighs against 'the great, disciplined, authoritarian structures' of Plato, Hegel and Marx, in which a particular ideal is presented with such strength that the violent suppression of alternatives seems a small price to pay (1969: 171). Berlin's emphasis tends to be on those views that elevate some conception of the common good or social justice to the detriment of personal liberty and freedom of choice, as in the two great mid-twentieth-century rivals to liberalism, state communism and fascism. But he also allows that individual liberty itself can be fetishized to a point where it too becomes a narrow and exclusive religion, excluding the proper recognition of other values, as in the extreme laissez-faire liberalism of the mid-nineteenth century (ibid.: xlvi). In recent times one might single out along similar lines the stronger forms of communitarianism, such as that of MacIntyre (1985, 1988), which seek a level of moral consensus that

DIVERSITY

presupposes something akin to pre-Reformation religious ortho-doxy. At any rate, although particular cases may be contestable, the general principle is clear that political views resting on relatively narrow conceptions of the good are likely to conflict with the outlook of pluralism.

Does it follow, however, that because we accept that relatively narrow views should be ruled out, we must accept the converse, that views at the wider end of the scale must always be superior? Is more *always* better? I believe the answer is, no. Although the idea of maximizing the range of available goods is a helpful first step towards defining the pluralist ideal of diversity, it is no more than a first step. Pluralist diversity raises not only quantitative but also qualitative considerations.

The notion of maximization needs to be qualified, for three reasons. The first of these has already been discussed, namely that a pluralist ethic cannot be a purely maximization ethic because maximization implies commensuration. Second, maximization can at best refer to the maximum range of values possible in the circumstances, and under no circumstances can a society accom-modate more than part of the full range of values known to human experience. To pursue one set of goods or excellences is often to close off, necessarily, the possibility of another set. This is true both in the life of an individual person and within the life of a society. As Gray writes: 'A priest cannot, compatibly with his avocation, adopt the virtues of a soldier, or a nun the excellences of a courtesan' (1993b: 301). Societies, too, develop in ways that permit or celebrate some ways of life and rule out others: 'The life of a medieval troubador could not be lived in ancient Egypt any more than the life of a temple courtesan could be lived in medieval Christendom' (ibid.: 1993b: 293). We cannot have everything; there is simply not enough 'space' within the life of an individual or a society to enjoy all the goods known to human experience. Choices must therefore be made, and choices among incommensurables involve qualitative considerations – which goods should we privilege, fitting within what background conception of the good? – that cannot be captured by a purely maximizing criterion.

Third, even within the limits of what is strictly possible, some individuals and societies may pursue *too many* different goods. As Kekes observes, there are 'lives that are too scattered. Projects are begun and then discontinued, enthusiasms ebb and flow, the attractions of many possibilities are perceived but too few of them

141

FROM PLURALISM TO LIBERALISM

are realized' (1993: 97–8). The problem with such lives is the very opposite of excessive narrowness. 'In such lives there are many values, but between their favorable evaluation and realization come the distractions of other values whose realization also recedes for the same reason' (ibid.: 98). Once again, merely to pursue as many values as possible is inadequate as an interpretation of pluralist diversity. First, the more values we pursue the greater the chances are that the realization of some will get in the way of others, so that to insist on chasing a very wide range of options may be self-defeating. Second, the pluralist point of view requires that we take values seriously as distinct goods worthy of concern even in those circumstances where we must choose against them. A life in which we pursue so many different goods that we do justice to none of them does not look like a good life from the pluralist viewpoint. Again, these points could be applied both to the life of an individual and to that of a society. Arguably, societies as well as individuals may dissipate their energies, cultural and ethical as well as physical, in a quest for too wide a range of goals.[3]

For these reasons the ideal of diversity implied by the pluralist outlook cannot be captured solely by the idea of maximizing a range of values. Once again there is a need for choices to be made, choices that require guidance of a qualitative nature. That is not to say that considerations of quantity are irrelevant to pluralist diversity, since the narrowing of available values to a very small range is clearly at variance with the pluralist outlook. Pluralist diversity implies support for at least some generous range of goods as available goals for individuals and societies. What exactly that range should be is, of course, not something that can be expressed in a precise formula applicable to all cases, but that does not undermine the basic principle. Beyond the initial requirement of a generous range, however, pluralist diversity cannot simply be about multiplication of options alone. What else, then?

The pluralist goal of a sheer range of values must be qualified by considerations of 'coherence' among those values. The available values must cohere with one another at least to the minimum degree necessary to avoid the problems identified above with sheer maximization. First, considerations of coherence fit with the pluralist approach to practical reasoning, which rejects abstract maximizing models in favour of a particularist process of weighing competing values in context. Second, the content of the values pursued must fit together within a horizon of real possibility for the

142

DIVERSITY

individual or society concerned, given the person's or the society's experience and identity. Third, in addition to being realistic prospects, the values in question should not be so widely scattered or fragmented that their pursuit can only be half-hearted or self-defeating. The goods should therefore cohere sufficiently that all may be taken seriously. Of course, there will always be conflict among different goods, such that in some situations one good can only be promoted at some cost to another. Indeed, the tension among competing goods may be a source of energy and inspiration. But there is a difference between a dynamic tension among competing goods and a situation where so many values of various kinds and weightings have some claim on our attention that dynamism is replaced by confusion and exhaustion.

Do considerations of coherence have any specifically political implications? In the same way that the quantification requirement of at least a generous range of goods rules out those political positions that take an excessively narrow view of value, might some other range of views not be ruled out by the qualitative requirement of coherence?

A leading candidate here, I believe, is the 'postmodernist' approach to politics. Postmodernism is strong on multiplicity, indeed to such an extent that it ignores coherence completely.[4] Despite the many difficulties in identifying what exactly such an approach entails, a common thread in postmodernist claims may be roughly traced as following from a sweeping rejection of universals across a range of fields and dimensions, including ethical universals such as those accepted by value pluralists. So far as there is a distinctively postmodernist outlook, it may be summed up in Jean-François Lyotard's formula, 'incredulity toward metanarratives', that is, scepticism about accounts of human history claiming the status of objective truth (1984: xxiv). Rather, postmodernists like Lyotard typically claim, such accounts should be regarded as no more than partial or relative narratives, possessing no better title to truth or authority than other such accounts. There are, simply, many different ethical perspectives, none privileged above others, all of fundamentally equal weight. So far as postmodernism can be said, consistently with its own relativism, to imply any sort of distinctive ethic of its own, that ethic is captured by Stephen White's phrase, 'fostering otherness', meaning the celebration of multiple ethical and cognitive perspectives and the witholding of a privileged status from any of them (1991: Chapter 7).

143

The extreme relativism of postmodernism makes it immediately objectionable from a pluralist point of view. First, pluralists must be concerned at the postmodernist rejection of universal values. Postmodernist writers often suppose they are making a case for respect for the otherness of groups and individuals who have been oppressed or silenced by dominant cognitive and ethical outlooks. But 'otherness' includes, on the face of it, the otherness of imperialists, racists and fascists: on what grounds can the postmodernist argue that these others should not be 'fostered' too? If the answer is that we ought to foster only those identities that themselves respect and foster the identities of others, then the postmodernist ethic turns out not to commend 'otherness' as such, but only a certain kind of otherness. How can that distinction be drawn without recourse to the kind of non-relative ethical judgement that postmodernists claim to have rejected? A consistent postmodernism thus suffers from the same problem as a consistent strong relativism: it leaves us no way of separating acceptable from objectionable identities and practices. From a pluralist point of view, postmodernism thus attracts the same objections as strong cultural relativism: it legitimates what cannot be legitimated, namely ethical and political schemes and practices that fail to respect universal values.

Second, postmodernism is objectionable from a pluralist point of view not only because it has no regard to the content of the values its logic endorses, but also because it has no regard to the relations among those values. Postmodernism, that is, leads to a problem of ethical incoherence. This is because some identities and practices, as well as being ethically objectionable, are in their very nature likely to collide destructively with others. Some identities or narratives, indeed, are identified precisely by their violent opposition to others – for example the religious and cultural fundamentalisms of the Balkans, Northern Ireland, the Middle East and elsewhere. An approach to politics that merely advocates the fostering of undifferentiated and unmediated 'otherness' is a hostage not only to ethically repugnant traditions, but also to the enmity of mutually hostile and destructive traditions. A politics that claimed to foster the otherness of both Jews and Nazis would be clearly, and disastrously, incoherent. Yet the logic of postmodernism, once one looks behind its superficially attractive celebration of multiplicity, gives us no principled way of rejecting such a self-destructive politics.

DIVERSITY

The excesses of postmodernism show, again, that the diversity implied by value pluralism cannot simply be a matter of promoting multiple values without regard to what these values are and how they relate to one another. The pursuit of many different values and ways of life will be futile and self-destructive unless contained by boundaries that are not wholly relative to the contending perspectives. The fostering of otherness or difference cannot by itself be an adequate criterion for public policy. Rather, it must be qualified for the sake of at least the minimal degree of coherence sufficient to make the realization of some generous range of values a real possibility – a possibility that is not undermined by its own excessive regard for multiplicity. The politics of value pluralism will therefore involve, as postmodernist politics cannot, a commitment not only to mutiplicity but to a set of limiting principles. That balance of commitments, I shall now argue, is best struck by liberalism.

6.3 From Diversity to Liberalism

The second step in the diversity argument is the claim that pluralist diversity is better accommodated by liberalism than by alternative political configurations. We have now seen that the diversity entailed by pluralism is not a matter of sheer multiplicity of goods alone, although a generous multiplicity is necessary. Rather, pluralist diversity requires a balanced combination of respect for many different goods and ways of life together with the containment or accommodation of those goods and ways of life within a coherent framework. That balance of commitments, we have seen, rules out certain prominent rivals to liberalism: on the one hand authoritarian, conservative and strong communitarian views which permit an undue narrowing of the range of values sanctioned by a society, and on the other hand postmodernist approaches that multiply values and ethical perspectives without regard to content or coherence. How does liberalism fare in this respect?

Liberalism has a strong claim to be seen as striking the required balance between multiplicity and coherence, and therefore to satisfying the requirements of pluralist diversity. As to multiplicity, the liberal emphasis on individual liberties and rights clears a private space for the pursuit of many different values, whether these are embodied in personal projects or collective ways of life. As

145

FROM PLURALISM TO LIBERALISM

Galston puts it:

> A narrow society is one in which only a small fraction of inhabitants can live their lives in a manner consistent with their flourishing and satisfaction. The rest will be pinched and stunted to some considerable degree. All else being equal, this is an undesirable situation, and one that is best avoided. To the maximum extent possible in human affairs, liberal societies do avoid this kind of pinching. This is an important element of their vindication as a superior mode of political organization. (1999a: 892)

On the score of coherence, those same liberal freedoms and rights place limits on the values, projects and ways of life that may legitimately be pursued within a society, limits designed to prevent these from coming into destructive collision with one another.

This account of liberalism as balancing multiplicity and coherence fits with the justificatory argument that liberalism is neutral among conceptions of the good, at any rate approximately neutral. Although not wholly neutral in impact or in the reasons offered for public policy, a liberal political order is as neutral as possible, and more neutral than the alternatives. As pointed out earlier, any society must make some choices as to what goods it will emphasize, since the range and diversity of human ends is such that not all of these can be accommodated within the space of a single society. The choice of one good will necessarily constrain or marginalize another. Given that such choices must be made, the pluralist outlook implies that the best choice is that which leaves room for the pursuit of the greatest possible diversity of values and ways of life. The liberal ideal of approximate neutrality is thus coextensive with the requirements of pluralist diversity.

To claim that liberalism is approximately neutral in these terms is to claim that it accommodates diversity better than rival political forms. On this point liberalism faces two broad lines of attack. On one hand, it might be claimed that liberalism sanctions too much multiplicity of value at the expense of coherence; on the other, that liberalism sacrifices legitimate multiplicity for the sake of its own vision of order.

The first sort of objection might be brought by monists of various kinds, both radical and conservative. Politically radical monists include most prominently the utopian thinkers discussed in Chapter 4, classical Marxists and anarchists, who look forward to the

146

DIVERSITY

complete transcendance of significant social conflict and the total harmonization of human values in a perfected society of the future. We have already seen why such a view must be rejected from a pluralist point of view, namely because of its failure to recognize the reality of value incommensurability with its implication that social and ethical harmony is an impossibility (4.3.1). This mistake is not made by liberalism, which attempts to contain or manage conflict rather than to transcend it (4.3.2).

What about forms of socialism other than Marxism and anarchism? Not all versions of socialism share the utopian hopes of these classic forms. Is pluralist diversity better served by liberalism than by socialism at large? This is a complex question, since there are so many varieties of socialism (and of liberalism). Here I can offer no more than the outline of a reply. I assume that at least one commitment that all socialist views have in common, and that distinguishes such views from those of liberals, is to public ownership or control of the economy (production, distribution and exchange). Liberals, by contrast, tend to favour private ownership or control, in effect a capitalist economic base. If that is so, I suggest that pluralist diversity will count in favour of liberalism in contrast with the stronger forms of socialism, that is, those that insist on a very extensive degree of public control. The Soviet-style command economy, at one end of the socialist spectrum, is manifestly inadequate as a vehicle for diversity. Such a system places all significant decisions, economic as well as political, in the hands of a few party bosses and bureaucrats, whose value preferences, often very narrow, dominate all others. The same cannot be said, however, of the other end of the spectrum, the mixed economy of Western social democrats. But then the latter advocate public control only as a qualification or correction to capitalism, rather than as an alternative. Social democracy is indistinguishable, at least for practical purposes, from 'social' or 'egalitarian' forms of liberalism.

My suggestion is that on the score of pluralist diversity the liberal endorsement of private property makes liberalism superior to most forms of socialism (and that those kinds of socialism of which this is not true are indistinguishable from species of liberalism). I have already argued that pluralist diversity is well served by liberal rights and liberties in general, since these create both spaces for the pursuit of multiple goods and ways of life and a coherent framework within which such pursuits can proceed effectively. We saw in Chapter 2 that among the most important liberal rights and

147

liberties are those connected with private property and the market. The liberties of property and the market open the way to the multiplication of different enterprises, both individual and collective, compared with the narrower prospects permitted by central planning. As Milton Friedman puts it:

> The characteristic feature of action through political channels is that it tends to require or enforce substantial conformity. The great advantage of the market, on the other hand, is that it permits wide diversity. It is, in political terms, a system of proportional representation. Each man can vote, as it were, for the color of tie he wants and get it; he does not have to see what color the majority wants and then, if he is in the minority, submit. (1982: 15)

Moreover, the market, it may be argued, generates not only multiplicity but also coherence. Friedrich Hayek, for example, describes the market as a 'catallaxy' or 'spontaneous order' (1967: 164). For Hayek, the market enables the unforced ordering of productive and service contributions from millions of individual agents, whose dispersed and often tacit knowledge cannot be comprehended by any central planning organization.[5] By effecting order as well as multiplicity, the capitalist market answers to the requirements of pluralist diversity in a way that socialist public control does not.

I should say immediately that the foregoing account of pluralist support for capitalism needs to be strongly qualified, since a wholly unrestricted capitalism (therefore laissez-faire liberalism) leads, as Berlin saw, to an anti-pluralist narrowness of its own. I shall argue this point later as part of my pluralist case for liberalism in a social or egalitarian form (9.2). My claim at present is that on the ground of diversity, the pluralist outlook supports private property and market capitalism at least as a *starting point* for economic distribution, in preference to the public control principle characteristic of socialism. For that reason pluralist diversity favours a broadly liberal form of politics as against a distinctively socialist one.

Returning now to the 'excessive multiplicity' objection to liberalism, another source of this might be a conservative view, according to which the liberal focus on individual rights and liberties is too weak to provide an adequate framework for ethical choice. Sense can be made of such choices, and reliable guidance

DIVERSITY

obtained, only by reference to a substantial local tradition. My reply to this objection was given in Chapter 5, where I argued that Kekes's conservative insistence on the authority of local tradition (also characteristic of Gray's middle period) rests on an unnecessarily narrow interpretation of the context required for pluralist choice, and is neglectful of universal norms. The coherence required by pluralist diversity cannot be identified with a rigid insistence on local tradition, and so the liberal answer to the question of coherence, namely the framework of individual rights and liberties, cannot be dismissed simply because it may come into conflict with tradition. Pluralist diversity requires that limits be placed on multiplicity, but existing traditions are not coextensive with those limits.

From a pluralist point of view, then, liberalism has the better of the argument with those who would claim that it fails diversity by over-emphasizing a multiplicity of goods at the expense of coherence. Rather it is the critics of liberalism on this score who are mistaken, either projecting a utopian harmony of values which is impossible (Marxism and anarchism), or constricting choice through extensive public ownership of control planning of the economy (stronger forms of socialism), or insisting on an adherence to local tradition which is excessively narrow (conservatism).

Might it then be objected that liberalism is inadequate for the opposite reason: that the liberal commitment to a coherent framework (of agreed and enforceable rights and duties) is too *restrictive* of multiplicity? One obvious source of this view is postmodernism, which I have already criticized on the score of incoherence (6.2) and need not discuss again. A second source is the pragmatism advocated by Gray. We saw in the last chapter how Gray interprets value pluralism as permitting only pragmatic settlements among incommensurable ways of life rather than any sort of politics that rests on a particular conception of the good. This is supposed to rule out liberal universalism as incompatible with pluralism. We also saw, however, that despite its initial appearance of capaciousness, Gray's notion of modus vivendi itself turns out to depend on either of two conceptions of the good, and that both of these are unacceptably narrow from a pluralist point of view. Gray's pragmatism assumes that conflicting values can either be commensurated in terms of self-interest or subordinated to the super-value of peaceful coexistence. Either way, settlements of this kind fail to satisfy the ethic of diversity implied by pluralism. But

149

what of the other side of Gray's case, his claim that pluralist diversity is curtailed by liberalism?

Gray argues that liberalism fails to maximize diversity because it accommodates different ways of life only at the cost of sanitizing them, reshaping them in its own image. 'Liberal societies tend to drive out non-liberal forms of life, to ghettoize or marginalize them, or to trivialize them'; traditional or non-liberal ways of life often 'linger on in liberal societies' only 'as shadows of their former selves' (Gray, 1995a: 154). A world in which liberalism is only one way of life among others, Gray argues, would be more diverse than one in which all cultures were subjected to liberal restraints, hence more desirable from a pluralist point of view. A pluralist could consistently be a defender of illiberal forms of life as contributing to an overall diversity of cultures. Pluralists need not, indeed should not, accept liberalism universally.

There are three possible replies liberal pluralists might make to Gray's objection. First, they might allow that liberalism does not maximize cultural diversity, but argue that this loss is outweighed by other benefits. Second, they might reply that even if liberalism does not maximize *cultural* diversity, it does maximally promote the diversity of values internal to cultures, which is the kind of diversity to which pluralists are principally committed. Third, they might argue that if liberalism maximizes the internal diversity of cultures, then it must maximize cultural diversity after all. (Note that I am not using 'maximize' here in a sense that involves commensuration, since 'diversity' is not a single, quantifiable good but rather the notion of a range of qualitatively distinct goods. To maximize diversity in the sense intended here is to promote the widest possible coherent range of goods.)

First, then, liberals could accept that liberalism does not maximize diversity, but argue that this is a small price to pay in return for the benefits. This is the line taken by Stephen Macedo, for example, who concedes that 'it would be wrong to identify the spread of liberalism with the maximization of diversity or the liberation of unlimited experimentation: liberal norms rule out many experiments in social organization, require a common subscription to liberal rights, and encourage a uniformity of tolerance, openness, and broad-mindedness' (1990: 278–9). Nevertheless, Macedo argues, the elimination of certain forms of diversity is a price worth paying for the extension of liberal community and peace. Liberals should admit that the extension of their form of

DIVERSITY

politics 'holds out the promise, or the threat, of making all the world like California' (ibid.: 278). But considering the alternatives, that fate is far from undesirable.

Compare this liberal trade-off with Gray's. In effect Gray recommends that some, indeed many people live under authoritarian regimes for the sake of (allegedly) greater cultural variety in the world as a whole. Some people, in other words, will have to pay the price necessary for others to enjoy a better world. Gray's view cheerfully violates the bedrock liberal principle of equal concern and respect: individual human beings possess a special moral worth that nothing else has, such that they should be treated, in Kant's phrase, always as ends, never as means only. Gray's is a view that allows some to be treated as mere instruments for the well-being of others. Indeed, the well-being we are talking about here seems to be chiefly aesthetic, since what is gained by the beneficiaries of Gray's more culturally various world, in return for the price paid by others, is nothing more than the pleasure generated by the agreeable prospect of cultural variety.

This reply to Gray is a strong one in liberal terms, but from a pluralist point of view it is question-begging. The reply presupposes a liberal commitment to equality of moral worth and equal concern and respect. But that begs the question of whether liberal values and principles ought to be privileged by pluralists. If we take pluralism seriously, then we must take seriously the ethic of diversity. And given the ethic of diversity, is Gray not right that liberalism can be no more than a part of that diversity?

The second reply to Gray therefore questions the sense of 'diversity' to which value pluralists are committed. Gray's claim that liberalism can be only part of a pluralist diversity might seem correct at first sight, since the world he advocates contains two sorts of society, liberal and non-liberal, while a liberal world would contain only liberal societies. But this is too simple. We should recall that 'diversity' in this connection is diversity in the specific sense implied by the outlook of value pluralism. Diversity in that sense has two key features which are crucial to the present discussion. First, as we have seen, pluralist diversity is not a matter of sheer multiplicity; it also contains a requirement of coherence (6.2). To promote diversity in the pluralist sense is not simply to multiply forms of life without regard to their content or to the relationship between them. The balanced outlook implied by pluralism, I have argued, is shared by liberalism. While liberal

151

constraints do place limits on cultures, they do so in order to enable the greatest possible range of cultures to coexist peacefully with others. Coexistence, on this view, is sought through a balance of multiplicity and coherence, rather than, as on Gray's account, through interest-driven bargaining or haphazard accommodation with no other end in view than stability at any price.

To the liberal solution there are two broad alternatives. The first is to bring all ways of life under a single non-liberal regime, an arrangement which Gray himself is unlikely to support as conducive to diversity. The second is to allow rival cultures to confront one another without any common political framework. The result of this latter opinion will be either the modus vivendi favoured by Gray, less accommodating than it appears, or open conflict in which the combatants are bound to be damaged and some may be extinguished altogether. In the absence of liberal restraints we should not expect a hundred flowers to bloom. This may be especially so in a modern world of increasing globalization, where different forms of life cannot simply avoid one another. The Balkan conflicts of the 1990s may serve as a dramatic recent example – in this respect echoing the wars of religion that gave birth to liberalism – of the potential of unrestricted multiplicity to destroy itself. On the other hand the historical record shows that there has never been a war between established liberal democracies (Doyle, 1983). A good case can thus be made for the view that the cause of pluralist diversity is better served by liberal containment, even recognizing the costs this brings, rather than by the unrestricted confrontation of different and often mutually hostile forms of life allowed by Gray's picture.

The second feature of pluralist diversity that bears on Gray's argument concerns the distinction, introduced in Chapter 3 and developed in Chapter 5, between pluralism at the level of cultures and pluralism at the level of values or goods (3.1.3, 5.3). Gray's claim that liberalism fails the test of diversity makes a crucial assumption, namely that the diversity to which pluralists are committed is solely or primarily a diversity of cultures or forms of life. That assumption in turn depends on the view that cultures are incommensurable in just the same way and to the same extent as values. It is because Gray sees cultures as incommensurable that he regards them as moral equals, as impervious to external criticism, and therefore as not subject to reasoned comparative evaluation or ranking. On this view pluralists must respect all cultures equally as incommensurable sites of value. A desirable world is one in which

152

DIVERSITY

there is maximum cultural diversity, regardless of the content of the cultures concerned. Liberal and non-liberal cultures amount merely to alternative ways of ranking human goods, none of these alternative rankings being inherently superior to others.

Gray's assumptions here are mistaken, and we have already seen why: they conflate value pluralism with strong cultural relativism (5.3). Cultures are not necessarily on a moral par from a pluralist point of view because they are not wholly incommensurable. Rather, they are partly commensurated by generic universal values. Recognition of and respect for universal values is mandated by the pluralist outlook, which thus acknowledges ethical criteria external to particular local cultures. It follows that on the pluralist view cultures are not wholly self-contained ethical authorities, but subject to comparison and critical evaluation in terms of universals. It follows further that the diversity to which pluralists are committed is not simply a diversity of cultures regardless of content. Pluralists cannot support a diversity of cultures which do not adquately respect universal values.

Moreover, pluralists cannot support a diversity of cultures which are not themselves internally diverse. That is because pluralism requires respect for a plurality of values, including universal values, in whichever culture or period they may be instantiated. The diversity to which pluralists are committed is therefore primarily a diversity of values or goods, which may or may not be adequately realized in particular cultures. To promote cultural diversity without regard to cultural content is to collapse the pluralist outlook into cultural relativism. A diversity of monistic cultures is intelligibly desirable from a relativist point of view, according to which evaluation is wholly internal to the cultures concerned. But a diversity of monistic cultures is not necessarily desirable from a pluralist perspective – or at any rate, a pluralist must rank a diversity of internally monistic cultures lower in value than a diversity of internally diverse cultures. It is not that cultural diversity has no value for pluralists. Rather, the value of cultural diversity follows as a consequence from the value of the diversity of goods. Pluralists, that is, will promote cultural diversity so far as it serves to increase the diversity of goods, including universal goods. The primary concern of the pluralist is to promote a diversity of values; cultural diversity is a secondary and contingent goal.

So, even if it were conceded that liberalism did not, on balance, maximize *cultural* diversity, it could still be argued that liberalism does maximize the kind of diversity commended by value pluralists, namely diversity of *goods* (which may themselves be complex). Cultures, or particular configurations of goods, are plural only in consequence of the plurality of their constituent values. Consequently, as we have seen, value pluralists may justifiably value some cultures more than others, namely those characterized by a greater diversity of goods. And it is precisely the opening up of traditional cultures to the possibility of the legitimate pursuit of a more diverse range of goods that has been the historical effect of liberalism. Even if it were true that liberalism did not maximize the diversity of cultures, it could still be argued that liberalism increases the diversity of goods within cultures and that this is what is most important from a value-pluralist point of view.

There is a third liberal response to Gray worth considering, however. This is that the diversity of values internal to cultures that is promoted by liberalism is in turn likely to lead to greater diversity *among* cultures. Liberalism, that is, maximizes cultural diversity after all. This is explained by David Johnston as follows:

> Diversity in individuals' projects and values – or conceptions of the good – will tend to generate diverse social worlds. Even if it should happen that the same set of conceptions of the good were held by the members of two different liberal societies at a given time, the openness of liberal societies to diversity would tend to pull the two societies in different directions over time. As individuals within the two societies move toward different projects and values, they would begin to act differently in their efforts to pursue those projects and to realize their values. As a result, the two societies would diverge. They would come to be quite different sorts of social worlds, even if both societies remained equally liberal. (1994: 27)

Because of their internal diversity, liberal societies will develop along different lines resulting in increased external diversity. A world composed entirely of liberal societies would still be a world in which societies are very different from one another. California is (whether mercifully or not) only one expression of liberalism among others, not the only one.

Even on the score of cultural diversity there is therefore more to be said for liberalism than Gray (or Macedo, for that matter) allows. Gray's argument that liberal universalism leads to a net reduction of

DIVERSITY

cultural diversity (compared with a partly non-liberal world) depends not only on a mistaken conception of pluralist diversity, but also on some questionable empirical assumptions. Part of what he seems to have in mind is the 'cultural globalization' thesis in which cultural uniformity is brought about by the forces of global market capitalism, of which liberalism is the ideological expression (Barber, 1995; Gray, 1998). This assumes, first, that liberalism is no more than the political arm of capitalism. Certainly the two have been linked historically and conceptually, but they are not invariable allies, as shown by the arguments of social or egalitarian liberals like Rawls, Ronald Dworkin and others. Many of the most significant qualifications to capitalism, including the welfare state and Keynesian planning, have been liberal in inspiration. Second, Gray's argument assumes that the phenomenon of capitalist globalization tends invariably to cultural homogenization. But the literature on the cultural effects of globalization is divided on this question, some commentators agreeing with Gray while others 'have linked globalization with enduring or even increased cultural diversity' (Scholte, 2000: 23).[6]

Third, Gray's view appears to rely on further assumptions that could be labelled 'essentialist' in an undesirable sense. For the picture he presents is of a series of discrete, self-contained, traditional cultures being confronted and overcome by a discrete, monolithic liberalism. There are two essentialisms at work here. The first is an essentialist view of cultures which supposes that liberalization must mean the destruction or at least corruption of cultural identity. The second is an essentialist view of liberalism as an intellectual entity necessarily irreconcilable with local conditions. A less polarized account would allow that the intersection of liberalism and non-liberal traditions is a two-way street giving rise to new, hybrid forms of both liberalized local cultures and localized liberalisms. Although it should not be pretended that nothing at all is lost in such a process, it is at least arguable that this kind of hybridization promotes cultural diversity on balance.

I conclude that there is a good case to be made on several grounds for liberalism as a promoter of the diversity required by pluralism. Liberalism gives political effect to the balanced goal of multiplicity and coherence through its maintenance of a framework of individual rights and liberties. The maintenance of a liberal framework is not without costs to global cultural diversity, but these are balanced and

FROM PLURALISM TO LIBERALISM

probably outweighed by gains in the diversity internal to societies, which itself will generate diversity among societies. The pluralist ethic of diversity thus converges with the liberal principle of approximate neutrality. In these various ways liberalism promotes diversity to a greater degree than its rivals. It is the latter rather than liberals who err in the direction either of excessive emphasis on moral coherence (Marxism, anarchism, conservatism, strong communitarianism, strong socialism), or excessive insistence on multiplicity (postmodernism). Gray's view is an odd amalgam of both of these excesses, since he advocates an unlimited multiplicity of cultures but is happy that many of these will be monistic. Contrary to Gray, diversity in the pluralist sense will be better served by liberal universalism, which promotes pluralist diversity more consistently. If liberalism is the best vehicle for diversity, and value pluralism gives us a reason to value diversity, then value pluralism gives us a reason to value liberalism.

Notes

1. Note the difference between this argument for peaceful coexistence or accommodation and that offered by Gray (5.2). Gray's argument conceives coexistence as an end or 'interest' common to all human beings, begging the classic pluralist question of why this particular end should be privileged universally in preference to other fundamental ends. The argument offered in the present chapter derives the goal of accommodation from the concept of value pluralism itself. See, similarly, the argument for accommodation by way of 'reasonable disagreement' in Chapter 7.
2. This is from one of the more liberal sections of Kekes's *The Morality of Pluralism*, 'The possibilities of life' (1993: 27–31; see also Chapter 6). Compare other passages in Kekes's work where the mood is more explicitly conservative and the emphasis is on the authority of received tradition (see 5.3 above). See also Galston, who argues that value pluralism entails 'a preference for social capaciousness over social narrowing' (1999a: 891). Raz makes a similar point, although he holds that 'an adequate range of options' is a necessary precondition not for the good life in general but for the good of personal autonomy in particular (1986: 373–7; and see Chapter 8 below).
3. See, for example, Arthur Schlesinger's critique of American multiculturalism as threatening to lead to 'the fragmentation, resegregation, and tribalization of American life' (1992: 18).
4. The contrasts (and some similarities) between value pluralism and

156

DIVERSITY

postmodernism are discussed by Crowder and Griffiths (1999). For a different view see McKinney (1992), who interprets Berlin's pluralism as a form of postmodernism, albeit an inconsistent one; but compare Berlin's reply (1992b).

5. Hayek writes: 'The central concept of liberalism is that under the enforcement of universal rules of just conduct, protecting a recognizable private domain of individuals, a spontaneous order of human activities of much greater complexity will form itself than could ever be produced by deliberate arrangements ...' (1967: 162). Note that there are hints in Hayek's work of an underlying value pluralism: 'The chief point about the catallaxy is that, as a spontaneous order, its orderliness does *not* rest on its orientation on a single hierarchy of ends' (ibid.: 164). That is, the spontaneous order achieved by the market emerges from the engagement of many different views about how values ought to be ranked. Echoing Berlin, Hayek describes a free society as one that does 'not enforce a unitary scale of concrete ends, nor attempt to secure that some particular view about what is more and what is less important governs the whole of society' (ibid.: 164–5). I sympathize with this element of Hayek's position, but criticize his attempt to link value pluralism with economic laissez-faire in 9.2 below.

6. See e.g. Chris Barker, who writes that 'the globalization of television is not best understood in terms of cultural imperialism and the homogenization of world culture. Rather, ... while forces of homogenization are certainly in evidence, of equal significance is the place of heterogenization and localization. Consequently, globalization and hybridity are preferred concepts to imperialism and homogeneity as we approach the end of the twentieth century' (1999: 58). See, similarly, Waters (1997), Holton (1998), Sheridan (1999).

CHAPTER 7

From Pluralism to Liberalism II: Reasonable Disagreement

In the previous chapter I argued that value pluralism generates a case for liberalism on the ground of diversity, principally of goods and secondarily of ways of life. In this chapter I construct a second argument from pluralism to liberalism, this time making the accommodation of a diversity of ways of life the principal focus. The argument here is based on the notion of 'reasonable disagreement'. My central claim is that if value pluralism is true, then we must accept that many (although not all) disagreements about the nature of the good life will be reasonable, and therefore that the state ought to accommodate such disagreements rather than attempt to eliminate them. The best political vehicle for accommodating disagreement about the good life is liberalism.

This argument can be brought into sharper relief by critically comparing it with Rawls's 'political' case for liberalism. As we saw in Chapter 2, Rawls's later political reformulation of his theory of justice is perhaps the most sophisticated, certainly among the most influential, of justifications of liberalism along neutrality lines. Rawlsian political liberalism thus provides a challenging standard against which to assess the contribution made by my pluralist case to the defence of liberalism. More specifically, I shall focus on a distinctively Rawlsian objection to attempts like mine to base liberalism on value pluralism. Charles Larmore has argued that pluralism cannot ground a case for liberalism as neutral among conceptions of the good because pluralism is itself a controversial conception of the good (1996: Chapter 7). Larmore seeks to draw a

158

sharp contrast between the contestable character of Berlinian pluralism and the uncontroversial nature of the 'fact of reasonable pluralism' that underlies Rawlsian political liberalism. The Rawlsian approach is superior, he argues, because its starting point is more widely acceptable. I argue that my pluralist case is no more controversial than the political liberalism of Rawls and Larmore, in part because the most fundamental assumption of political liberalism, that of reasonable disagreement about the good life, actually presupposes value pluralism. Moreover, although value pluralism may be controversial in the sense that many people would currently reject it, that does not mean they have good reason for doing so. Pluralism may be too controversial to justify liberalism on the basis of popular consensus, but it may still ground a reasoned case for liberalism that takes issue with consensus. Indeed, the pluralist case for liberalism is superior to Rawls's political argument, since its foundations are deeper and more explicit, and it rightly recovers both liberal universality and philosophical regard for truth, both of which are commendable from a pluralist point of view.

The chapter is divided into four sections. The first of these places Larmore's objection in the context of Rawlsian political liberalism, which I compare and contrast with the value-pluralist approach. I consider some initial replies to Larmore before turning to my principal response in 7.2. There, the claim that the Rawlsian idea of reasonable disagreement presupposes value pluralism sets up the central thesis of the chapter, the argument from pluralism to liberalism by way of reasonable disagreement, which is developed in 7.3. In the final section I argue that the pluralist case is not only no more controversial than the political approach but superior to it.

7.1 Political Liberalism and Value Pluralism

Larmore argues that the justification of liberalism can and should do without value pluralism. Pluralism is 'too controversial a doctrine, far too exclusive of many views well represented in our culture, to have a rightful place among [liberal] principles' (1996: 155). Liberalism is properly founded not on value pluralism but on the Rawlsian notion of 'reasonable disagreement' as to the nature of the good life. Pluralism, by contrast, is a view of the ultimate nature of the good about which reasonable people may disagree. It cannot be a focus for what people have in common.

Larmore's objection emerges out of his defence of Rawlsian political liberalism (ibid.: Chapter 6). According to Larmore, liberal theories were developed historically as a solution to a particular problem, and their adequacy must be judged according to their success in solving that problem. The problem is how to identify principles for political association, justifiable to all members of the association, given a background assumption of widespread and permanent disagreement among the members as to the nature of the good life – given, that is, widespread and permanent 'plurality of belief', as I have been calling it. Note that the kind of disagreement which liberalism presupposes, according to the Rawls–Larmore thesis, is not merely current disagreement that may be resolved in the future, but disagreement that is expected to be permanent. Disagreement about the nature of the good is expected to be permanent because such disagreement is 'reasonable'. Even when people are being reasonable, that is, judging in accordance with human reason and in good faith, they may still disagree about the good; reasonableness alone cannot compel agreement on this matter. Modern societies must nevertheless accommodate many individuals and groups who disagree reasonably with one another in this way.

How can we arrive at principles that all citizens can accept, as required by the liberal commitment to equal concern and respect, in the face of reasonable disagreement about how to live? On the Rawls–Larmore view, the liberal solution is the doctrine of neutrality. This involves formulating a 'core, minimal morality which reasonable people can share, given their expectedly divergent religious convictions and conceptions of the meaning of life' (ibid.: 152). Only this minimal morality should be declared and enforced by the state. To be the object of agreement, the minimal morality cannot favour any particular conception of the good life over others. This does not mean that the citizens of a liberal state cannot pursue their own conceptions of the good in private. On the contrary, the whole purpose of liberal neutrality is to enable them to do so without colliding harmfully with other people doing the same thing. Rawls and Larmore draw a sharp distinction between a public sphere governed exclusively by 'public reason', or principles which all citizens can accept, and a private sphere in which people are free to form and pursue their own view of the good. Public reason emerges from an 'overlapping consensus' among reasonable private conceptions of the good, that is, from the point at which such conceptions converge. Rawls presents this view as 'political' in three senses (1993: 11–15). First, the principles of liberal justice need be accepted only in the realm of public policy, not necessarily in the personal or private dimension of life. Second, liberal justice is 'freestanding', or independent of any 'comprehensive moral doctrine' or conception of the good life. Third, it is derived from the contents of the public political culture shared by all citizens of modern democracies, whatever their private conception of the good.

It seems to follow that liberal neutrality cannot involve appeal to the notion of value pluralism. That is because while liberalism, addressing the problem of reasonable disagreement, aims at neutrality among conceptions of the good, pluralism 'is precisely a deep and certainly controversial account of the nature of the good, one according to which objective value is ultimately not of a single kind but of many kinds' (ibid.: 154). Such an account would be rejected, for example, by followers of 'religious orthodoxies that have sought in God the single, ultimately harmonious origin of good' (ibid.). Pluralism is itself a controversial conception of the good of the kind that Rawlsian liberalism aims to accommodate at arm's length rather than to endorse. On the Rawls–Larmore view, liberalism cannot base itself on value pluralism; rather, its fundamental assumption is that of reasonable disagreement. 'This expectation of reasonable disagreement, to which liberalism does appeal, lies at a different, one might almost say more "impartial" level than pluralism' (ibid.: 167). Liberalism presupposes the truth of reasonable disagreement, not value pluralism.

Larmore's argument appears to be a powerful one. He is certainly right to point out that any defence of liberalism on the basis of Berlinian value pluralism will be importantly different from the Rawlsian 'political' approach. What exactly the differences are, however, and how they should be evaluated is another matter. The contrast Larmore draws between political liberalism as usefully neutral and value pluralism as unhelpfully controversial is one I shall challenge in due course. To begin with, though, let us consider some other points of comparison and contrast between the two approaches.

First, the pluralist argument argument in Chapter 6 is, like Rawls's political liberalism, neutrality-based. But there is a difference in the kind of neutrality sought in each case. While Rawls seems to maintain a commitment to a thoroughgoing neutrality of reasons, I have presented the pluralist case as requiring only the less demanding standard of approximate neutrality. No case for liberalism, it seems to me, can meet the requirements of a strict neutrality of reasons; on the other hand no case for liberalism needs to meet those requirements. Liberals neither can show nor need to show that their principles are limitlessly accommodating of different ways of life; they need only show that their principles are more accommodating than the alternatives.

However, the more significant difference between the pluralist case for liberalism and Rawls's turns on the distinction between universalist and particularist approaches, or 'comprehensive' and 'political'. Of the three senses in which Rawls's liberalism is said to be 'political', only one clearly applies to the pluralist argument as so far formulated: the pluralist argument, like Rawls's, addresses only 'the basic social structure'. That is, the case I have set out for ranking the goods characteristic of liberalism (personal autonomy, toleration, etc.) above other goods applies only in the public realm, the realm of those institutions that form and execute public policy. It is no part of the argument, as stated so far, that the goods of liberalism must be preferred to the alternatives in the decisions made by individuals and groups in the private sphere. Consistent with the operation of the public liberal framework of rights and liberties, people can rank goods as they please. (Even this claim on the part of the pluralist case to count as 'political' in Rawls's terms is one I shall qualify later, in Chapters 8 and 9. My overall case does not rely on any sharp distinction of this kind between public and private realms.)

In the other two senses of 'political' identified by Rawls, the pluralist case seems not to be political but, rather, comprehensive. Indeed, it is certainly not political in the particularist sense of being drawn from the contents of a public political culture. The operative principles of the pluralist argument for liberalism in its universalist form (so far, respect for universal values, recognition of incommensurability, and promotion of diversity) are derived not from any cultural contingency but from the formal features of value pluralism, which is a theory of the real nature of value. In contrast with the particularism of Rawls's political liberalism, therefore, the pluralist case is a universal one, generating principles that, if valid, are valid independently of local culture. What about Rawls's claim that his theory is political in the sense of 'freestanding', or not reliant on any particular comprehensive moral doctrine? Whether the pluralist argument is political in this sense depends on whether or not value pluralism counts as a comprehensive moral doctrine.

REASONABLE DISAGREEMENT

Larmore argues that pluralism is indeed a comprehensive moral doctrine, or controversial conception of the good, and that this distinguishes the pluralist approach from Rawls's political route. He claims, moreover, that this is what makes the pluralist case a more contestable and hence less viable way of arguing for liberalism than Rawls's political method. But these claims are themselves controversial, and I shall argue against them in a moment.

To summarize, the chief points of comparison between the pluralist and political approaches are as follows. While both are attempts to justify liberalism along neutralist lines, Rawls insists on a strict neutrality of reasons while the pluralist case works with the more relaxed standard of approximate neutrality. More importantly, while Rawls's argument is particularist because based on the contents of a public political culture, the pluralist case is universal because grounded in an account of the nature of value.

Which approach is better? More specifically, is Larmore right to reject the pluralist approach because of its allegedly more controversial nature? I begin by reviewing some preliminary responses before setting out my main reply in the next section. First, pluralist liberals could challenge Larmore's characterization of the liberal project. He assumes that *the* problem that liberalism sets itself is how to accommodate multiple competing conceptions of the good within a single political association. This, it is true, is *one* of the problems liberals have historically tried to solve, but it has not been their only concern. As we saw in Chapter 2, another theme that has been central throughout the history of liberal thought has been the liberation of the individual (2.2.3). For Kant and Mill, the best polity is that which secures the emancipation and flourishing of the individual person conceived as strongly autonomous. That ideal confronts and excludes conceptions of the person as properly heteronomous, legitimately governed by received traditions and customs. The liberalism of Kant and Mill is consequently perfectionist rather than neutralist, since it effectively asserts the superiority of a particular conception of the good life. Such a view is necessarily controversial, and arguably as controversial as any argument made on the basis of value pluralism. Whereas a pluralist argument for liberalism takes issue with conceptions of the good based on monist outlooks, such as monotheistic religions, the perfectionism of Kant and Mill takes issue with conceptions of the good that value or permit heteronomous personality. Both approaches controvert conceptions of the good that stress the

163

FROM PLURALISM TO LIBERALISM

authority of certain kinds of tradition, and it does not seem that in this regard value pluralism is obviously more controversial than Kantian or Millian perfectionism.

Larmore could respond that this is precisely why liberals should turn away from perfectionist justifications towards a neutralist strategy (1996: 127–32). Yes, the liberal repertoire does include a perfectionist tradition, but the neutralist approach is preferable because less exclusive and controversial. But then, the neutralist strand is preferable only on the assumption that the only, or at least the most important, problem to be solved is the problem of accommodation. This begs the question against the problem of liberation, which is arguably just as important if not more so. The fact is that the liberal tradition is concerned with both of these problems equally, and that, as a consequence, neutrality and perfectionism both capture vital aspects of the liberal outlook, even though they are in tension with one another. Liberalism cannot be identified wholly with the neutralist strain to the exclusion of the perfectionist. And so far as liberalism is a perfectionist enterprise, it is liable to rest on a conception of the good as controversial as anything in value pluralism.[1]

However, let us set aside the perfectionist strain in liberalism for the present and focus on the liberal aspiration to neutrality. Let us suppose, furthermore, that Larmore is correct in his characterization of value pluralism as a controversial conception of the good, or in Rawls's term a 'comprehensive moral doctrine', and therefore subject to reasonable disagreement. Even conceding that the liberal goal is neutrality and that pluralism is a controversial conception of the good, pluralism may still contribute to the justification of liberalism by providing at least one route to a Rawlsian overlapping consensus. That is, even supposing that Larmore is correct, and value pluralism is no more than one comprehensive moral doctrine among others, it may be a comprehensive moral doctrine that supports liberalism (as against, for example, conservatism). Indeed, this seems to be Rawls's own thought. Rawls himself gives 'a pluralist view', defined along value-pluralist lines, as one of the participant views in his 'model case' of an overlapping consensus, or point of agreement among different comprehensive views (1993: 145). On this account pluralism is not the only route to liberalism, or even the best, but it is one route among others. If pluralism is subject to reasonable disagreement, then not everyone can be reasonably expected to accept it, but those who do will have a reason to accept liberalism.[2]

7.2 Reasonable Disagreement and Pluralism

Might it be possible, however, for pluralist liberals to make a stronger claim? Might they claim that pluralism is not merely one controversial route to liberalism among others based on rival comprehensive moral doctrines, but rather an argument for liberal neutrality that is no more controversial than the political argument of Rawls and Larmore? Pluralist liberals can indeed make this claim. To show this, I shall compare the pluralist argument with the Rawls–Larmore argument at their respective starting points, in the pluralist case 'value pluralism', in the Rawls–Larmore case 'reasonable disagreement'. I shall argue that the pluralist case is no more controversial than the Rawls–Larmore thesis because the idea of reasonable disagreement turns out on inspection to depend on that of value pluralism.

Recall that reasonable disagreement involves more than mere de facto plurality of belief. The mere fact that different people believe different things is thoroughly uncontroversial, but nothing much follows from it. As we saw in connection with Walzer's argument discussed in Chapter 1, plurality of belief may attract many logical responses ranging from acceptance and even celebration of that plurality to a determined attempt to challenge and replace it with a single orthodoxy (1.1). The neutralist liberal response of accommodation becomes compelling only if we add to the bare fact of disagreement the expectation that the disagreement will be permanent so that attempts to remove it will be costly and futile. Thus Rawls and Larmore argue that disagreements about the nature of the good are not only pervasive in the modern world but can be expected to be permanent. Why can they be expected to be permanent? Because they are reasonable. 'Reasonable people tend naturally to differ and disagree about the nature of the good life' (Larmore, 1996: 122). We must expect people to diverge over such matters not just because of prejudice and ignorance, which could in principle be dispelled by enlightenment, but because even when people are being reasonable they may still disagree about the good.

But why, one may ask, may even reasonable people disagree about the good? Rawls's answer, endorsed by Larmore, takes the form of an account of 'the sources, or causes, of disagreement among persons so defined', namely 'the many hazards involved in the correct (and conscientious) exercise of our powers of reason and judgment in the ordinary course of political life' (Rawls, 1993: 55–6). These 'burdens

FROM PLURALISM TO LIBERALISM

of judgment' are as follows:

a The evidence – empirical and scientific – bearing on the case is conflicting and complex, and thus hard to assess and evaluate.

b Even where we agree fully about the kinds of considerations that are relevant, we may disagree about their weight, and so arrive at different judgments.

c To some extent all our concepts, and not only moral and political concepts, are vague and subject to hard cases; and this indeterminacy means that we must rely on judgment and interpretation (and on judgments about interpretations) within some range (not sharply specifiable) where reasonable persons may differ.

d To some extent (how great we cannot tell) the way we assess evidence and weigh moral and political values is shaped by our total experience, our whole course of life up to now; and our total experiences must always differ. Thus, in a modern society with its numerous offices and positions, its various divisions of labor, its many social groups and their ethnic variety, citizens' total experiences are disparate enough for their judgments to diverge, at least to some degree, on many if not most cases of any significant complexity.

e Often there are different kinds of normative considerations of different force on both sides of an issue and it is difficult to make an overall assessment.

f Finally, as we note in referring to Berlin's view (V: 6.2), any system of social institutions is limited in the values it can admit so that some selection must be made from the full range of moral and political values that might be realized. This is because any system of institutions has, as it were, a limited social space. In being forced to select among cherished values, or when we hold to several and must restrict each in view of the requirements of the others, we face great difficulties in setting priorities and making adjustments. Many hard decisions may seem to have no clear answer. (Rawls, 1993: 56–7)

Note that the burdens of judgement are meant to explain how reasonable people can be expected to disagree about the nature of the good, even though they can agree on other matters such as the claims of the natural sciences. Rawls and Larmore are not endorsing

REASONABLE DISAGREEMENT

a general scepticism – that would be at odds with liberalism, which requires the possibility of reasoned agreement about the need for and contents of the liberal framework. Rather, they are trying to explain why questions of the good in morals and politics are peculiarly liable to provoke disagreement even among reasonable people. But as Rawls himself observes (and Larmore acknowledges), items (a) to (d) are 'not peculiar' to 'moral and practical' questions; rather, they 'apply mainly to the theoretical uses of our reason' (ibid.: 56). If moral and practical questions are especially prone to attract disagreement, then that special feature must be explained by those burdens of judgement that distinguish such questions from others. Only burdens (e) and (f), then, are strictly relevant to the question of disagreement about the good, that is, to what it is about questions concerning the good life that makes them peculiarly contestable.

Two problems arise here for Larmore's argument. First, (e) and (f) are burdens of judgement applying to 'moral and practical' questions generally, that is, they apply not only to questions of the good but also to questions of 'the right' or 'the minimal morality' to which Larmore appeals as neutral ground (Johnston, 1994: 37). If so, Larmore's attempt to separate liberal neutrality from theories of the good like value pluralism is compromised, since it is not only theories of the good that are subject to reasonable disagreement but also theories of the right of the kind necessary to inform neutrality. Larmore might reply that although the burdens of judgement do extend to questions of the right, in that connection those burdens are not as severe as they are in questions of the good. Such a reply would be plausible, but would entail a concession that theories of the right are less controversial than conceptions of good only as a matter of degree. Merely to identify value pluralism as a conception of the good would not be sufficient to show that it is more controversial than the Rawlsian notion of the right. The Rawlsian notion of the right would be controversial too; the only question would be why and how far the Rawlsian approach is less controversial than the pluralist.

That question is answered by a second point. The Rawlsian approach is no less controversial than the pluralist because the two burdens of judgement that crucially explain reasonable disagreement about the good, namely burdens (e) and (f), are in effect formulations of value pluralism. Reasonable disagreement turns out, on the account given by Rawls and Larmore themselves, to

167

FROM PLURALISM TO LIBERALISM

presuppose value pluralism. The Rawls–Larmore thesis can be no less controversial than the value pluralism it depends on.

Burden (e) is the incidence of 'different kinds of normative consideration of different force on both sides of an issue', such that it is 'difficult to make an overall assessment' (ibid.: 57). Fleshing out this idea in a footnote, Rawls refers to Thomas Nagel's article, 'The fragmentation of value' (1991), which argues that there are basic conflicts of value where the values appear to be 'incomparable: they are each specified by one of the several irreducibly different perspectives within which values arise; in particular the perspectives that specify obligations, rights, utility, perfectionist ends and personal commitments. Put another way, these values have different bases and this fact is reflected in their different formal features' (ibid.: 57, note 10). The idea of there being 'irreducibly different' bases for value judgement such that there may be cases where 'overall assessment' is difficult is precisely the central thesis of value pluralism. Rawls sees that this view amounts to a controversial conception of the good ('a comprehensive moral doctrine'), and so offers it as merely a 'not implausible' account of the claim made in (e), remarking that 'it suffices for our purposes simply to assert (e)' (ibid.). But since he suggests no alternative account of (e), one must suppose that this is the best he has to offer. Moreover, a monist version of (e) would be hard to imagine, since by definition the values concerned would be, at least in principle, subject to a principled ranking or trade-off in terms of the relevant super-value or common denominator. As we have seen, a distinguishing feature of monist views is that they hold out the promise of a relatively unproblematic solution to value conflict by reference to a single formula applicable to all cases (3.1.3, 4.3.1). But it is precisely the implausibility of that idea that Rawls is getting at in (e). If (e) rules out monism, then it implies pluralism.

Value pluralism is also entailed by burden (f). Under this heading 'we face great difficulties' when we are 'forced to select among cherished values' (ibid.). Again, this would be hard to square with a monist view, which by definition involves the availability in principle of a clear decision-procedure in cases where we must rank some values ahead of others. In this connection, indeed, Rawls explicitly cites with approval the authority of Berlin: 'As Berlin has long maintained (it is one of his fundamental themes), there is no social world without loss: that is, no social world that does not exclude some ways of life that realize in special ways certain

168

fundamental values' (ibid.: 197). Moreover, the fact 'that there is no social world without loss is rooted in the nature of values and the world, and much human tragedy reflects that' (ibid.: 197, note 32). In this reference to 'the nature of values and the world' it is hard to imagine a clearer indication that Rawls's case appeals to the idea of value pluralism as I have been defining it, namely as a theory of the nature of the good. Since burden (f), along with (e), is crucial to Rawls's explanation of how disagreement about the good can be reasonable – the central observation to which his neutralist liberalism responds – then it is hard to avoid the conclusion that the neutralist liberalism of Rawls and Larmore, although immediately addressing reasonable disagreement, presupposes the truth of value pluralism. At this point one is tempted to reverse a famous Rawlsian dictum. At least in the limited sense that value pluralism is a 'metaphysical' doctrine because it is a conception of the good, Rawls's liberalism is 'metaphysical, not political'. At any rate, Rawlsian political liberalism is no less controversial than the value-pluralist case for liberalism, since it presupposes value pluralism.

Could reasonable disagreement about the good be explained in some way other than value pluralism? Rawls says that his list of the burdens of judgement is incomplete and 'covers only the more obvious sources', but he offers no suggestion as to what the less obvious sources might be (Rawls, 1993: 56). Larmore believes that burden (d), the great variety of life experiences created by modern society, 'provides the key to explaining the phenomenon' (Larmore, 1996: 170). But he gives no reason why (d) should be preferred to any of the other explanations. Moreover, his belief seems ill-founded since he accepts Rawls's observation that (d) is among those burdens on the list that 'are not peculiar to reasoning about values, and so fall short of the explanation we seek' (ibid.). Larmore goes on to suggest that what really needs explaining is not disagreement about values but agreement in the sciences. 'Reasonable disagreement in the handling of complex questions is perhaps just what we should expect ... and the extraordinary fact is that this phenomenon has largely ceased to occur in the natural sciences' (ibid.: 171). This evades the issue. The fact that we would like to explain agreement in the natural sciences does not reduce the need to explain disagreement about values: the two issues are obviously aspects of the same overall question, namely why there is apparently less agreement about values than there is about the claims of the natural sciences.

FROM PLURALISM TO LIBERALISM

Could Rawls and Larmore reply that reasonable disagreement does not depend on value pluralism but merely the *appearance* of value pluralism? Perhaps the combined effect of all the burdens of judgement is that we could always disagree reasonably about the good even if value monism were true. On this view values may not be radically plural in actual fact, but such are the difficulties in the way of reaching reasoned agreement about moral questions that we had better act as if they were. The Rawlsian commitment to reasonable disagreement about the good would then rest not on the metaphysical claim that value pluralism is true, but on the empirical claim that, when it comes to moral questions, the burdens of judgement have the same effect on our efforts to reach agreement as if pluralism were true.

This possibility cannot be ruled out altogether, but there is something rather strained about it. If the best explanation for reasonable disagreement is the appearance of value pluralism, then the most natural explanation of the appearance of value pluralism is the truth of value pluralism. Rawls himself tends in this direction in his references to Nagel and Berlin. If monism were true, then there would always be the possibility that the monist structure would be discovered and provide the means for reasoned agreement about the good life. In fact there is no sign of this happening. That could be because of the burdens of judgement (a) to (d), but these have not prevented widespread reasoned agreement in the case of the natural sciences. The likelier explanation is provided by burdens (e) and (f), those closest to the idea of value pluralism.

I conclude that, on the account given by Rawls and Larmore themselves, value pluralism is the best explanation for reasonable disagreement about the good. Reasonable disagreement therefore presupposes value pluralism. This amounts in effect to a further argument for the truth of value pluralism to set beside those given in Chapter 3. Even if I am wrong about this, however, the foregoing discussion is sufficient to support the two claims I am principally concerned to establish in the present chapter. First, a case for liberalism based on pluralism is at least no more controversial than one based on reasonable disagreement. Even if reasonable disagreement does not presuppose pluralism, Rawls's burdens of judgement apply to his notion of 'the right' as well as the good. Moreover, as we saw in Chapter 2, the idea of the right as the basis for public policy requires people with non-liberal conceptions of the good to keep these private, a position which is itself controversial for non-liberals

170

(2.2.2). Second, the discussion suggests a second argument from pluralism to liberalism to add to the argument from diversity, namely an argument from reasonable disagreement.

7.3 Accommodating Reasonable Disagreement

Even if reasonable disagreement does not presuppose pluralism, pluralism may still be true. If pluralism is true, it implies widespread reasonable disagreement about the good life. Reasonable disagreement ought in turn to be accommodated, and is best accommodated by liberalism. The claim suggests an argument in three main steps: from pluralism to reasonable disagreement, from reasonable disagreement to accommodation, and finally from accommodation to liberalism.

First, how does pluralism imply reasonable disagreement about the good life? On the pluralist view, many different values make distinctive claims on us and we must choose among those claims in particular situations. Where the context for choice can be closely specified, it may be (although this is not necessarily so) that one ranking is clearly more rational than others. For the judge presiding at a trial, for example, justice should clearly come before other values. But we often try to rank values in a more general way, such that the ranking is intended to apply across many different situations. This is what we do when we formulate a conception of the good life; such a conception is in essence a ranking of goods intended to apply generally – throughout the life of an individual or of a society. In this more general kind of case there is clearly more room for people to decide, for good reason, on different priorities. The life of the dedicated artist and unfaithful lover may be the only rational life for Picasso, but not everyone is Picasso. Under pluralism, different ways of ranking goods in general, including different conceptions of the good, may be equally (or incommensurably) reasonable. Moreover, these may come into conflict. This is especially true of conceptions of the good, such as religious conceptions, which lay down desirable patterns of life for all human beings, each claiming an authority which excludes that of its rivals. The Roman Catholic conception of the good would conflict with a view that everyone should live like Picasso. Where a conception of the good is both highly general and claims exclusive authority for itself, there we will likely have not merely divergence but disagreement. Moreover, that disagreement will be reasonable if each of the rival conceptions is reasonable on its own terms, which is possible under pluralism.[3]

This implication suggests a further general principle implicit in the notion of pluralism – in addition to respect for universal values, recognition of incommensurability, and promotion of diversity. The principle that we should acknowledge reasonable disagreement among conceptions of the good draws on two elements of pluralism in particular, namely conflict and incommensurability. From the potential for conflict among plural goods follows the necessity of choice (3.1.4). From the incommensurability of goods it follows that choice cannot, on the face of things, be mandated by a single absolute or general ranking applicable to all or most cases (3.1.3). That is, no such single ranking is mandated by reason.

Note that the argument is not that pluralism implies that *all* conceptions of the good are equally reasonable. Such a view would undermine liberalism rather than support it, since it would admit conceptions of the good which are hostile to fundamental liberal values. Moreover, such a view would be more in keeping with a subjectivist or relativist outlook than with value pluralism. The pluralist view is not that all conceptions of the good are equally reasonable, because some may violate the pluralist principles of universality, incommensurability, diversity, or indeed reasonable disagreement. Rather, the pluralist view is that a certain range of conceptions of the good is reasonable, namely those compatible with the principles of pluralism, and that within that range there is room for reasonable disagreement among them.

So far as disagreement about the good life is reasonable, that disagreement must be accommodated. This is the second step in the argument. Pluralism gives us reason to disagree about some things, but also to agree about others. In particular, pluralism gives us reason to disagree about the substantive content of the more general conceptions of the good. But that very fact gives us reason to agree on the need for a framework to contain such disagreements peacefully.

An objection suggests itself here. Could we not acknowledge the fact of reasonable disagreement and respond not by accommodating the disagreement but by trying to enforce orthodoxy – an illiberal response? Here we should remember that we are dealing not just with de facto disagreement but with reasonable disagreement. With this in mind, one answer, given by liberals like Rawls and Larmore,

REASONABLE DISAGREEMENT

is that to enforce agreement in this situation would be to violate the basic Kantian principle of respect for persons, since it would amount to ignoring people's status as rational moral agents. To be legitimate, principles of justice must be acceptable to reasonable people. A problem with this answer from a pluralist point of view is that it assumes commitment to a liberal ranking of values, but such a ranking cannot simply be assumed by pluralists. Liberal pluralists could respond in two ways. First, they could rely on other pluralist arguments for a liberal ranking: the 'diversity' case already made (Chapter 6), and the 'virtues' argument to come (Chapter 8). The latter argument in particular would be effective here, since, as we shall see, it connects pluralism with personal autonomy. The trouble with this move is that the argument from pluralism to liberalism by way of reasonable disagreement would then have to be seen as dependent on the other two arguments rather than providing a separate line. This would leave the overall pluralist case for liberalism somewhat weaker than if reasonable disagreement provided independent support for it.

Liberal pluralists may therefore be better off taking a second option, which is to pursue the Lockean line that if disagreement about the good is reasonable, then it cannot be overcome by force. Attempts to compel agreement on matters that attract disagreement among reasonable people will be not only costly but futile, because outward practice can be compelled but not inner belief. Some writers have argued that this claim is not wholly convincing, since even if belief itself cannot be enforced, the conditions giving rise to it may be (Waldron, 1991). Moreover, there are historical examples of the forcible conversion of whole peoples from one religious orthodoxy to another over the course of several generations (Barry, 1991). But if it is not strictly true that reasonable disagreement *cannot* be overcome by force, liberal pluralists can reply that, historically, this has been possible only at massive cost in terms of resources expended and suffering endured. The question then arises, what can justify this? The typical answer has been precisely the kind of 'pursuit of the ideal', to use Berlin's term, that pluralists reject. It is when the goal of policy is conceived as a super-value to which all else is subordinated that attempts are most frequently made to justify the enforcement of orthodoxy. The rejection of accommodation, in other words, fits better with a monist than a pluralist outlook. The latter counsels moderation, as Berlin suggests: 'Revolutions, wars, assassinations, extreme measures may in

173

FROM PLURALISM TO LIBERALISM

desperate situations be required. But history teaches us that their consequences are seldom what is anticipated; there is no guarantee, not even, at times, a high enough probability, that such acts will lead to improvement' (1992a: 17). For pluralists, the costs of attempting to eliminate rather than accommodate disagreement are likely to outweigh the benefits.

Supposing that reasonable disagreement requires accommodation rather than transformation, the third step in the argument takes us from accommodation to liberalism. The argument is entailed by that of Chapter 6, where liberalism was presented as the likeliest political vehicle for accommodating the maximum practicable diversity of goods and ways of life. To accommodate a diversity of ways of life is necessarily to accommodate disagreement where these conflict.

The argument can be seen as a development of one of the strands in the anti-utopian case presented by Berlin (Chapter 4). Recall that for Berlin one of the key implications of pluralism is that in ruling out the possibility of an absolute ranking of values, it eliminates the possibility of a 'final solution' in politics. Notions of an ultimate political order in which all significant conflicts will be solved, as in classical Marxism and anarchism, must be rejected as utopian. Rather, we must reconcile ourselves to forms of politics that accept moral conflict as permanent and that work to manage rather than transcend it. The argument from reasonable disagreement takes much the same line. Pluralism shows that much disagreement about the good life is permanent because reasonable, and therefore cannot be overcome, only contained. But reasonable disagreement provides a more complete case for liberalism than Berlin's anti-utopianism. Berlin's case, I argued, takes us only part of the way from pluralism to liberalism, since its anti-utopian conclusion could also be satisfied by conservatism or pragmatism (4.3.2). My main reasons for rejecting conservatism and pragmatism from a pluralist point of view have already been set out in Chapter 5, but reasonable disagreement adds a further consideration. All political systems presuppose some conception of the good, but this may be more or less receptive to the notion of reasonable disagreement. A political system that is appropriately sensitive to reasonable disagreement will be one grounded in principles sufficiently capacious to accommodate a diversity of rival conceptions of the good. That requirement is better satisfied by liberalism than by conservatism or pragmatism. As I argued in Chapter 5, both Kekes's conservative

174

REASONABLE DISAGREEMENT

pluralism and Gray's pragmatic pluralism depend on conceptions of the good that are universal in ambition but narrow in content: in Kekes's case adherence to local tradition, in Gray's the privileging of self-interest or peace. The relative narrowness of these conceptions contrasts with the liberal good, with its concern for a diversity of both goods and ways of life. The pluralist argument from reasonable disagreement, supported by the argument from diversity, thus completes that side of Berlin's case that emphasizes the permanence of moral conflict in human affairs. The idea of reasonable disagreement takes us from pluralism to anti-utopianism in a specifically liberal form.

7.4 Is Pluralism too Controversial?

If my argument in this chapter is successful so far, I have shown that there is a pluralist case for liberalism by way of reasonable disagreement, and that this is no more controversial than the Rawlsian political case. However, it might now be objected that this merely places the two on the same problematic level. Larmore's point remains valid, it might be claimed, that value pluralism is strategically unsatisfactory as a basis for liberalism because it is too controversial. Even if pluralism does provide good grounds for liberalism, that will not help because too few people can be expected to accept value pluralism as a starting point. All I have established is that Rawlsian political liberalism is in this connection just as limited. In this section I shall reply to this objection, arguing for three main points. First, although value pluralism may be too controversial to serve as a focus for a consensus-based justification of liberalism (in which the Rawlsian argument is no more successful), it is not too controversial to ground a persuasive philosophical or truth-based justification. Second, if philosophical justification is the goal, then the willingness of pluralists to put their 'metaphysical' claims on the table makes their approach superior to that of Rawlsian political liberalism, because it makes explicit the kind of argument that Rawls tries to avoid but cannot, and because it rightly restores to the liberal project its traditional universality. Third, the justification of liberalism ought to be philosophical rather than consensus-based, both for liberal reasons and from the perspective of value pluralism.

Value pluralism should be conceded to be 'controversial' in two

175

FROM PLURALISM TO LIBERALISM

senses. The first may be called the 'de facto' sense: many people at present do not believe that pluralism is true or have beliefs that rest on monistic assumptions at variance with pluralism. Thus, Larmore argues that pluralism is at odds with many religious views, especially those of monotheistic religions which insist that all values are ultimately united in the will of a single God.[4] Supposing that this is true, what are its implications? It follows, as Larmore says, that pluralism cannot be the basis for a widespread acceptance of liberalism in the manner of Rawls's 'overlapping consensus' argument. Such an argument takes existing reasonable beliefs about the good as given and seeks to show that these converge at a set of points which imply a conception of liberal justice. If pluralism is accepted by relatively few people at present, it clearly cannot provide such a point of overlap. It does not follow, however, that de facto disagreement about pluralism is reasonable, in the Rawls–Larmore sense of the permanent 'reasonable disagreement' to which liberal neutrality responds. Although it may be that many people currently reject pluralism, it may also be that reasonable people ought to accept it.

There are indeed good reasons to believe that value pluralism is true, as I argued in Chapter 3 and again, in connection with reasonable disagreement, in section 7.2. I also conceded that these arguments do not amount to a watertight case or complete philosophical demonstration. This is the second sense in which pluralism is controversial: it is philosophically controversial. All the arguments for its acceptance are vigorously contested. But to say that a claim is philosophically controversial is consistent with allowing not only that there are strong arguments for the claim, but also that the claim is likely to be true on balance. This is the conclusion I reached in Chapter 3. The case for the truth of pluralism is not watertight, but it is persuasive none the less. It is not a case that convinces all philosophers, but it is more plausible than the alternatives. At the very least it ought to be seriously entertained by reasonable people.

Value pluralism, then, is controversial in the de facto and philosophical senses, but these are compatible with holding that there is good reason to accept its truth on balance. If so, then pluralism should be recognized as a plausible basis for a reasoned justification of liberalism. This will not be a justification based on consensus, since (I have assumed) there is no public consensus in favour of pluralism. Rather, it will challenge consensus, asking

REASONABLE DISAGREEMENT

people to reflect on and question their beliefs, and to draw out the implications of what they can believe for good reason. The 'controversiality' of the pluralist case should not be a bar to its being persuasive for reasonable people.

In this connection it is important to acknowledge a sense in which value pluralism is not controversial. A crucial assumption of Larmore's argument is that value pluralism is a controversial conception of the good on a level with religious conceptions, for example, and therefore subject like them to reasonable disagreement. But although value pluralism is a conception of the good in the sense that it makes claims about the nature of the good, it is not a substantial conception of the *good life*. Pluralism is not, to use Rawls's term, a 'comprehensive moral doctrine'. Although pluralism gives an account of values as having certain features and interrelations, it does not provide a specific prescription for how to live a good life in the manner of substantial conceptions of the good such as religious conceptions. It is true, as I have argued, that pluralism implies certain normative principles for assessing the value of individual lives and social and political arrangements. The principles so far derived from pluralism (respect for universal values, recognition of incommensurability, promotion of diversity, and acknowledgement of reasonable disagreement) are strong enough to determine a broadly liberal political settlement. But within that framework there is space for individuals and groups to pursue many different versions of the good life. This is, of course, precisely the idea of liberal neutrality. The point is that value pluralism, although undeniably a conception of the good, is not on all fours with the kind of substantial conception that neutralist liberals are typically concerned to bracket off from the public realm of the state. Not all conceptions of the good need rule out neutrality, sensibly interpreted.[5]

Larmore might reply, as before, that even if value pluralism is not quite on a level with substantial religious conceptions of the good, it remains a highly controversial doctrine which many people can be expected to reject. But again, the fact that pluralism is incompatible with the existing beliefs of many people and currently disputed by philosophers shows only that pluralism cannot at present be the focus of popular or philosophical consensus; it does not show that pluralism cannot ground a reasoned argument that challenges consensus. Indeed if my argument in the previous section was correct, the idea of reasonable disagreement itself suggests that

177

FROM PLURALISM TO LIBERALISM

reasonable people must at least engage seriously with the idea of pluralism. Either one accepts the idea of reasonable disagreement or one does not. If pluralism is presupposed by reasonable disagreement, then someone who accepts reasonable disagreement must also accept value pluralism. What if reasonable disagreement is rejected? Here again there are two possibilities. Someone might deny that his conception of the good is subject to reasonable disagreement because, at least when it comes to that conception, he denies the authority of reason. Obviously no rational argument can persuade this person of the truth of pluralism. But that is because he has placed himself, in this respect, beyond the reach of any rational argument; it is not because there is no such argument to be made. Alternatively, someone might deny that her conception of the good is subject to reasonable disagreement because, she believes, that conception is required by reason. If this person is sincere, she is open to rational persuasion. Even if she rejects pluralism at present, that need not be permanent if the case for pluralism is (as I have argued) favoured by reason, at least on balance.

I conclude that although we can, for the present, expect de facto and philosophical controversy about value pluralism, that controversy is consistent with our allowing that the case for value pluralism is plausible and persuasive on balance. Value pluralism is not endorsed by current consensus – neither is the Rawlsian case. But pluralism is not controversial in the same way as substantial conceptions of the good life. It does not propose a specific ranking of values (beyond the implicit liberal framework) that would inevitably attract reasonable disagreement. Rather, it is a meta-ethical theory of the good which implies a politics of accommodation. Pluralism is a sound basis for liberalism, one that reasonable people can and should accept, even if they disagree about much else.

The second main point I wish to make in this section is that if truth rather than consensus is the goal, then pluralism is a more compelling basis for justifying liberalism than is the Rawlsian political argument. That is partly because the pluralist case, while no more controversial than political liberalism, is more forthcoming about its own foundations. The Rawlsian case purports to be wholly 'political', but if reasonable disagreement presupposes pluralism then that case rests ultimately on pluralism too. Pluralism might thus be said to *support* Rawls's argument by completing it. But once 'political' liberalism is seen to rest on value pluralism, the argument is transformed: it can no longer be seen as political in all of the

178

senses Rawls intends. Specifically, it can no longer be seen as appealing only to de facto beliefs drawn from the public political culture of a particular society. The further, deeper level of value pluralism transforms the argument from a particularist case into a universalist one.

This universalist transformation should not be seen by neutralist liberals as a cause for consternation. The partly submerged role of pluralism in Rawls's argument shows that his particularist turn is unsuccessful, but also unnecessary. Rawls's particularism is unsuccessful because it conceals a dependence on universalism at a deeper level. It is unnecessary because it is not needed to achieve Rawls's goal of preserving neutrality. Neutrality is not destroyed by the pluralist argument for two reasons. First, the pluralist argument aims only at approximate rather than complete neutrality. Second, Rawls himself sees that the neutrality aimed at does not exclude reliance on all ideas of the good. Rather, the goal is neutrality among 'comprehensive moral doctrines' or controversial 'conceptions of the good' on a par with religious prescriptions for the good life. But pluralism, I have argued, is not a conception of the good in that category, and therefore is not itself a view towards which a liberal state must be neutral. Pluralism is a view of the good, but not one that must attract permanent because reasonable disagreement. The justification of liberalism on pluralist grounds is compatible with approximate neutrality.

If my argument is correct, it is only by appeal to pluralism that a neutrality defence of liberalism can be completed. Without its subterranean appeal to pluralism Rawls's case would not succeed, since it could give no adequate account of why the disagreement it addresses must be permanent. On the other hand, once Rawls's reliance on pluralism is acknowledged, the particularism of his distinctively 'political' argument falls away as unnecessary. I conclude that compared with the Rawlsian argument the pluralist case is the stronger. It makes explicit what is partly concealed in political liberalism, namely how to explain the crucial notion of reasonable disagreement. In doing so, moreover, it frees liberal argument from the constraints of particularism. The pluralist case restores the traditional liberal aspiration to universality while at the same time preserving the ideal of neutrality in a sensibly modest form.

My final claim in this section is that the pluralist approach is also preferable to the Rawlsian political line at a more general level, namely its implications for the proper role of political philosophy in a modern liberal democracy. The traditional, 'Socratic' task of philosophy is the pursuit, through reasoned argument, of the truth. The later Rawlsian political case for liberalism, however, subordinates the search for truth to the achievement of consensus. The goal is the identification of the contents of an 'overlapping consensus' among as many as possible of the various beliefs contained within the public political culture of a constitutional democracy. Whether those beliefs are justified is not questioned. The pluralist approach, by contrast, is in this sense squarely 'metaphysical', since it is founded on claims about the nature of value. It restores the traditional role of philosophy as an inquiry into truth. This is not to say that agreement is not important on this view, rather that what is important is agreement on the truth.

Why should pluralist metaphysics be preferred to Rawlsian consensus? Some answers are implicit in points already made. First, there is little to be gained from the consensus approach. If existing beliefs must be accommodated 'as is', then the area of overlap among them is likely to be small. This expectation is borne out by the thinness of Rawls's own account of the overlapping consensus (Scheffler, 1994). Second, the consensus approach does not appear to avoid metaphysics in any case, as several commentators have suggested (2.2.2) and as I have argued in the case of its implicit reliance on value pluralism. Third, there is no good reason why political philosophers should avoid metaphysical questions and good reason why they should pursue such questions. This point is well made by Jean Hampton (1989). Part of the reason why Rawls wants to eschew such issues is in order to express a principle of toleration of and respect for people holding divergent conceptions of the good. But, as Hampton points out, respecting persons does not require that we accept without criticism everything they believe or say: philosophical argument is compatible with respect for persons. Indeed, true philosophical argument positively entails respect for persons, since it implies that one recognizes the person one is trying to persuade as a rational agent worthy of reasoned argument rather than merely an appropriate object of coercion or manipulation or patronizing mollification. 'Such respect is the foundation not only of philosophy but also of liberal society; it is that upon which we must insist if we are to have either' (ibid.: 812). If toleration and respect are desirable goals, then philosophical pursuit of the truth is a positive value rather than something to be avoided.

Are there any distinctively *pluralist* reasons for public appeals to truth rather than consensus? An interesting suggestion is made by Bernard Williams:

> The consciousness of the plurality of competing values is itself a good, as constituting knowledge of an absolute and fundamental truth. This is a good which, in the name of honesty, or truthfulness, or courage, may be urged against someone who recommends simplification of our values ... [O]ne who properly recognises the plurality of values is one who understands the deep and creative role that these various values can play in human life. In that perspective, the correctness of the liberal consciousness is better expressed, not so much in terms of truth – that it recognises the values which indeed there are – but in terms of truthfulness. It is prepared to try to build a life round the recognition that these different values do each have a real and intelligible human significance, and are not just errors, misdirections or poor expressions of human nature. To try to build a life in any other way would now be an evasion .... (1980: xviii)

A willingness to acknowledge the true nature of human values, including their pluralism if that is the case, contributes to any good life for human beings. This is so both for its own sake, since knowledge is an intrinsic human good, and for the practical contribution this particular kind of knowledge makes to the living of a good life, which will be a life in which distinct values will be recognized for what they are. A society in which the idea of value pluralism is at least on the agenda for public discussion is one that opens up the possibility of good lives for more of its citizens than a society that confines such matters to the private discussions of philosophers.

Perhaps a Rawlsian might reply as follows. Yes, knowledge or truth, including knowledge or truth concerning values, is a genuine value, important because universal. But on the view of pluralists themselves, truth can only be one such important value among others. It may come into conflict with other goods – Williams elsewhere allows that truth may undermine pre-reflective moral certainties (1985: 148, 167–9). In some cases truth may be outweighed by other values. Indeed, our present circumstances amount to such a case. In the context of a modern constitutional democracy characterized by widespread reasonable disagreement

FROM PLURALISM TO LIBERALISM

about the good life, what is most important is not pursuing the truth, which may be unattainable, but reaching consensus on a framework for fair co-operation. Agreement is prior to truth in this particular case.

Pluralists have two rejoinders. First, they can point out, as before, that not all disagreement about the good is equally reasonable, consequently not all conceptions of the good have an equal claim to being accommodated. In particular, there is good reason to argue against those conceptions in conflict with value pluralism, since there is good reason, on balance, to accept the pluralist account of the good as true. Indeed, once more, value pluralism will be unusually hard to reject if it is presupposed by the idea of reasonable disagreement itself. Second, pluralism gives us an important reason to be prepared to challenge people's beliefs rather than just accommodate them. This is that pluralists should want people to be critically reflective in outlook rather than uncritically receptive or heteronomous. Pluralists, in short, should place considerable weight on the value of personal autonomy. If that is so, then the kind of critical inquiry involved in philosophical argument in pursuit of the truth becomes again a salutary stimulus rather than an obstacle. On the contrary, it is the purely consensus-building approach that, on this view, is inadequate, since it does nothing to question existing beliefs and so nothing to encourage autonomy rather than conformism. Why is autonomy such an important value from the point of view of pluralism? That is a question for the next chapter.

To summarize, this chapter has dealt with a number of complex, interconnected issues, and it may be helpful to separate out my main conclusions as follows.

(1) Value pluralism implies an argument for liberalism by way of 'reasonable disagreement'. If values are plural and incommensurable, then we should expect reasonable disagreement, within certain limits, about the nature of the good life. That disagreement ought to be accommodated, and is best accommodated politically by liberalism.

(2) Contrary to Larmore, this argument is no more controversial a basis for liberalism than that of Rawlsian 'political' liberalism, which depends on (a) the notion of reasonable disagreement, which presupposes value pluralism; and (b) conceptions of the good, that are no less controversial.

182

REASONABLE DISAGREEMENT

(3) Pluralism is in any case not a controversial conception of the good on a level with religious and other substantial conceptions of the good life that are subject to reasonable disagreement. On the contrary, the case for pluralism, although not watertight, ought to be found persuasive by any reasonable person.

(4) The pluralist case for liberal neutrality is superior to Rawlsian political liberalism because it makes Rawls's pluralist foundations explicit without undermining the goal of neutrality.

(5) The pluralist approach is superior to the Rawlsian approach more generally, because it restores the traditional role of philosophy as a critical inquiry into the truth rather than a vehicle for obtaining consensus among unexamined beliefs.

Notes

1. Indeed, I shall argue later that from the pluralist point of view it is the perfectionist (autonomy-based) approach to liberalism that ought to be accorded priority over the neutrality approach (based on diversity and reasonable disagreement); see 9.1 below.

2. In the model case, Rawls describes an overlapping consensus among (1) a tolerant religious doctrine, (2) 'a comprehensive liberal moral doctrine such as those of Kant or Mill' and (3) a view containing both 'the political values formulated by a freestanding political conception of justice' and 'a large family of nonpolitical values. It is a pluralist view, let us say, since each subpart of this family has its own account based on ideas drawn from within it, leaving all values to be balanced against one another, either in groups or singly, in particular kinds of cases.' Rawls argues that all these views 'lead to roughly the same political judgements and thus overlap on the political conception' (1993: 145–6).

3. For a similar explanation of how conflict arises among conceptions of the good under pluralism, see MacKenzie (1999: 330–1), interpreting Berlin: 'In order to demonstrate the assumption of conflict in the doctrine of value-pluralism Berlin begins with the notion that an individual's value system is encapsulated in their "model of man". This "model of man" is constituted by the extrapolation of familiar moral experiences into generalized explanatory frameworks. Given that people view moral situations in a variety of ways the "model of man" they generate from those experiences will vary. Moreover, they will necessarily come into conflict. As each model is conceived as a generally applicable frame of reference they exclude others derived from different experiences of different "interpretations" of the same experience ... The conflict of values arises with the generalization of these models.'

183

4. This claim has been interestingly contested by Galston: 'In my view, this is a verbal difficulty that disappears when we examine the concrete experience of faith communities over time. Even when a religion appears to assert a dominant end, on closer inspection it turns out that each religious doctrine, or concept of God, establishes a complex field of values, the relations among which are contestable and contested. There is an inner logic that leads to pluralism within, and not just between, religions' (1999a: 880). Acceptance of value pluralism may be compatible with religious conceptions of the good, even monotheistic ones, since these too may add to our sense of ethical experience as a field of potentially conflicting incommensurables. Even if one believes that all values harmonize within the mind of God, one could consistently accept the idea of pluralism as accurately capturing the nature of human moral experience.
5. Compare Rawls's recognition that his own theory of political liberalism employs several 'ideas of the good', and that this is consistent with his goal of neutrality (1993: Lecture V).

CHAPTER 8

From Pluralism to Liberalism III: Virtues

In this chapter I set out the third of my principal arguments from pluralism to liberalism. The first was the diversity argument, the second the argument from reasonable disagreement. Both of these imply a case for liberalism that is accommodationist in character: liberalism is justified along these lines as approximately neutral among different conceptions of the good. I shall now argue that pluralism also implies a case for liberalism as the best political vehicle for the development and practice of certain 'pluralist virtues' or traits of character, in particular personal autonomy.[1] My basic claim is that these are virtues required for practical reasoning under pluralism, and that they are best promoted by a liberal form of politics. On this view, liberalism becomes not only a political framework for a society containing diverse and conflicting conceptions of the good life (Chapters 6 and 7), but also an ethical framework for those conceptions themselves. This virtues-based argument consequently suggests a form of liberalism that is broadly 'perfectionist' rather than neutralist, that is, based on a conception of the good which it is the legitimate business of the state to protect and promote. A question then arises as to the relation between this approach and that of the previous two chapters, since the two appear to be in tension, but I shall postpone that issue until the next chapter (9.1).

My discussion is divided into four sections. First, I give an account of the virtues required for reasoned choice making under pluralism. Second, I show how those virtues are promoted by

185

liberalism through a corresponding set of characteristically liberal virtues and attitudes. My contention that the pluralist virtues do best under liberalism is reinforced by my focus, in the third section, on the link between pluralism and personal autonomy, the liberal virtue par excellence. In the final section I make some general points about the scope and implications of the virtues argument, including its place in the pluralist case for liberalism overall.

8.1 Pluralist Virtues

I start with a passage from Michael Walzer:

> I don't know anyone who believes in value pluralism who isn't a liberal, in sensibility as well as conviction ... You have to look at the world in a receptive and generous way to see a pluralism of Berlin's sort ... And you also have to look at the world in a skeptical way, since the adherents of each of the different values are likely to rank them very high on a scale designed for just that purpose. And receptivity, generosity, and skepticism are, if not liberal values, the qualities of mind that make it possible to accept liberal values (or better, that make it likely that liberal values will be accepted). (1995: 31)

For Walzer, liberalism is linked to value pluralism not so much by a logical relationship as by 'informal' or 'pragmatic' arguments. In a similar vein, Galston notes 'the common fundamental orientation that gives rise to both' (1999b: 777). On this view, to connect pluralism with liberalism it is enough to point out that most pluralists are liberals, while a great many monists are not. A person who subscribes to the pluralist outlook is likely to accept the liberal outlook too – at any rate is more likely to do so than a monist. There seems to be a natural affinity between pluralism, with its picture of a multiplicity of genuine goods and ways of life, and liberalism, with its commitment to toleration and constraints on political power. Pluralist and liberal temperaments are likely to overlap.

Walzer's point possesses limited force as it stands, but it is also helpfully suggestive. As with his similarly pragmatic argument discussed in Chapter 1, his observation is true as far as it goes, but complacent in its implication that this kind of loose affiliation is an adequate substitute for attempts at a tighter justification. If Gray and Kekes are right, then even if pluralists tend to be liberals temperamentally, they ought not to be liberals either philosophically or politically. The truth of Walzer's observation does not preclude the need for liberals to look for a more rigorous case for liberalism on the basis of pluralism. But his remark is also helpful to the more rigorous pluralist case for liberalism, because it suggests another way (in addition to the diversity and reasonable disagreement arguments already discussed) in which that case may be made out. If the general attitudes characteristic of pluralism and liberalism are so sympathetic in practice, might they not be mutually supportive in principle? Specifically, might it not be the case that the pluralist outlook involves 'qualities of mind' or virtues that flourish best within a liberal political framework? I shall argue that this is indeed so. First, I shall show that pluralism implies a commitment to a particular set of virtues; second, that those virtues are best realized under liberalism.

How does pluralism imply a set of virtues? The short answer is that if values are plural and incommensurable, then when they come into conflict in particular cases we can choose rationally among them only by engaging in the particularistic kind of practical reasoning described by the Aristotelian tradition. To be successful in that kind of practical reasoning requires the development of certain virtues. Recall that in Chapter 3 I set out two ways of reasoning in the face of pluralism, particularist and universalist. The second of these has been my main concern over the preceding chapters: we can seek the guidance of general principles derived from reflection on the elements of value pluralism itself. The principles so far identified include respect for universal values, recognition of incommensurability, promotion of diversity, and accommodation of reasonable disagreement. I have argued that, taken together, these principles are sufficient to identify liberalism as the best *political framework* for pluralist choice. But what about such choices themselves? *Within* the political framework already identified, that is, in the particular situations that confront us in our lives, how can we choose rationally among competing incommensurables? The commitment to a liberal framework scarcely answers all our questions about how we should live: what occupation we should enter, whom we should choose as a marriage partner, which religion we should practise. As Nussbaum puts it: 'A general account may give us necessary conditions for choosing well; it cannot by itself give sufficient conditions' (1992b: 93). Particular questions of the kind just mentioned can only be answered by particularist practical reasoning. This was the first form of guidance for pluralist choice that I identified in Chapter 3 (3.2). But the need for such an approach when plural values conflict in particular cases is also a general principle implied by the nature of pluralism.[2]

Once again, the key elements of value pluralism at work here are conflict and incommensurability. The unavoidability of conflicts among plural values requires that we must often choose among them, and the incommensurability of values ensures that such choices are 'hard' in the sense that they are not resolvable by any single, straightforward formula. In such cases reasons to choose one course rather than another are provided not by reference to a general rule which is regarded as authoritative across many different situations, but rather by attending to the particularities of the decision context. Attention to the context of our decision enables us to specify the elements of that context, its constitutive facts and values, and so to specify what matters most to us in that situation: which values should come first and in what combination. Especially important among the value components of a choice context is the chooser's background conception of the good life. This is the principal backdrop against which the values at stake can be weighed against one another and ranked without recourse to (impossible or superficial) commensuration – although of course it is possible that one's conception of the good will itself be revised as part of the deliberation.

This kind of particularist ethical reasoning requires, as Aristotelians are well aware, certain skills or excellences or 'virtues'. Taking Nussbaum's version of Aristotle as my model, I list four of these as follows: generosity, realism, attentiveness and flexibility.

8.1.1 Generosity

In order to reason successfully under value pluralism we must first have an appreciation of something of the great range of values that are part of human experience, and so potentially available to be pursued. This appreciation may be termed (following Walzer) *generosity*. As Stephen Macedo puts it:

> If our world really is one of incommensurable basic goods then one who is knowledgeable and articulate about these different basic values, one who possesses a language of qualitative

VIRTUES

contrasts and a broad experience of the nature of basic goods and the different ways of participating in them, understands the world better than shallow reductionists and those uncritically wedded to a narrow, parochial way of life. (1990: 219)

A person who can conceive of no more than a narrow range of values, or who has only a vague notion of all but a few limited ends, cannot cope well with the demands of rational choice under value pluralism. Such a person would be unaware of, or would ignore, genuinely valuable options.

The person of practical wisdom under pluralism consequently needs to have an awareness of the diversity and incommensurability of universal values, and of the forms taken by those values in different ways of life. This awareness includes, first, a basic notion of the generic human goods, that is, of those goods that are essential to any form of human flourishing. Second, the pluralist chooser must also appreciate that the values from which one must choose are not only multiple but radically distinct from one another — that is, incommensurable. Pluralist choosers must therefore have a capacity to appreciate each value in its own right and for its own sake. Third, some appreciation would be needed of the multiplicity not only of human goods but also of legitimate ways of life in which those goods are instantiated. As argued in previous chapters, value pluralism does not imply a duty to endorse existing ways of life to the same extent as it implies respect for human values. The general principles of value pluralism already discussed (universality, incommensurability, diversity and reasonable disagreement) all place limits on what can count as a desirable form of life from a pluralist point of view. But within those limits an appreciation of the range of legitimate forms taken by human life must be part of the pluralist outlook, if only as a consequence of the necessary grasp of the plurality of goods.

It follows that the pluralist person of practical wisdom will need those qualities or dispositions of mind that enable him or her to achieve the necessary appreciation of the diversity of values and ways of life. These qualities will include knowledge, experience and what may be called 'moral imagination', or the ability to conceive of goods or forms of life as valuable even when one does not pursue them oneself. Pluralist persons of practical wisdom must therefore be generous in the sense that they are capable of envisaging a range of values and ways of life as genuinely good, and as comprising a number of irreducibly distinct goods, even though these are not their own values or ways of life.

8.1.2 Realism

A second set of virtuous dispositions necessary for good choice under pluralism can be labelled the virtues of *realism*. When incommensurable values come into conflict, one of the senses in which choices among them are 'hard' is that there can be no complete compensation for whatever value or combination of values is chosen against. Where such values are very important, pluralist choices can be genuinely tragic; even in less momentous cases inescapable choices among competing plural values can be cause for regret despite one's best efforts. The clear-headed pluralist is thus, as Nussbaum observes, faced with the experience of 'vulnerability to loss' (1992b: 67): in having to choose among important plural values, we cannot escape forgoing some genuine good. 'Aristotelianism fosters attention to the ways in which the world can impede our efforts to act well; it indicates that caring about many things will open us to the risk of these terrible situations' (ibid.: 64).

The quality of mind required for this aspect of the pluralist outlook is honesty or even courage. Those who genuinely adopt a pluralist point of view cannot fool themselves that conflicts of this kind can be resolved without ultimate, perhaps tragic, cost. Rather, they must face the depth and permanence (as well as the pervasiveness) of value conflict and the absolute nature of the losses that result from it. They are 'realists', in contrast with the 'utopians' discussed in Chapter 4 who deal in final solutions and complete compensations. The virtue of realism in this sense is thus akin to the 'skepticism' associated with the pluralist outlook by Walzer (see also Galston, 1999b: 777). It should be added, though, that this will be a moderate scepticism directed primarily against excessively ambitious goals of moral and political perfection, rather than a thoroughgoing denial of the role of reason in ethics. An extreme scepticism of the latter kind would be at odds with the pluralist outlook.

VIRTUES

8.1.3 Attentiveness

Third, rational choice under value pluralism requires *attentiveness*. We have seen that reasoned choice among plural and incommensurable values can be guided by general rules only at a general level, the level of the political framework. Particular decisions in such cases must be determined by a particularist approach, one in which close attention is paid to the particulars of the concrete situation. It is only by specifying the precise facts and values that constitute the context for choice that the pluralist chooser can specify what is most important to him or her in the situation. Only then can the chooser arrive at reasons to subject the contending considerations to some kind of ranking.

The idea of particularist attentiveness can be seen to have different aspects or levels, three of which can be distinguished as follows. First, attention must be paid to the distinctive character of the different goods involved in a choice situation. 'The Aristotelian agent scrutinizes each valuable alternative, seeking out its distinct nature' (Nussbaum, 1992b: 63). Second, the agent must attend to the distinctive particularity of the situation, which is constituted partly by the values at stake but also by the relevant facts. For the pluralist or Aristotelian chooser, 'the subtleties of a complex ethical situation must be seized in a confrontation with the situation itself' (ibid.: 69). Third, again closely connected with the first two aspects, we must attend to the individual persons involved in the situation, to their claims and needs. As Nussbaum reminds us, we should beware of losing sight of the human reality behind conflicts of values, and of allowing 'numbers and dots' to take the place of real men and women (ibid.: 101).[3]

8.1.4 Flexibility

The final virtue required for pluralist practical reasoning is *flexibility*. Having attended to the particulars of the concrete situation in which she finds herself, the pluralist chooser must be able to respond flexibly. That is, she must not insist on trying to resolve the situation by rigid application of a general rule, but rather be prepared to reach a balance between general rule and particular judgement tailored to the circumstances. Illustrating the idea of ethical flexibility, Nussbaum recounts Aristotle's metaphor of the

'Lesbian Rule'. The person who persists in choosing according to a rigidly predetermined standard is like an architect who tries to apply a straight ruler to a fluted column. The architect who knows his business will use the Lesbian Rule, a flexible ruler that 'bends to the shape of the stone and is not fixed'. Nussbaum concludes that 'good deliberation, like the Lesbian Rule, accommodates itself to the shape that it finds, responsively and with respect for complexity' (ibid.: 70).

Again, this does not mean that rules are irrelevant and that pluralist choices must be arbitrary or ad hoc. Even in the strongly particularist account of practical reasoning presented by Nussbaum, general rules have an important role to play as useful summaries of decision-making experience. But rules will not by themselves *determine* particular decisions. Rather, such decisions will require a process of 'interplay' or 'conversation' between general rules and concrete particulars in which each may be modified by the other (ibid.: 94–5). Especially important here is the 'evolving picture of the good or complete human life' that the agent brings to the situation. 'She views the good particular judgement as a further articulation of this evolving conception of the human good – or as a revision of it, if it should seem defective. Nothing is unrevisable' (ibid.: 95).[4]

The habit or cast of mind necessary for thinking and choosing in this way is that of flexibility. The pluralist chooser must be prepared to balance background commitments, including those summarized in the form of general principles or a conception of the good life, against considerations brought forward by attention to the concrete situation. Achieving such a balance means being open to reconsidering and revising either principles or particular judgements. The pluralist chooser must be flexible enough to consider changes in either direction.

8.2 Liberal Virtues

Having shown how pluralist practical reasoning requires certain virtues, I shall now argue that those virtues flourish best under a liberal form of politics. Liberalism promotes values and attitudes, indeed virtues, that in various ways complement or support the pluralist virtues identified in the previous section. I shall proceed by

VIRTUES

reviewing each of the pluralist virtues and articulating its connections with attitudes distinctively promoted by liberalism.

8.2.1 Broad-mindedness

First, the generosity required by the pluralist outlook is virtually identical with the kind of *broad-mindedness* encouraged by liberalism at its best. We have seen that to be genuinely conscious of the plurality of values is to acknowledge as legitimate and valuable something of the range of distinct (incommensurable) goods and ways of life pursued not only by oneself but also by others. The same sort of generosity is a virtue of liberalism. It is true, as Galston points out, that liberals can sometimes be 'decidedly ungenerous when faced with traditional ways of life they regard as stultifying and benighted' (1999b: 777). But at its best liberalism is guided in part by its foundational commitment to the peaceful accommodation of multiple forms of life. The attitude encouraged by this commitment is one 'receptive to a wide although not unlimited range of value-based claims. It will be generous to ways of life that reflect unusual but not indefensible choices among, or orderings of, basic values' (ibid.). A similar point is made by Macedo: 'The character that flourishes in a liberal, pluralistic social milieu, will have broad sympathies' (1990: 267). This is because a liberal politics is one which balances the acceptance of disagreement with the acknowledgement of human commonalities. Liberals will acknowledge that although others may pursue different goods and ways of life from their own, those others are still, like themselves, moral agents worthy of respect and therefore that their choices are also worthy of respect, at least prima facie. 'As we come to realize that those who engage in lives different from our own are nevertheless like us in important ways, we may come to sympathize not only with these persons but also with their projects and commitments' (ibid.). Liberal respect for persons leads at least to toleration of other cultures, and perhaps to a more positive celebration of cultural diversity.

Liberal broad-mindedness will not be unlimited, since it cannot embrace those choices and ways of life that are themselves hostile to toleration and respect for persons. But the liberal outlook is likely to be superior on this point to the viable alternatives. This is essentially the same point as that made in Chapter 6 under the heading of diversity (6.3). On the score of diversity, liberalism is superior to those conservative or strong communitarian approaches that sanction the political enforcement of a single local tradition. The politics of postmodernism or 'difference' may be in a sense even more broad-minded than liberalism, but that is only because it lacks the limits that would make it coherent.

8.2.2 Moderation

The second virtue required for pluralist reasoning, realism, overlaps and is supported by the liberal virtue of *moderation*. Pluralists accept that incommensurable values will sometimes come into conflict and that such conflict will result in uncompensated, perhaps tragic, losses. Consequently, pluralists are realists in the sense that they accept that the harmonious realization of all genuine values is not to be achieved in human life, either the life of an individual person or of a society. Liberals, similarly, accept the inevitability of conflict, loss and personal and social imperfection – the theme emphasized by Berlin (4.3) and confirmed by the argument from reasonable disagreement (Chapter 7). The good political system, for liberals, is one that accommodates and contains conflict rather than trying to transcend it. It follows that the liberal outlook is moderate in two senses. First, liberalism is not excessively demanding or ambitious; it does not expect moral or social perfection. Second, those principles to which liberals are committed are themselves held and pursued subject to revision rather than with single-minded fanaticism.

Both of these dimensions of liberal moderation are reinforced by the pluralist outlook. First, the inevitability of value conflict and loss, and the impossibility of perfection, will be a strong reason to limit the ambitions of the state. While it is true that some liberal reformers have been highly optimistic, that optimism always stops short – so far as we are still talking about a liberal position – of utopian hopes for achieving a society that is 'perfected' in the sense just mentioned. The best reason for this self-restraint is not moral scepticism or indeterminacy – a shaky basis for liberalism, as we have seen in several places. The reason is the expectation of reasonable disagreement about the good, of which the deepest explanation, we saw in the previous chapter, is value pluralism (7.2). If values are plural and incommensurable, we must expect that (within the liberal political limits already set out) there can be many

VIRTUES

legitimate forms of the good life corresponding to multiple legitimate ways of ranking incommensurable goods. The reason why these should be at least tolerated by the state is not scepticism but its opposite: the pluralist realization that the suppression of any of these legitimate forms is a real and irreplaceable loss of something valuable. Consequently, from both pluralist and liberal points of view, state programmes should tread warily, acknowledging and taking seriously the force of disagreement and the destructive effects of hard choices. A self-conscious value pluralism gives liberals good reason for the traditional moderation of their expectations concerning the state.

Moderation in this sense is a virtue for both citizens and leaders in a liberal society, and in both cases moderation is underscored by pluralist realism. In his virtues-based defence of liberalism, Galston lists several 'virtues of citizenship', among which is the requirement that liberal citizens 'be moderate in their demands and self-disciplined enough to accept painful measures when they are necessary' (1991: 224–5). According to Galston, this virtue is especially important in counteracting a besetting vice of popular governments, namely their 'propensity to gratify short-term desires at the expense of long-term interests and the inability to act on unpleasant truths about what must be done' (ibid.: 224). The insistence that 'unpleasant tuths' about the costs of our decisions be faced honestly is precisely the message of pluralist realism. Moderation in the demands of liberal citizens must be complemented by moderation in the conduct of their leaders. The citizenry must not ask for too much, but the leadership must not promise too much. In addition, Galston argues that liberal leaders must exhibit virtues of patience in accepting the limitations of a diverse society, and integrity in resisting the temptation to curry favour 'by pandering to immoderate public demands. Against desire liberal leaders must counterpoise restraints; against the fantasy of the free lunch they must insist on the reality of the hard choice ...' (ibid.: 226). Here again, in the emphasis on 'the reality of the hard choice', liberal moderation and pluralist realism overlap.

Another dimension of overlap between pluralist realism and liberal moderation is the *provisional* nature of liberal commitment. The experience of value conflict and loss that results from value pluralism may be 'internalized' (to borrow a term from Macedo, 1990: 238) at either of two levels. First, it may be internalized by a society as a whole, with the effect already discussed, namely

195

moderation in the sense of realistic social and political expectations. Second, value conflict and loss may be internalized by individual persons. The effect of this is also to encourage moderation, this time in the sense of moderating or qualifying the nature of one's commitments. If pluralism means that the particular way a person ranks goods is only one legitimate way among others, then to appreciate that is to see that one's preferred ranking might have been otherwise, and may yet be open to revision. To see this is to be discouraged from regarding one's commitments as incontestable absolutes, and so to make it less likely that those commitments will be held fanatically, to the detriment of every other concern and to the concerns of others. Pluralist realism will thus lead to liberal moderation. Conversely, living in a liberal society characterized by diversity and toleration encourages the thought that such features are justified by an underlying value pluralism: liberal moderation in this sense reinforces pluralist realism.[5]

8.2.3 Attention to values, situations and persons

We come now to the third of the central virtues implied by pluralist practical reasoning, namely *attentiveness*. Due regard to value pluralism means that reasoned choices among conflicting plural values cannot be wholly determined by general rules, since general rules imply abstract rankings of values that pluralism questions. The elements of pluralism themselves imply a set of general principles that together add up to a broadly liberal political framework for pluralist choice. But within that framework pluralist practical reasoning must be particularist, or attentive to the particularity of the case in hand. I distinguished three aspects of this attentiveness, namely attention to the particularity of values, of situations, and of persons.

Is pluralist attentiveness promoted by liberalism? At first sight it may seem that attention to particularity is not one of liberalism's strong points. Liberal thought places a strong emphasis on the acceptance of general rules, derived by abstraction from particular cases and uniformly applicable across a range of such cases. One thinks immediately of principles such as the rule of law and universal rights. But while liberal commitments to rules and to generality cannot be denied, that does not mean that liberalism neglects the virtue of attentiveness altogether. In fact liberalism

VIRTUES

promotes attentiveness in all three of the respects listed earlier.

First, attention to the range and distinctiveness of values is already implied by the 'generosity' or broad-mindedness common to both pluralism and liberalism (8.2.1). Second, attention to the particularity of concrete situations is present in the liberal outlook in two ways. To begin with, general rules, whether liberal or non-liberal, are usually themselves the product of reflection on concrete situations. As Nussbaum points out, Aristotelian particularism can accept a universal rule as authoritative 'insofar as it is a summary of wise decisions' (1992b: 69). Many liberal principles are defensible in just this way. For example, the notion of human rights can be defended as encapsulating many particular judgements made in the past to the effect that in concrete situations more good comes of allowing people certain claims and liberties than of witholding these.[6] This aspect of rules is not, of course, peculiar to liberal rules. More distinctive of liberalism is the way rules are applied in particular situations – the second sense in which the liberal outlook implies attention to concrete situations – but this involves the notion of personal autonomy, which I shall come to in a moment.

The third aspect of pluralist attentiveness was attention to the individual persons affected by one's decision. In this respect liberal attentiveness is perhaps at its strongest, since the idea that individual persons matter, and matter equally, is the most fundamental of all liberal commitments (2.1). Among pluralist liberals, the ideal of respect for persons is seen, for example, in Berlin's attack on those versions of positive liberty that make it possible for leaders 'to ignore the actual wishes of men or societies, to bully, oppress, torture them in the name, and on behalf, of their "real" selves' (1969: 133). Nussbaum's warning against treating individual human beings as if they were 'numbers and dots' is another powerful expression of an attitude that is both pluralist and liberal (1992b: 101). Note also the link between liberal attention to persons and pluralist realism. What motivates attention of this kind is the 'vulnerability to loss' that pluralism implies, in this case the sense that each human being is something both valuable and irreplaceable.

It might be objected that what is being respected here is not so much the particularity of the persons concerned as the universal attributes of which persons are merely bearers.[7] But this objection has more force against some versions of liberalism than against others. The Kantian notion of respect for persons, it is true, takes as

197

the focus of respect the capacity for moral autonomy that is possessed by all normal mature adult human beings equally. For Mill, on the other hand, liberty is to be defended in part as instrumental for 'individuality', the sense that as well as possessing a common humanity each individual human being is unique (1974: Chapter 3). In this notion of the human person as valuable in a way that is irreplaceable because incommensurable with the value of any other human being, the liberal view once more coincides with the pluralist.[8]

8.2.4 Personal autonomy

So far I have argued that the pluralist virtues of generosity, realism and attentiveness are promoted by liberalism through the corresponding liberal virtues or attributes of broad-mindedness, moderation and respect for persons. The question arises whether forms of politics other than liberalism may have the same effect. I believe I have already done enough to show that the claims of liberalism in this regard are superior to those of any rivals. This is true, for example, of a comparison between liberalism and its closest competitors from a pluralist point of view, conservatism and modus vivendi pragmatism. Conservatism may run liberalism close on the score of realism and moderation, but on the remaining criteria liberalism clearly has the stronger claim. The conservative stress on local tradition makes it less generous or broad-minded towards different goods and ways of life, and perhaps less attentive to the particularities of different situations. Similarly, Gray's modus vivendi approach, although alive to uncompensated loss and attentive to context, is paradoxically ungenerous in its narrow insistence on self-interest or peace at any price as the ethical bottom line.

If any doubt remains, however, liberalism decisively shows its advantages over its rivals in relation to the fourth of the pluralist virtues, namely flexibility (8.1.4). If pluralism requires that we attend to the particularities of concrete situations rather than insisting always on the application of general rules (including those implicit in Gray's notion of modus vivendi), then we need to be able to respond flexibly to those situations. Corresponding to pluralist flexibility is the liberal celebration of *personal autonomy*. Since autonomy is the most distinctive of liberal virtues, a link between autonomy and flexibility will be the strongest of links between pluralism and liberalism.

The essence of the idea of personal autonomy is the notion of making one's own life. 'The autonomous person is a (part) author of his own life. The ideal of personal autonomy is the vision of people controlling, to some degree, their own destiny, fashioning it through successive decisions throughout their lives' (Raz, 1986: 369). For liberals, autonomy is a virtue, perhaps the paramount virtue. As Mill puts it: 'Where not the person's own character but the traditions and customs of other people are the rule of conduct, there is wanting one of the principal ingredients of human happiness, and quite the chief ingredient of individual and social progress' (1974: 120). To be autonomous contrasts with being coerced or manipulated. It also contrasts with the uncoerced and unmanipulated acceptance of what Mill calls 'the despotism of custom', the uncritical reception of prescriptive tradition as one's ethical standard. 'The despotism of custom is everywhere the standing hindrance to human advancement, being in unceasing antagonism to that disposition to aim at something better than customary, which is called, according to circumstances, the spirit of liberty, or that of progress or improvement' (ibid.: 136). To be autonomous is to act on standards that are 'one's own' in a strong sense. It is to deny that value conflicts can be resolved simply by the mechanical application of traditional or other rules. Thus far autonomy, in its opposition to unquestioning adherence to custom, is immediately on the side of flexibility against rigidity in ethics.[9]

Might autonomy not involve its own form of rigidity, however? If autonomy means living in accordance with 'one's own plan of life', might that plan not involve an inflexible commitment to a monist ethical principle, say a form of utilitarianism? Such a life would seem to count as autonomous, yet would be as rigid as a life based on unquestioning adherence to tradition. If so, liberal autonomy would not necessarily intersect with pluralist flexibility.

In reply, we should distinguish two cases. First, a person may have a plan of life that is rigid at the point of conception. A person might make a once-and-for-all decision to live according to some monist standard, say a form of utilitarianism, which will henceforth not be questioned. In such a case the person may be autonomous in making the decision, but his life thereafter is not autonomous. That is because, as described, his life lacks the dimension of critical reflection that is essential to autonomy. One might autonomously decide to surrender autonomy, but having done so (supposing this can be done[10]) one necessarily ceases to be autonomous. As Raz points out, the image that the metaphor of the autonomous person as 'part author of his life ... is meant to conjure up is not that of the regimented, compulsive person who decides when young what life to have and spends the rest of it living it out according to plan ... the ideal of personal autonomy is not to be identified with the ideal of giving one's life a unity' (1986: 370). In this first case, then, autonomy does not involve rigidity, since rigidity has excluded autonomy.

A second case, however, is that of a person who maintains an attitude of critical reflection towards her commitments yet with the result that she periodically reaffirms her adherence to a monist rule. Such a person does seem to be both autonomous and committed to an approach to ethics that is in the relevant sense rigid: autonomous inflexibility is in this sense possible. But this sort of case is likely to be uncommon. As Raz argues, although some autonomous approaches to life may be like this, 'most are not of this kind. They allow for variations, encourage spontaneity, and some of the conventions governing their form delineate the (often plentiful) circumstances and reasons which are legitimate occasions for changing one's mind and abandoning the pursuit, without any whiff of failure in the air' (ibid.: 384).

Moreover, even so far as some autonomous persons may fail to be flexible, that shows only that autonomy is not a *sufficient* condition for flexibility. But all flexible choosers are autonomous: autonomy is a *necessary* condition for flexibility. That is, to be flexible in responding to concrete situations is necessarily to be involved in making one's own life. The reason is that to be flexible in the required sense is to reject the mechanical or unquestioned application to every situation of traditional and other rules. To reject the authority of external rules is to be thrown back on the resources of one's own judgement, and so to become the author of one's own life. Or rather, it is to be committed to self-authorship as an ideal. A person could fail to achieve autonomy and, for example, just drift through life. But drifting would not be flourishing, according to the standards either of liberalism or pluralism. The anomic drifter would not be a good or successful chooser from the pluralist point of view because he would not be exhibiting the pluralist virtue of flexibility. Rather than responding flexibly to a situation, he would be permitting himself to be dominated or

VIRTUES

pushed about by it. Autonomy does not necessarily oblige us to be flexible (although autonomy will usually involve flexibility), but being flexible obliges us to be, or try to be, autonomous. While the relations between flexibility and autonomy are not wholly symmetrical, they overlap significantly. We arrive once more at an important convergence between the general attitudes of pluralists and liberals. Pluralist flexibility requires liberal autonomy as a matter of necessity, while liberal autonomy will usually encourage pluralist flexibility. I shall examine this link more closely in the next section, where I inspect the relation between pluralism and autonomy more generally.

To summarize the central argument of the chapter so far: pluralist and liberal virtues are mutually reinforcing, such that liberalism is the best political form for equipping people to choose well (that is, for good reason) under value pluralism. We have noted four such points of mutuality: pluralist generosity and liberal broadmindedness, pluralist realism and liberal moderation, pluralist attentiveness and (in particular) liberal respect for persons, pluralist flexibility and liberal autonomy. This last connection is especially important because of the centrality of the position occupied by autonomy in the liberal scheme of values. Since the value liberals place on autonomy is one of the main features that sets liberalism apart from other political views, it is worth pursuing the relation between pluralism and autonomy further.

8.3 Pluralism and Autonomy

In this section I develop the connection already outlined between pluralism and autonomy. In so doing I shall be strengthening further the links between pluralism and liberalism. My argument, in brief, is that to choose among plural and conflicting plural and incommensurable values is a demanding task that involves actively creating one's own plan of life, that is, it involves the exercise of personal autonomy. We have already seen the beginnings of this argument in the connection drawn in the last section between liberal autonomy and pluralist flexibility. Further resources for the argument are to be found in the accounts of the relation between pluralism and autonomy given by Raz and Macedo, which I examine first. I then set out my own version of the argument, concluding by comparing it with the cognate strand in Berlin.

201

FROM PLURALISM TO LIBERALISM

8.3.1 Raz on pluralism and autonomy

We saw in Chapter 2 that personal autonomy, or making one's own life, is the central value in Raz's particularist–perfectionist defence of liberalism (2.2.4). Raz rejects neutrality as a possible goal for any form of politics, since any form of politics, liberalism included, presupposes some conception of well-being for its citizens, that is, some conception of the good life. Liberal politics is justified by its active promotion of a conception of well-being based on personal autonomy. It is in this (Rawlsian) sense that Raz's liberalism is 'perfectionist'. Consequently, Raz is likely to be criticized by neutralist liberals for supporting the enforcement of a specific conception of the good when modern societies are characterized by widespread disagreement about the nature of the good. On the neutralist view Raz's liberalism is both authoritarian and unlikely to be accepted by many citizens. To this objection Raz makes, in effect, two replies. First, he presents the liberal autonomy-based notion of well-being as historically and socially relative rather than universal in derivation and application. The autonomous life is not that of all people at all times, but rather a social ideal only for modern industrial societies. In such a society, characterized by conditions of fast technological and social change, being able to make one's own life, rather than being reliant on traditional norms, is the only way to flourish. It is in this sense that Raz's liberalism is not universalist but 'particularist'.

Raz's second line of reply is that the conception of well-being promoted by his liberal state is not narrow and 'rigoristic', like that of an authoritarian state, but 'pluralist', embracing many different goods and 'forms of life'. Autonomy, although an essential part of any good life under this conception, is not so much a substantive form of life in competition with others, as a way in which to approach many different ways of living. Moreover – and this is Raz's most important argument for my purposes – the existence of a plurality of values within the liberal conception of well-being follows from the special place in that conception occupied by autonomy itself. That is, Raz argues that to value autonomy as liberals do is necessarily to presuppose 'moral pluralism'.

Raz's innovative linking of pluralism and autonomy has frequently been noted, but it is less frequently observed that he outlines two different versions of the link. The version usually acknowledged (e.g. Mulhall and Swift, 1996: 323–6) goes as

202

VIRTUES

follows. To value autonomy is to presuppose moral pluralism because 'autonomy is exercised through choice, and choice requires a variety of options to choose from' (Raz, 1986: 398). To be autonomous is to make choices about how to live one's life; a person with no real choice about what to do cannot be autonomous. Autonomy is not necessarily valuable: that a wrong action is performed autonomously does not increase its value, indeed the reverse. Autonomy is valuable only when directed to valuable ends. Therefore, autonomy is to be valued only when it involves a choice among multiple valuable options. Valuing autonomy implies 'an adequate range' of goods to choose from, that is, a conception of moral pluralism (*ibid.*: 372).

Note, however, that the 'moral pluralism' implied by valuing autonomy in this first version of Raz's argument is (as he recognizes) pluralism only in a 'weak' sense, not the full sense of Berlinian value pluralism (*ibid.*: 398). Moral pluralism here means only 'a variety of conflicting considerations' presupposing 'choices involving trade-offs' and different forms of life with distinctive virtues (*ibid.*). This involves only plurality and potential conflict, which are indeed sufficient for the kind of choice among multiple goods implied by valuing autonomy. But this conception of moral pluralism does not entail incommensurability of values, the hallmark of genuine (in Raz's terminology 'strong') value pluralism. Therefore, this first version of Raz's argument takes us only from autonomy to weak pluralism; it is not an argument for strong or full value pluralism.

However, Raz also mentions another version of his argument, this time moving from autonomy to value pluralism proper. 'If valuing autonomy commits one to the creation of value which in turn presupposes strong pluralism, then assuming the value of autonomy one can prove strong value-pluralism' (ibid.). The pivotal phrase is 'the creation of value', to which valuing autonomy commits us, and which presupposes genuine value pluralism. Earlier Raz explains that value is 'created' when a person becomes committed to the various goals that give shape to one's life: 'one creates values, generates, through one's developing commitments and pursuits, reasons which transcend the reasons one had for undertaking one's commitments and pursuits. In that way a person's life is (in part) of his own making. It is a normative creation, a creation of new values and reasons' (ibid.: 387). New choices shape our lives in ways that generate new considerations for further choices. For example, if I choose to become a lawyer rather than a doctor, then that choice of

203

occupation will influence the considerations I bring to decisions later, since those decisions will be made against a background of legal rather than medical experience.

It is easy to see how the creation of value in this sense is involved in autonomy, less easy to see how it presupposes value pluralism. To be autonomous, actively to make one's own life, is necessarily to create value in the sense Raz describes. But how does the creation of value as understood here imply not only the plurality but also the incommensurability of values? Raz does not pursue this connection, so it may be that he could complete the argument, but it is hard to see how. Values could be created in Raz's sense even if they were not incommensurable. For example, suppose that values could be commensurated through the common denominator of utility, and I apply the utilitarian standard to determine the choice of one occupation over another. My choice of occupation, although determined by utility, will still shape the course of my life so as to generate further goals and considerations that were not part of my original decision. Raz's notion of creation of value does not seem to depend on value pluralism.

On the face of it, then, Raz's argument from the value of autonomy may seem to be of little help in linking autonomy with value pluralism and thus reinforcing the pluralist case for liberalism. Neither version of Raz's argument seems to establish the connection sought between autonomy and value pluralism. The first version links autonomy only with pluralism in a weak sense, the second does refer to value pluralism proper but fails to complete the connection. Moreover, even if the Razian connection were made, and value pluralism was seen to be implied by valuing autonomy, that would still amount only to a liberal case for pluralism, not a pluralist case for liberalism. (Of course, the latter is my goal, not Raz's.) Even if Raz were correct that the liberal commitment to autonomy presupposes value pluralism, it could still be asked what justifies the liberal commitment to autonomy. Raz's answer, as we have seen, is not value pluralism but the contingent circumstances of modern industrial society.

Despite these difficulties, Raz's argument contains some of the seeds of the case I have in mind. As far as I am aware, Raz is the first writer to see that there is a significant link to be made between value pluralism and autonomy. Moreover, he provides an important clue to what that link might be in his idea that both pluralism and autonomy involve 'the creation of value'. I shall shortly set out my own view of what the creation of value involves. First, however, I turn to another helpful source.

8.3.2 Macedo's argument

Another argument that assists the case I am constructing is to be found in the work of Macedo (1990). Responding to the communitarian criticisms of the 1980s, Macedo argues that liberalism need not be identified with instrumental reasoning, moral scepticism, social atomism or superficial conceptions of community. Disagreement about the good is a crucial starting point for liberalism, leading to the liberal emphasis on personal liberty. But liberalism is not about disagreement and fragmentation alone; it also stands for a shared set of values and virtues. 'Liberals can articulate worthy and attainable ideals of human flourishing, virtue, and community' (ibid.: 205). The question is how the positive, shared aspects of liberalism can be established in the face of the fact of disagreement with which liberal thought starts. Here Macedo seeks to turn an apparent weakness into a strength: disagreement and diversity are not merely 'problems' to be overcome but sources of convergence on the central liberal commitment. 'A pluralistic social milieu positively encourages the reflective capacities defining moral personhood and those more extensive capacities composing the ideal of liberal autonomy' (ibid.: 234). Disagreement and diversity are positives because they encourage people to take a critically reflective view of their commitments, hence to be autonomous rather than heteronomous. Moral pluralism generates a need for liberal autonomy.

This link between pluralism and autonomy is developed by Macedo as follows. 'Social pluralism' generates 'a number of live ethical options. In a pluralistic and sufficiently tolerant social milieu one may seriously consider and actually choose among a variety of options and lifestyles' (ibid.: 235). Awareness of multiple options leads to the realization that one's own way of life is one option among others, a thought that encourages critical reflection on one's own choices and situation, which could be otherwise. Further, critical reflection on the options facing one calls forth the 'strong evaluation' of those options. Strong evaluation is 'the capacity critically to assess and even actively shape not simply one's actions, but one's character itself, the source of our actions' (ibid.: 216).

FROM PLURALISM TO LIBERALISM

Strong evaluators make choices not merely on the basis of their desires but according to 'second-order' standards (such as their conception of the good life) according to which their desires themselves may be evaluated. Moreover, the strong evaluator 'fashions a coherent pattern of second-order desires into an ideal of character, and is capable of weighing one ideal against another' (ibid.: 217). That is, to be a strong evaluator is to be autonomous, a person engaged in making her own life rather than merely living according to norms that are already given, whether by external tradition or internal desires.[11]

In short, liberal autonomy is stimulated by the pluralist outlook because being alive to the plurality of values encourages us to adopt an attitude of critical reflection towards our own values, which leads to autonomy in choice and conduct. 'Social pluralism penetrates to the core of the liberal personality, provoking the inner experience of value conflict and stimulating critical reflection . . . We may say that the "internalization" of value pluralism and conflict is part of the liberal ideal of autonomy – part, perhaps, of being fully conscious of the moral complexity of our world' (ibid.: 237–8). Conversely, the experience of liberal autonomy encourages us to see choices among contending values and ideals as a normal part of life. 'The autonomous character is capable of affirming rather than bemoaning liberal modernity, with its many possible ways of life, the openness of all choices, and its protean ideal' (ibid.: 269). Although Macedo does not quite say so, this suggests that liberal autonomy may encourage us to be more open to the possibility of deep value pluralism as a likely source of our pervasive experience of moral conflict. Pluralism and autonomy are mutually supporting by way of critical reflection and strong evaluation.

Macedo's argument comes close to a persuasive pluralist case for liberalism by way of autonomy but for one problem: it is not clear that by 'social pluralism' Macedo always means value pluralism in the sense that concerns us here. It is true that he explicitly endorses Berlin's conception of pluralism, including value incommensurability (ibid.: 236).[12] But that endorsement is not well integrated into his account of 'pluralism' and its implications. Apart from the gesture in Berlin's direction, what Macedo usually seems to understand by pluralism is what I have called 'pluralism of belief', in Macedo's formulation 'disagreement about what the good life consists in', leading to the existence of 'a variety of options and lifestyles' (ibid.: 234, 235).

206

On the other hand, Macedo's argument does not really work unless pluralism means value pluralism. Mere plurality of belief does not by itself encourage critical reflection and strong evaluation. The bare fact that different people value different things need not lead me to question my own values unless I take those other values seriously as genuine goods I might pursue too. Macedo is aware of this point: 'What is needed is not only competition among ideals, but respectful competition and a certain attitude toward change: a mutual willingness to try new things, to entertain various ideals' (ibid.: 235). What is needed, in other words, is something like the value-pluralist virtue of generosity discussed earlier in connection with the coextensive liberal virtue of broad-mindedness (8.1.1, 8.2.1). Consequently, although Macedo's argument is not as clearly value-pluralist as it might be, it would not take much to make it so. Macedo provides us with the general shape of an argument from pluralism to liberalism by way of autonomy. Moreover, he provides us with much of the substance of that argument, which needs only a more explicit emphasis on what is distinctive about the pluralist outlook.

8.3.3 From pluralism to liberal autonomy

Given the contributions of Macedo and Raz, I am now in a position to assemble my own argument from pluralism to liberal autonomy. The basic claim is that in order to choose rationally among contending plural values one needs to be autonomous. The reason is that such choices are demanding. To adopt the pluralist outlook is to recognize that in a particular situation one may have to choose from several incommensurable goods. Such choices are 'hard', as we have seen, in part because they cannot be determined by the universal application of simple rules such as those proposed by utilitarians and other monists. Pluralist choosers must therefore be flexible in their practical reasoning, attending and responding to the particulars of the situation. Rules may be useful as rough summaries of wise decision making in past experience, but they cannot be regarded as decisive. Still less can pluralists allow their unexamined desires to decide value conflicts for them, since that would amount to treating the satisfaction of de facto preferences as commensurating all other values – another essentially monistic approach. Rather, pluralist choosers are obliged to adopt a critically reflective attitude

FROM PLURALISM TO LIBERALISM

towards both their own desires and those rules and traditions that come to them from their social milieu. They are obliged, that is, to be strong evaluators, indeed extra-strong evaluators, as I shall argue in a moment. They are thus obliged to be autonomous, or self-creating, indeed autonomous in a strong sense. It is perhaps something like this connection that Raz has in mind when he refers to 'the creation of value' as a link between the value of autonomy and pluralism.

The link between autonomy and the exigency of pluralist choice can be brought out more clearly if we distinguish three levels of evaluative capacity, to which correspond three levels of self-direction. First, 'weak' evaluation occurs when a person chooses in accordance with unexamined desires. The weak evaluator is weakly self-directing in the sense of 'autarchic', that is, having the capacity to identify and reflect on his own desires to some degree, as well as to act on those desires. But autarchic persons may be heteronomous, 'conformists or "slaves" to fashion or to conventions, acting from standards, ideals, and values taken over uncritically from others' (Macedo, 1990: 216). Autarchy falls short of autonomy. A person who decides to become a doctor rather than a lawyer just because that is the unquestioned family tradition is to that extent autarchic rather than autonomous.[13]

Autarchic agents are therefore only weakly self-determining in comparison with those capable of the second level of evaluation, namely the 'strong' evaluation already discussed. The strong evaluator, again, is a person capable not only of identifying and acting on given desires but of reflecting critically on those desires, calling them into question, and rejecting or revising them in accordance with second-order critieria such as a background conception of the good. The strong evaluator is thus autonomous, in the sense that she actively shapes her own life, in comparison with the relative heteronomy of the merely autarchic person. The autonomous agent will not rest satisfied, for example, with family tradition as the decisive reason for choosing medicine rather than law. She will subject the claims of tradition, along with any first-order inclinations she may have, to a process of critical reflection. The possession of autarchic capacities is sufficient for a person to count as a bearer of moral personality and therefore the fundamental liberal right to equal care and respect. But the liberal ideal of personal autonomy is met only by those who realize the capacity for strong evaluation. All persons normally possess the potential to be

208

VIRTUES

strong evaluators, and the liberal ideal is to realize that potential as far as possible.

To be a rational chooser from the pluralist point of view, however, requires an even stronger level of evaluation and therefore of self-direction than that of strong evaluation and liberal autonomy. There is, therefore, a third level of evaluative and self-directive capacity that is required by pluralist practical reasoning. That is because strong evaluation and autonomy are still compatible with a monist outlook. The person choosing between medicine and law, for example, could be an autonomous utilitarian, taking as his critical standard for strong evaluation a version of the injunction to maximize human happiness or the satisfaction of preferences.[14] But a genuinely pluralist chooser cannot accept as decisive any such predetermined rule of conduct. The pluralist chooser must go beyond even the autonomous acceptance and application of such rules, and must ask questions at a deeper level still: 'Why should I prioritize human happiness in this case rather than some other value? How far does utilitarianism answer to my background conception of the good life?' Pluralists must be prepared to interrogate not only their desires but also the authority of rules that purport to regulate desires. Pluralists must therefore be self-directing at a deeper level still than strong evaluators.[15]

To choose rationally among competing plural values requires a stronger degree of self-direction than autonomy as so far defined, or at least it requires autonomy in an especially strong form. There is thus an asymmetry between the liberal ideal of autonomy and the pluralist ideal of strong autonomy. Pluralists are more demanding on this score than liberals. But this asymmetry does not upset my argument. On the contrary, if liberalism is the best political form required for the promotion of personal autonomy, then the case for liberalism is still stronger where the goal is the realization of an especially strong form of autonomy. Although liberal autonomy in its standard form is not sufficient for the degree of autonomy required for rational choice under pluralism, liberal autonomy remains a necessary condition for that kind of choice. This conclusion is consistent with my earlier concession that a liberal form of politics cannot be expected to guarantee the making of wise choices among plural values in particular cases in private life. Nevertheless, liberalism best promotes those capacities that make such wise choices possible.

The argument I present here may be regarded as a development of the second of the two main lines from pluralism to liberalism implicit in Berlin. The first line, by way of reasonable disagreement, was completed in Chapter 7. The second line takes its cue from Berlin's claim that it is because choice among conflicting values is a necessity that the freedom to choose is so valuable. The necessity of choice is said to imply a case for freedom of choice, hence for a form of liberalism based on negative liberty. We saw in Chapter 4 that this argument is flawed as it stands, since the necessity of choice does not make choice – or therefore the freedom to choose – valuable (4.1.2). But the argument can now be restated more successfully in terms of autonomy. To appreciate the plurality of values is to accept that we must choose among them when they conflict. Moreover, it is to accept that such choices will be hard, in the relevant sense, since plurality includes incommensurability. Consequently, to adopt the pluralist outlook commits us to meeting the necessary conditions for making hard choices. Prominent if not pre-eminent among those conditions is personal autonomy. It is not choice alone that imposes this requirement, but the peculiarly demanding nature of choice under value pluralism.

Note, however, that this argument gives us a further reason to correct Berlin's blanket preference for negative liberty over positive. I noted in Chapter 4 that his suspicion of the positive idea properly attaches only to those versions that are linked with ethical monism and that invite authoritarian interpretation. At least some positive conceptions of liberty have a legitimate role in liberal politics (Crowder, 1988; Christman, 1991). We can now see, in addition, that at least one kind of positive liberty is commended by pluralism itself. Pluralism leads us to value personal autonomy, but personal autonomy falls within the positive rather than negative family of freedoms: it is a positive capacity for strong self-direction rather than mere absence of interference. Berlin's argument from choice can be reconstructed to take us from pluralism to liberalism, but by way of positive liberty, not negative. This is not to say that negative liberty has no value from a pluralist point of view. The 'accommodation' arguments, from diversity and reasonable dis-agreement, indicate the importance on pluralist grounds of social spaces within which individuals and groups may pursue their conceptions of the good unimpeded. Rather, pluralism provides grounds for valuing *both* negative and positive liberty, and both (suitably understood) have important contributions to make to liberalism. All this follows from the logic of Berlin's own view.

VIRTUES

Just as the pluralist outlook leads to liberal autonomy, liberal autonomy promotes the capacity to choose rationally among plural values. It does so in several ways. As we have just seen, a strong form of autonomy is necessary for people to cope rationally with the exigency of choices which cannot be decided by the straightforward application of simple rules. Autonomy can also be seen to enhance each of the pluralist virtues. We saw earlier that autonomy answers to pluralist flexibility, required by the need to respond to the particulars of the choice situation (8.2.4). It follows that autonomy also reinforces the pluralist virtue of attentiveness to the details of the situation and the persons in it.[16] Another pluralist virtue stimulated by liberal autonomy is generosity towards different goods and ways of life. As both Raz and Macedo point out, to count as autonomous a person needs a range of valuable options to choose from, and that is not simply a matter of knowing that her society contains a plurality of beliefs and value judgements. It also requires that she take those beliefs and value judgements seriously as reflecting the existence of options that are genuinely valuable rather than merely believed by others to be so. It requires, that is, a generous appreciation of a range of goods and ways of life other than her own. Finally, liberal autonomy is also a stimulus to pluralist realism. The broad-mindedness and critical reflection required for autonomy enable people to recognize that hard choices among basic values involve genuine and perhaps tragic losses. Moreover, the same features of autonomy encourage people to distance themselves from their commitments sufficiently to recognize them as liable to revision in favour of alternative views. From this aspect of liberal moderation it is a short step to seeing the alternatives on offer as underwritten by value pluralism.

8.4 Implications of the Virtues Argument

To summarize, in this chapter I have argued the following. Practical reasoning under value pluralism involves the exercise of certain 'pluralist virtues', namely generosity, realism, attentiveness and flexibility. These pluralist virtues are promoted by liberalism through the cognate or overlapping liberal virtues of broad-mindedness, moderation, respect for persons and personal autonomy. Liberalism is superior to rival forms of politics in its support for the pluralist virtues, especially through the link between

FROM PLURALISM TO LIBERALISM

pluralist flexibility and the key liberal commitment to autonomy. There is an especially strong link of mutual support between pluralism and liberal autonomy because of the distinctively demanding nature of pluralist choice. The connection between pluralism and autonomy provides both support for and correction of the choice-based argument from pluralism to liberalism proposed by Berlin.

How does this argument fit within the value-pluralist case for liberalism overall? In particular, how does it relate to the accommodationist or neutrality arguments of Chapters 6 and 7? Most importantly, the virtues argument deepens the sense in which, on the pluralist view, liberalism should enter into people's lives. In Chapters 6 and 7 I argued that pluralism recommends liberalism as a political framework for accommodating diverse and conflicting conceptions of the good life. The effect of the virtues argument is that liberalism is now presented, in addition, as involving values which ought to be *part of* those conceptions of the good. To live well under pluralism requires choosing well (i.e. for good reason) when plural values conflict, which in turn requires the practice of liberal virtues, including personal autonomy. In short, the best lives under pluralism are liberal lives. This is not to say that under pluralism there is only one way to live. Rather, there are many different legitimate conceptions of the good on the pluralist view, but the best of them have liberal components, namely the virtues required for pluralist choice. In other words, liberalism provides not only a political framework for a pluralist society, but also an ethical framework for the best ways of life under pluralism. The best lives under pluralism are liberal lives, but these come in many varieties.

Does the foregoing argument apply to all good lives, or only to those lived in acknowledgement of value pluralism? It might be tempting, in line with the current widespread sympathy with cultural relativism, to suppose that only those people whose outlook includes acceptance of the plurality and incommensurability of values need practise the pluralist-liberal virtues in order to live the best lives possible for them. In this way the pluralist and liberal virtues could be relativized to self-consciously pluralist ways of life. This may be a more comfortable view for some people, but it is not supported by the logic of pluralism. True, from a pluralist point of view the relevant virtues apply most obviously and immediately to the life of the self-conscious pluralist who is aware of the exigency of the some of the choices she faces. But the full scope of the argument

212

VIRTUES

is wider than that. Value pluralism is an account of the objective nature of values and the relations among them; its central thesis is that some human values are plural and incommensurable independently of the contingent beliefs of particular individuals and groups. It follows that conflicts among such values are objective phenomena too. People may be faced with pluralist choices whether or not they recognize them as such. If so, then the virtues necessary to make such choices well also apply regardless of whether those concerned are clear-headed pluralists. Pluralist choices may arise under any way of life, and so the qualities of mind requisite to coping well with those choices will always be desirable, even if not recognized as desirable, and even if not always realizable in practice. So far as the pluralist virtues overlap liberal virtues, the latter must, on the pluralist view, be part of the best life for any human being. I do not wish to say that a life that lacks the pluralist or liberal virtues, or that does not acknowledge the plurality and incommensurability of values, cannot be a good life in some, perhaps many, respects. There are good lives other than liberal and self-consciously pluralist lives, and good lives lived in ignorance of significant truths. If value pluralism is true, however, such lives will not be among the best possible.[17]

This raises again the question of how the virtues argument fits with the accommodationist line of Chapters 6 and 7. The perfectionism of the one may seem to conflict with the approximate neutrality of the other. Pluralism appears to commend liberalism as on one hand a particular conception of the good, and on the other a political container for many such conceptions. How can such a position be coherent? I have already provided the materials for my answer, especially in referring to liberalism as an ethical *framework* for the good life, and to the variety of liberal lives, but I shall gather these materials together in the next chapter.

Notes

1. On virtue ethics in general see Foot (1978), MacIntyre (1985), Casey (1990), Slote (1992), R. Crisp (1996). The relation between the virtues and liberalism is examined by Macedo (1990), Galston (1991) and Berkowitz (1999).
2. It might be objected that I have assumed too readily that to choose 'successfully' among conflicting incommensurable values necessarily means

FROM PLURALISM TO LIBERALISM

to choose rationally. On a pluralist view, practical reason is itself only one component of the human good, possessing no greater intrinsic value than other goods. If so, then might one not cope with conflicts among incommensurables just as satisfactorily by choosing wilfully or on the basis of arbitrary preferences? My answer, following Nussbaum, is that practical reason occupies a special place among the human goods as one of two 'architectonic' functions (the other being 'affiliation') that 'organize and arrange all of the others, giving them in the process a characteristically human shape' (1990: 226). Practical reason enables us to make choices among conflicting plural goods in a way that is coherent and makes sense of our lives by doing justice to the goods we aim at. In its absence, our choices are likely to be either too narrow or too fragmented and self-defeating (see the argument for 'coherence' in pluralist choice at 6.2 above). To 'cope well' with choice under pluralism is therefore to choose for good reason, i.e. for reasons which are likely to yield a coherent and fulfilling result.

3. This aspect of attentiveness is emphasized by writers influenced by Simone Weil, including Iris Murdoch (1970), and proponents of 'care' ethics such as Sarah Ruddick (1980) and Joan Tronto (1993).

4. The idea is similar to Rawls's notion of 'reflective equilibrium', in which one works towards an adequate theory of justice by testing the theory against one's particular 'considered judgements' or intuitions, progressively bringing theory and judgements into line with one another by a process of mutual revision (Rawls, 1971: 19–21, 48–53).

5. A similar argument is put forward by Macedo, who suggests that the internalization of value conflict by the individual could both encourage critical reflection on his or her conception of the good, and 'also help brake what would otherwise be a fanatical commitment to a perfectly consistent and comprehensive set of harmonious values. The inner experience of value conflict encourages a degree of tentativeness in our commitment to any set of values, and this provides room for reflection, self-criticism, toleration, moderation, and an openness to re-evaluation and to change ... The internalization of diversity and conflict allows the reflective self to maintain some distance from any single end, or the values of any particular community' (1990: 238–9). Macedo overstates the 'tentativeness' of liberal commitment, conceding too much to those who would define a liberal as someone who will not take his own side in an argument. Liberals can, indeed should, be committed to the values and principles of liberalism deeply and intensely without becoming fanatics. The difference between the liberal and the fanatic turns not so much on depth and intensity of belief as on the recognition of revisability and change. Liberal commitments are 'provisional' not in the sense that they are weak or 'tentative' but in the sense that liberals regard them as always open to re-examination and revision. Indeed, Mill argued that it is by holding beliefs

214

VIRTUES

provisionally in this sense, by regarding them as permanently subject to reassessment, that we make them stronger. It is when beliefs are allowed to harden into unquestionable dogmas that they atrophy and lose their vivacity and force (1974: Chapter 2). It is therefore in the sense that beliefs and values, even the most fundamental, are always regarded as open to reconsideration and revision, that the liberal view of commitment is moderate. And once again, the liberal view and the pluralist are mutually supportive.

6. See Lukes (1993) for an argument along these lines. Lukes defends human rights by imagining a series of societies (admittedly caricatured) in which human rights are not respected, for reasons characteristic of the particular society. A similar understanding of general rules as the result of reflection on concrete experience is articulated by Rawls's notion of 'reflective equilibrium'; see note 4 above.

7. See the distinction drawn by Charles Taylor between two kinds of respect or 'recognition', one based on universal attributes, the other on particular identities, giving rise to the politics respectively of 'equal dignity' and 'difference' (1994: 37–9).

8. Even liberal respect for persons interpreted on the Kantian or universalist model implies a significant element of particularism, since respect for individuals for whatever reason is an invitation to attend to their claims in particular situations. The principle of equal concern and respect does not require identical treatment regardless of circumstance, as Ronald Dworkin has argued in several places (1977, 1985).

9. This is not to say that autonomy must be seen as wholly opposed to membership of, and identification with, a tradition or culture; see 8.3 and 9.3 below.

10. Compare Robert Paul Wolff (1970), who argues that one cannot surrender autonomy. This view depends on Kantian assumptions about the essential nature of moral agents that Wolff does not make explicit. But if Wolff's view were right, it would not upset my basic argument here. It would follow only that the first of the two cases distinguished here is not really a possibility, i.e. that people cannot really be inflexible in their commitments in quite this way.

11. The distinction between 'weak' and 'strong' evaluation comes from Charles Taylor's essay 'What is human agency?' (1985).

12. Macedo recommends this as a 'deeper' and 'truer picture of the nature of moral value and the experience of living in a liberal pluralistic society' than what he sees as the more 'superficial' kind of pluralism supported by Charles Taylor, who proposes a 'plurality of moral perspectives' (Macedo, 1990: 236–7). This is unlikely to be a fair account of Taylor, who is not in any straightforward sense an ethical or cognitive relativist.

13. This distinction between autarchy and autonomy is derived from Benn (1976, 1988), Taylor (1985) and Macedo (1990).

FROM PLURALISM TO LIBERALISM

14. The classical anarchist William Godwin (1976), for example, combines an ideal of autonomy ('private judgement') with a commitment to (act) utilitarianism. See Crowder (1991: Chapter 2).

15. This is the point at which Gray's notion of modus vivendi most clearly fails to satisfy the pluralist ideal of personal autonomy. Although modus vivendi seems to involve a flexible response to value conflict on the face of things, we have seen that on Gray's account it rests on a monistic commitment to either self-interest or peace, unqualified by any other consideration (5.2). The very strong form of autonomy required for pluralist practical reasoning would not permit such simple norms to go without critical challenge and revision in accordance with the circumstances. While Gray's modus vivendi calls for a flexible response to the situation subject to the narrow ends he stipulates, pluralist autonomy goes further in requiring a critically reflective approach to those ends themselves.

16. In this connection it is worth noting that liberal autonomy need not assume a radical separation of individuals from their social context. Although the liberal conception of autonomy is often identified with the Kantian idea of self-direction in accordance with pure reason, a realistic liberal autonomy is better understood on something closer to the Millian model, as a mode of response – reflective, critical and potentially revisionary – to one's ethical and cultural surroundings. This is well brought out by Macedo, who describes liberal autonomy as involving deliberation on the standards and ideals of one's own community: 'Deliberation is conducted in an inherited moral language: the repository of a shared culture composed of a plurality of communities and ideals. Liberal autonomy is not a matter of transcending contingency or inhabiting a world beyond our own; it is not a way of standing outside one's own community, much less all communities. Autonomy is a way of comporting ourselves in our liberal, pluralistic, community – critically playing off one aspect of our culture against other aspects and against our own experience' (1990: 218).

17. This view is supported by Bernard Williams's argument from 'truthfulness' discussed in the previous chapter (7.4): that a good life for human beings must, on a pluralist account, include a willingness to appreciate human values for what they really are and to build a life accordingly.

216

CHAPTER 9

Pluralist Liberalism

I have argued that value pluralism supports a case for liberalism by way of three main routes. First, pluralism implies a commitment to diversity that is best satisfied by the approximate neutrality of which liberalism is capable. Second, this relative neutrality also meets' the pluralist requirement that the desirable political system accommodate reasonable disagreement among conceptions of the good. Third, to engage successfully in practical reasoning in the light of pluralism requires a certain set of virtues, most notably a strong form of personal autonomy, which again flourish best in a liberal political order.

My question in this chapter is, what kind of liberal order will this be? First, I consider its general character in terms of the categories established in Chapter 2: univeralist or particularist, neutralist or perfectionist? I argue that while pluralist liberalism is clearly universalist in character, the issue between neutrality and perfectionism is more complex, since pluralism generates both kinds of justification for liberalism. While the arguments from diversity and reasonable disagreement point to a neutralist conception of liberalism, the virtues-based argument suggests a perfectionist view. My conclusion, however, is that although the accommodation aspect remains important, the perfectionist strand takes priority. Pluralist liberalism is broadly universalist and perfectionist in outlook. Second, having captured the general tenor of pluralist liberalism, I consider its implications for two major areas of public policy: economic distribution and cultural rights. I argue

217

FROM PLURALISM TO LIBERALISM

that, contrary to some views, the pluralist outlook does not support laissez-faire or minimal government in either of these fields. Rather, pluralism implies the need for state intervention for the purpose of redistribution and compensation for cultural disadvantage. Finally, I consider the implications of pluralism for the process by which public policy is decided. My argument here is that pluralist liberalism is likely to favour constitutional safeguards rather than, as proposed by some theorists, trusting wholly to political negotiation. Where compromise is unavoidable, this should be structured by the pluralist–liberal virtues.

9.1 What Kind of Liberalism?

In this section I consider the general character of pluralist liberalism in terms of the way different kinds of liberalism are distinguished and categorized in the contemporary literature. In the literature, different forms of liberalism emerge from different lines of justification. Current justificatory theories of liberalism have diverged, as we saw in Chapter 2, over two principal issues: first, whether liberalism can be defended on a universal basis or only as the politics of a particular form of social life; second, whether liberalism should be presented as neutral among competing conceptions of the good life or as expressing or promoting one particular conception of the good. The interplay of these various approaches produces four main positions (see Chapter 2, Table 1): universal neutrality (the earlier Rawls), particularist neutrality (the later Rawls), universal perfectionism (Kant, Mill, Galston), and particularist perfectionism (Raz). Consequently, the first task will be to clarify and consolidate the nature of the pluralist justification of liberalism in these terms. Is the pluralist case universalist or particularist, neutralist or perfectionist? The answer to that question will shape my account of the kind of liberalism thus defended.

This inquiry will involve discussion of two further (and related) issues. First, I shall be concerned with the question raised in Chapter 2 of the bearing of value pluralism on what I called there the current 'impasse' of liberal justificatory theory. Among the four identified approaches, I suggested that the existing literature reveals none to be clearly superior to its rivals. The question I am now in a position to consider is whether the pluralist arguments might break this deadlock. Second, I have so far offered as independent paths to

218

PLURALIST LIBERALISM

liberalism arguments that employ two distinct strategies, one broadly neutralist and the other perfectionist. An obvious question is whether these do not pull apart from one another rendering the case I have constructed incoherent. I acknowledged this as a natural and important question in Chapter 8, but postponed discussion of it. That discussion now falls due.

9.1.1 Universalism or particularism?

To the question of whether the pluralist case is universalist or particularist in character, it should be clear by now that my answer is, universalist. The principal defence of liberalism proposed in this book is not bounded by any particular culture or historical epoch. Rather, it is implicit in the notion of value pluralism, which is a theory of the nature of moral value across all human cultures and periods. If value pluralism as I have defined it is true, then the plurality and incommensurability of value is part of the moral experience of all human beings at all times. That experience may not be recognized as such in every case; indeed, the conscious recognition of value pluralism is of very recent origin, Berlin being the first to formulate the idea as we now possess it. As noted earlier, however, there is evidence of the experience of value pluralism, albeit not understood as such, in the pre-modern world as well as the modern – the *Antigone* of Sophocles is a familiar example, pagan polytheism perhaps another (Chapter 1, note 2; 3.3). We have also seen that an essential feature of the pluralist outlook, distinguishing it from ethical relativism, is that at least some goods are universal, that is, part of the best life for any human being. The notion of value pluralism is deeply universal in the sense that it describes universal features of the ethical experience of human beings.

The universality of pluralism implies a universal case for liberalism. This is not as obvious as it might seem. Value pluralism is a meta-ethical theory, that is, a theory of the form of moral judgement rather than a theory of the content of morality, and meta-ethical theories might make universal claims yet imply no universal prescriptions for politics – indeed imply that there can be no such universal prescriptions. Cultural relativism, for example, involves universal claims about the nature of moral judgement to the effect that such judgements are relative to a particular culture. Similarly, it might be argued that even if plurality and

219

FROM PLURALISM TO LIBERALISM

incommensurability are universal features of moral experience, the implication is that rational choices among conflicting plural values can only be worked out within particular contexts and that such choices cannot be guided by universal principles. In fact something like this was the view of the anti-liberal critics considered in Chapter 5: that if value pluralism is true then choice must be guided principally by local tradition or modus vivendi settlement and the universal principles of liberalism must be rejected.

I have argued, however, that it is the anti-liberal view that should be rejected. If pluralism is true then its formal features themselves imply a set of principles that apply regardless of context. Rational choice among plural goods requires respect for the universality of some goods, recognition of incommensurability and its implications, promotion of a diversity of goods and ways of life, accommodation of reasonable disagreement about the good, and the exercise of the pluralist virtues, especially personal autonomy, in practical reasoning. Together these principles amount to a broad framework for any particular choice under pluralism. It is also true that precise choices under pluralism must be strongly particularistic, in the sense that they cannot rely wholly on rules (let alone universal rules) but involve close attention to context (3.2, 8.1). Nevertheless, the particularism implied by pluralism is always bounded or limited by the framework of principles. Those principles are sufficient to identify the framework as, politically, a liberal one.

I conclude that the case for liberalism generated by the pluralist outlook is a universal case. That is, the argument is not limited to the point of view of any particular culture or historical period but is rooted in the moral experience of all human beings. If pluralism is true, then reasoned choice among plural values should always be bounded by a set of principles that imply the desirability, in principle, of a liberal form of politics. This amounts to a revival of a traditional liberal aspiration. In contrast with those recent forms of liberalism which have retreated into particularism, often framing their claims within the limits of existing liberal democracies, pluralist liberalism reasserts the traditional liberal project of speaking to humanity at large.

9.1.2 Neutrality or perfectionism?

The question of whether the kind of liberalism implied by value

PLURALIST LIBERALISM

pluralism is neutralist or perfectionist is more difficult. We have seen that arguments from pluralism to liberalism can be constructed along lines of both neutrality (Chapters 6 and 7) and perfectionism (Chapter 8). How do these two strategies relate to each other? There are three main possibilities. First, the two strategies might be reconciled so that they both converge on the same form of liberalism after all. Second, it might be claimed that reconciliation is impossible and that the two strategies stand in irresolvable and permanent tension with one another, leading to a permanent tension between two forms of liberalism. Third, it could be that the two strategies, and the liberal forms to which they correspond, come into conflict with each other but that one has priority over the other. I believe all three of these possibilities contain elements of the truth, but that the third comes closest to a comprehensive view.

First, then, the neutrality and perfectionist approaches, as generated by pluralism, may be reconciled to a degree. This may seem unlikely because neutrality and perfectionism appear, according to their standard definitions, to be opposites. While the neutral state is standardly defined (by Rawls, for example) as not enforcing or supporting any particular conception of the good life, the perfectionist state does precisely that. But these are ideal types rather than actual working systems, which (as Aristotle knew) are usually mixed. Moreover, the ideals themselves can be seen to require qualification when viewed through the lens of value pluralism. We saw on the one hand that the kind of state neutrality commended by the pluralist ethic of diversity is only 'approximate', not absolute. The claim to approximate neutrality is the moderate claim that the political system in question is more neutral than its rivals, or more accommodating than they are of a diversity of goods and ways of life. Approximate neutrality is thus a realistic goal, consistent with recognizing, as pluralists must, that any political system will involve the promotion of some goods and ways of life to the exclusion of others. It is never possible for a state to reduce such exclusions to zero, to be infinitely accommodating or absolutely neutral. On the other hand, the perfectionism implied by pluralism is not narrow but capacious. We saw that the pluralist outlook implied, by way of the pluralist approach to practical reasoning in particular cases, commitment to a certain set of virtues including personal autonomy. Together these commitments add up to a distinctively liberal conception of the good life, or to a range of such conceptions, which excludes rival conceptions. But the liberal conception of the good thus defined contains space for many different ways of living such a life, and for the possibility of creating new hybrid forms through the liberalization of different cultures. This relates to the point as that made by Raz (1986) when he argues that the valuing of personal autonomy presupposes an adequate range of good options (8.3.1). The liberal commitment to autonomy is a commitment to a society containing a diversity of goods and ways of life to choose from, or to influence the choices we have.

Between realistic neutrality and capacious perfectionism there is a significant area of overlap. A pluralist political system will accommodate, within its liberal framework, a greater diversity (bearing in mind the complex meaning of that word: 6.2) of goods and forms of life than its rivals. The liberal framework will naturally tend to favour those goods and forms of life that are liberal rather than non-liberal in character – a tendency that is not only natural but positively desirable from a pluralist point of view – but the range of liberal or liberalized goods and lives is not narrow. There are many projects and plans of life that can be approached and pursued autonomously. Approximate neutrality and capacious perfectionism converge in their accommodation of multiple goods and ways of life, an accommodation which is not unlimited but which is greater than that offered by non-liberal forms of politics.

There are limits, however, to the degree to which neutrality and perfectionism can be reconciled. Neutrality inevitably suggests a greater range of accommodation than perfectionism. Although neutrality involves the enforcement of a liberal framework and the limits that implies, the aspiration of the neutrality approach is to make that framework acceptable not only to liberals but also to non-liberals. The claim of neutralist liberals like Rawls is that someone with a non-liberal comprehensive moral doctrine can still accept a liberal framework for specifically political purposes. Perfectionist liberalism, on the other hand, since it involves the active promotion of liberal comprehensive moral doctrines, is more exclusive of, or at least places more pressure on, non-liberal ways of life. Neutrality and perfectionism, although convergent to a degree, diverge at this point.

The pluralist outlook to some extent confirms the conflict between neutrality and perfectionism as irresolvable and permanent. This is the second of the three possible accounts of the relation between the neutrality and perfectionist arguments from pluralism. From the pluralist point of view some degree of tension between the

PLURALIST LIBERALISM

two should be seen as appropriate since they represent, in effect, distinct and incommensurable values. The aspiration to neutrality implies a commitment to values of toleration and diversity. Liberal perfectionism, by contrast, expresses the goal of individual liberation in the shape of the realization of personal autonomy and the liberal virtues. On both sides of the conflict are important goods of a fundamental nature, each of which must be taken seriously. To take fundamental goods seriously, according to the pluralist outlook, is to acknowledge that choices among them are 'hard' as I have defined this term – that is, not resolvable by any simple rule, and involving real loss which cannot wholly be compensated. Pluralism itself therefore gives us reason to expect that the neutrality and perfectionist approaches to liberal justification can never be harmonized completely.

The pluralist outlook also acknowledges, however, that although choices among conflicting plural values may be hard, such choices must sometimes be made. Hence the third possible relationship between the neutrality and perfectionist arguments: one of these may have to be given priority. There may be cases where the tension between neutralist and perfectionist forms of liberalism will have to be resolved in favour of one or the other. For example, liberal states may sometimes have to decide whether or how far to tolerate non-liberal practices or forms of life within the state's jurisdiction. Here, in particular, it will make a difference whether the liberalism in question adopts the neutrality or the perfectionist model. Can the pluralist outlook offer any guidance to the making of that kind of decision?

So far as the balance between neutrality and perfectionism must be struck more in one direction than the other, I believe that the logic of the pluralist outlook favours a *perfectionist* emphasis. This may seem surprising given the pluralist emphasis on the plurality of genuine goods and, consequently, legitimate ways of life. But although value pluralism implies grounds for acceptance of neutrality as a minimum, it implies more than that; it implies grounds for accepting liberal principles as promoting a particular conception of the good life. Pluralism *at least* supports liberalism as an approximately neutral political framework for the coexistence of multiple conceptions of the good. But if pluralism also implies a case for liberal perfectionism, then there is no need for liberals to rest satisfied with neutrality, the weaker claim, except as a minimal or fall-back position.

FROM PLURALISM TO LIBERALISM

The same features of pluralism that support approximate neutrality as a minimal defence of liberalism also suggest a stronger justification of liberalism, as the best form of politics for realizing a superior conception of the good. This can be seen most clearly in the case of the pluralist argument for liberal neutrality by way of reasonable disagreement (Chapter 7). If pluralism is true, then we have reason to disagree about the precise nature of the good life, since many different views of how to rank goods in general will be reasonable – hence the need for a political order that remains approximately neutral among such views. But pluralism, as we saw, gives us reason to agree as well as disagree. The very fact of reasonable disagreement about the content of the good life gives us reason to agree on the need for an accommodating political framework. Pluralism gives us a reason to accept liberalism as such a framework. However, if pluralism is true, then we have reason to agree on more than this. We also have reason to agree that any conception of the good that is pursued in the light of value pluralism must exhibit certain virtues, including 'flexibility', which requires personal autonomy (Chapter 8). Since the virtues in question are largely coextensive with distinctively liberal virtues, and since personal autonomy is a central liberal value, pluralism in effect gives us reason to promote characteristically liberal or liberalized forms of the good life. We can still expect reasonable disagreement about the good, and that disagreement ought to be accommodated. But the legitimate range of disagreement will be within a spectrum of conceptions informed by the fundamental values of liberalism. Pluralism gives us reason to disagree about the precise *content* of the good life, but to agree that the good life will take a liberal *form* – or at least develop within a liberal ethical framework. If pluralism implies liberal neutrality at least, it also implies more than that: the desirability of liberal conceptions of the good. The stronger claim supersedes the weaker. To the extent that a choice must be made between neutrality and perfectionist forms of liberalism, pluralism pushes us towards perfectionism.

9.1.3 Pluralism and universal perfectionism

To sum up the general character of the liberalism implied by a commitment to value pluralism, this will be, as indicated by the justificatory arguments I have developed, liberalism in a strong

224

PLURALIST LIBERALISM

form: universal and (predominantly) perfectionist. To accept value pluralism is not merely to allow that there are many genuine goods and valuable ways of life. It is to recognize that certain ways of life are more desirable than others because they meet more completely the normative criteria implied by value pluralism itself. To adopt the pluralist outlook is therefore to commend a certain range of goods and virtues as desirable for human flourishing. The range of good lives commended by pluralism is bounded politically by liberalism as a limiting and enabling framework (the neutrality case). Also, and more strongly, pluralism indicates liberalism as tending to promote the substantive goods and virtues necessary to the best of those lives (the perfectionist case). Pluralism, that is, commends the promotion of liberal or liberalized ways of life. From a pluralist point of view, therefore, a liberal state (or other institution) may legitimately be a perfectionist state, not aspiring to neutrality among conceptions of the good but actively engaged in promoting liberal forms of the good.

Even from within the liberal tradition these strong pluralist claims on behalf of liberalism will be met by two main objections, echoing the objections to universalism and perfectionism outlined in Chapter 2. Enough has been said in the ensuing chapters, however, to suggest pluralist answers. First, particularists will object to the universalist component that there is more than one legitimate conception of the good life, and that the range of legitimate good lives extends beyond the liberal range. To this, pluralist liberals can reply that they accept that there is a range of good lives for human beings, and that the range of good lives extends beyond the boundaries of liberalism. Nevertheless, if value pluralism is true, then the best of those lives will be informed by the pluralist-liberal virtues, and so the best human lives will be liberal lives of one kind or another.

Second, neutralists will object to the perfectionist component of pluralist liberalism. They will say that the state endorsement of certain conceptions of the good in preference to others flies in the face of the endemic, because reasonable, disagreement about the nature of the good in modern societies. To this we now have several replies to make, accumulated from previous discussions. First, some such preference is unavoidable, since any political system involves a ranking of goods at least for public purposes. Second, the liberal ranking is a relatively capacious one that accommodates a wide range of good lives, indeed wider than anything available under

225

alternative systems. Third, the fact of reasonable disagreement does not extend to the notion of value pluralism itself in the same way that it applies to substantive conceptions of the good life such as those based on religious belief – indeed, reasonable disagreement presupposes pluralism. If pluralism is not subject to reasonable disagreement, then neither is what follows from pluralism, and this includes a commitment to a set of liberal virtues, among them personal autonomy.

All of these points have been made in greater detail in preceding chapters. Here I add a final consideration. Given that a state has a right, even a duty, to promote a certain (liberal) range of conceptions of the good, it does not follow that the best way of fulfilling that right or duty will be heavy-handed enforcement. That the massive use of force can be both a cruel and unproductive way of advancing a vision of the good is itself an insight of both liberalism and pluralism (7.3). Liberal perfectionism, in other words, need not be identified with coercion and imperialism, indeed it ought not to be so. More consistently with the principles of liberalism, the liberal good is better pursued through argument, education and lived examples of actual liberal lives. Pluralist liberalism, then, although tending towards the more militant end of the liberal spectrum, should not be thought of as ruthless and aggressive. It will nevertheless be staunch in defence of liberal values in contrast with the claims of anti-liberal or non-liberal ways of life. This will be a form of liberalism that dares speak its name. Let us now consider how this kind of liberalism will respond to more specific issues of public policy.

9.2 Economic Distribution

As we saw in Chapter 2, one of the major divisions within liberalism is over the legitimate role of the state in the distribution of economic resources (2.1). All liberals endorse private property, and by extension the capitalist free market, as at least a necessary starting point in this field. But they differ over whether and to what extent capitalism should be qualified or corrected. Classical or laissez-faire liberals favour a highly restricted role for government, leaving individuals maximally free to compete for resources through the market. Social or egalitarian liberals reply that free market distribution is not an adequate basis for justice in distribution or for genuine freedom for all. Rather, justice and freedom require active state intervention to correct market distribution. Which of these views is more likely to be favoured from a value-pluralist perspective?

An argument attempting to justify the classical viewpoint from a starting point in value pluralism is provided by Friedrich Hayek in *The Road to Serfdom* (1944). Although Hayek does not expressly use the terms 'value pluralism' or 'incommensurability', the account he gives of values and the problem of ranking has a pluralist understanding of goods at its base. Commencing his case against socialist planning, Hayek observes that all such plans take as their objective 'a definite social goal' (ibid.: 42). This goal is variously understood or formulated as the 'common good' or the 'general welfare' or the 'general interest'. However formulated, the goal 'cannot be adequately expressed as a single end, but only as a hierarchy of ends, a comprehensive scale of values . . .' (ibid.). Thus,

> to direct all our activities according to a single plan presupposes that every one of our needs is given its rank in the order of values which must be complete enough to make it possible to decide between all the different courses between which the planner has to choose. It presupposes, in short, the existence of a complete ethical code in which all the different human values are allotted their due place (ibid.: 42–3).

However, Hayek writes: 'No such complete ethical code exists.' This is true in the sense that we are simply unaware of any such 'all-inclusive scale of values', but also in the sense that there cannot be any such final scheme. 'Since, strictly speaking, scales of value exist only in individual minds, nothing but partial scales of values exist, scales which are inevitably different and often inconsistent with each other' (ibid.: 44).

Hayek's view rests on a notion of value pluralism: there are many different ends, and these cannot be ranked absolutely. It follows, he argues, that there is no objective truth about the proper ranking of different goods and that rankings are purely subjective. His political conclusion is that there is therefore no good reason for a government planning authority to demand that people comply with its plan, since that plan will presuppose a ranking of values that they may not and need not accept. Rather, 'individuals should be allowed, within defined limits, to follow their own values and preferences rather than somebody else's, [and] within these spheres the individual's

FROM PLURALISM TO LIBERALISM

system of ends should be supreme and not subject to any dictation by others' (ibid.: 44). Value pluralism implies economic laissez-faire.

Hayek's argument for laissez-faire is open to several objections from a value-pluralist point of view. The most obvious is that it amounts to a version of the 'argument from indeterminacy' which I have already considered and rejected as a pluralist case for any kind of liberalism (1.1, 4.1.1). The basic claim is that value pluralism implies that (1) competing goods cannot be ranked objectively, and that therefore (2) such ranking ought to be left to individuals. But we have seen that (2) does not follow from (1), and (1) does not follow from value pluralism. Pluralism does not imply wholesale moral indeterminacy, and even if it did, that would not ground a case for liberalism. If the ranking of plural values were wholly subjective, as Hayek supposes, then it would be a wholly subjective matter whether we should privilege the values of classical liberalism, including individual liberty. In any case pluralism does not lead to subjectivism in this way, since we have seen that there are several respects in which judgements under pluralism can be objective, either in context or in accordance with the general norms implicit in pluralism itself. From a pluralist point of view Hayek is therefore mistaken to suppose that 'scales of value exist only in individual minds' if this means that they are wholly subjective.

Indeed, Hayek's subjectivism here is at odds with his own classical liberalism, which in effect accords certain goods an objective priority, that is, a priority independent of the wishes of 'individual minds'.[1] Hayek's argument gives the initial impression that a regime of laissez-faire is neutral among possible rankings of competing plural values, but on inspection it is clear that laissez-faire involves its own distinctive ranking. Two main kinds of goods are privileged by laissez-faire, namely goods of personal security and goods of the market. Personal security is an objective priority for classical liberals like Hayek, since external defence and internal law and order must be secured by any liberal state regardless of individual preferences or of context. Security is valuable for its own sake as a necessary part of the good life for any person, and also instrumentally as essential to the normal functioning of the most important of all institutions on the classical liberal view, the market. Classical liberalism, since it relies on the market as the dominant means of distribution, effectively privileges those values that are characteristic of the market. These include individual

228

PLURALIST LIBERALISM

choice, freedom of contract, self-reliance and utility. More than any of these, however, what counts in the market is material wealth: money and tradable commodities. Money in particular becomes a dominant value, not so much a good desirable for its own sake but a universal solvent, the medium through which wants are satisfied or disappointed.

The price mechanism itself has a price, however, which is that the influence of the market tends to neglect or marginalize or distort other genuine and important human values. A dramatic expression of this in political theory is provided by Robert Nozick (1974), who offers a defence of market laissez-faire on the basis of absolute individual rights to non-interference to the exclusion of any other moral consideration. As H.L.A. Hart writes:

> The moral landscape which Nozick explicitly presents contains only rights and is empty of everything else except possibly the moral permissibility of avoiding what he terms catastrophe. Hence moral wrongdoing has only one form: the violation of rights, perpetrating a wrong to the holder of a right. So long as rights are not violated it matters not for morality, short of catastrophe, how a social system actually works, how individuals fare under it, what needs it fails to meet or what misery or inequalities it produces.... . In particular the State may not impose burdens on the wealth or income or restraints on the liberty of some citizens to relieve the needs or suffering, however great, of others. (1979: 81)

Indeed, Nozick's ethical basis is not only restricted to individual rights but to a narrow conception of rights as both inviolable and strictly negative. It is this narrow starting point that enables him to argue for a rigorously minimal state and to reject redistribution as unjust.

While any political system involves some costs in terms of values forgone or down-played, the particular costs imposed by laissez-faire violate all five of the universal principles implicit in the pluralist outlook.[2] First, the values of the market are on their own too narrow to do justice to the pluralist ideal of *diversity* (and therefore the liberal ideal of approximate neutrality). I argued earlier that the liberal endorsement of private property and the market is likely to serve pluralist diversity better than the public control advocated by socialists (6.3). But I also said that this point, true as far as it goes, would need to be qualified: the market is a necessary but not a

229

sufficient condition for diversity in the pluralist sense. Indeed, unrestricted market distribution leads to the neglect or downgrading of an unacceptably wide range of values. In particular, three categories of value come to mind as especially ill-served by laissez-faire.

The first is that of 'public goods'. 'National defence, law and order, lighthouses, streets and street lighting are examples of goods which are called "public" because they can't be supplied to anybody without being available to everybody, and their individual users can't be made to pay for them' (Stretton and Orchard, 1994: 54). Because of this problem of 'externalities' there is no incentive to supply such goods through the market, and the result is market failure in that respect. A supporter of laissez-faire might reply that if goods of personal security and perhaps infrastructure are neglected by the market, they could legitimately be provided by the minimal state that laissez-faire permits. But the minimal state could by definition do little more than this. Other public goods, such as clean air and the protection of the ozone layer, would face a precarious future. Moreover, if we extend the idea of public good beyond the strict economists' definition to include benefits such as public health care, education, housing and transport, provided free or below cost to those who cannot afford market rates, the price of laissez-faire becomes still more pronounced.

A second group of goods pushed aside by the market includes those championed by the socialist tradition. Consider the classic socialist trinity of 'liberty, equality, fraternity' (Crick, 1987: Chapter 6). In the culture of laissez-faire, liberty tends to be interpreted narrowly as a strictly negative absence of coercion, excluding concern for a broader conception of freedom as positive capacity (Hayek, 1960: Chapter 1). Similarly, equality, on the laissez-faire view, translates in the distributive field into a formal 'equality of opportunity', understood negatively as the absence of legal impediments to enterprise. This takes no account of a more substantial conception of opportunity as 'fair' only where a person has the means to take advantage of it (Rawls, 1971: 73). Fraternity, or solidarity, has little place in the laissez-faire order, since this is undermined by the vast inequalities and consequent class divisions that result from market allocation when it is unqualified.

Third, laissez-faire has little room for the promotion of the kind of values advanced in recent years by the contemporary communitarian movement: the satisfactions and dignity associated with a

PLURALIST LIBERALISM

stable cultural identity and sense of a common good, moral certainty and perhaps spiritual fulfilment (MacIntyre, 1985 and 1988; Sandel, 1982; Taylor, 1989b). This communitarian complaint is typically brought against all forms of contemporary liberalism, not just laissez-faire. But it is the latter, more than the social or egalitarian strand of liberalism, that is more open to the charge of excessive emphasis on private rather than public interests, and on individual liberty rather than the cultural basis of liberty. (Kymlicka's development of egalitarian liberalism in the direction of concern for cultural membership is a topic I shall consider in the next section: 9.3.)

The second pluralist principle to be violated by laissez-faire is that of the accommodation of *reasonable disagreement* about the good life. Because laissez-faire has such a restrictive effect on a society's potential for promoting a diversity of goods, it inevitably limits that society's diversity of conceptions of the good or ways of life too. Such a society is one that strongly favours those ways of life that are in tune with success in the market. A concomitant range of virtues will be privileged – enterprise, self-reliance, material ambition – together with whatever talents and skills happen to command a premium in the market at the time. Other ways of life and other virtues, no matter how reasonable, will be discouraged or pushed to the margins. Even the favoured forms of life will be unevenly distributed, since these will not be equally accessible to everyone. (I shall argue in a moment that laissez-faire fails to provide for all citizens a fair opportunity to acquire the pluralist–liberal virtues.) Moreover, when the market narrows the range of conceptions of the good realistically available to people, it also stifles reasonable *disagreement* as to what the good consists in. It becomes harder to dissent from (or even adequately to defend) market-oriented ways of life when these are the only ones realistically possible. The tendency of market hegemony is to diminish legitimate moral conflict, not by dramatically transcending it in the revolutionary manner imagined by the utopian radicals, but by suffocating it with the quietly repeated insistence that (in Mrs Thatcher's phrase) 'there is no alternative'. The result is a society lacking in the kind of healthy debate over the good commended by Mill, a situation also antipathetic to the outlook of pluralism.

Among the long list of goods that are neglected or downgraded by laissez-faire, several have a plausible claim to be counted as values that contribute to the good life for any human being. Consequently, laissez-faire is likely to violate a third general requirement of the pluralist outlook, namely respect for *universal* values. Examples of the values likely to fall into this class can be drawn from each of the groups listed above. Levels of health care, housing and education that are reasonable relative to the standards of one's society, personal freedom and equality of opportunity of a more than merely formal kind, and cultural resources sufficient to enable people to make sense of their life options – all these may be fairly described as making any life go better than it would otherwise. But all are at serious risk under laissez-faire, since in that kind of society a person's enjoyment of them is dependent on her success in the market. To allow the market the unrestrained dominance it enjoys under laissez-faire is to subordinate many goods that contribute to human flourishing.

Fourth, where the values of the market are allowed to predominate to the extent permitted by laissez-faire, not only are non-market goods neglected and devalued but the distinct character of some goods is distorted. Unrestricted laissez-faire does not adequately recognize the *incommensurability* of values. Under a laissez-faire regime money and commodities tend to be treated as commensurating all other goods. Where the market is a dominant institution it tends to commodify everything in its path, that is, to encourage people to accept that virtually anything can be traded. Values become dollar values. What is wrong with this from a value-pluralist point of view is that certain goods lose their distinctive character when they are treated as commodities. Justice and loyalty, for example, are no longer justice and loyalty once they are bought and sold. The tendency of the market is therefore, unless checked and balanced, to distort our understanding of important human goods by converting them into commodities. This point is strongly expressed by Walzer:

> Money is insidious, and market relations are expansive. A radically *laissez-faire* economy would be like a totalitarian state, invading every other sphere, dominating every other distributive process. It would transform every social good into a commodity. This is market imperialism. (1983: 119–20)

Walzer's reference to 'spheres' comes from his explicitly 'pluralist' *Spheres of Justice* (1983). For Walzer, there is a plurality of principles of just distribution corresponding to the plurality of goods to be distributed. Each kind of good possesses a distinct meaning or character that identifies it as occupying its own 'sphere of justice'. Walzer lists several such spheres, namely those of membership, security and welfare, money and commodities, office, hard work, free time, education, kinship and love, divine grace, recognition, and political power. Each of these spheres possesses, through its distinct meaning, its own distributive rules, and injustice occurs when the distributive principles of one sphere invade or 'dominate' another sphere. Among the most familiar instances of injustice in this sense is where other spheres are invaded or dominated by that of money and commodities. Walzer gives the example of health-care, the meaning of which in the contemporary United States requires distribution according to need, but which is at present dominated by the alien user-pays principles of the market. The distinct meaning of a good like health-care is expressed in part by its own distributive principle. When that principle is subverted or denied, as it is in the case of health-care in the United States, the distinctive meaning or character of the good is correspondingly subverted. It is, to that extent, conflated with other goods, its incommensurability denied.[3]

The kind of denial at work here is similar to that involved in preference-utilitarianism (3.1.3). In effect, money is treated as a common denominator in the sense of a commensurating medium. Money is 'the universal pander', writes Walzer, quoting Marx. 'Wherever money is used, it panders between incompatible things, it breaks into "the self-subsistent entities" of social life, it inverts individuality, "it forces contraries to embrace"' (ibid.: 95, 96). This is a weak form of commensuration compared with the commensurating claims of those who argue for a *summum bonum* or super-value. Money is usually said to 'represent' other values only in the superficial sense that it is a convenient medium through which they can be exchanged. This becomes objectionable, from a pluralist point of view, only when people lose sight of the fact that money is no more than a convenient medium, and come to regard it as desirable for its own sake and as containing, or as a substitute for, other goods. This, however, is a real danger in a laissez-faire society where the market is so dominant. It is in such a society that people are most likely to come to see all or most goods as tradable commodities. To take such a view is to blind oneself to the distinct natures of different goods, that is, to value pluralism.

Such a blinkered outlook is undesirable not only for its own sake, but because of what it leads to, namely, attitudes and policies that fail to appreciate the true nature of the trade-offs involved. Where goods are believed to be quantifiable in monetary terms, conflicts appear to be readily resolvable: one simply chooses the option that will yield the greater value for money. What this ignores, of course, is that there may be more at stake in such decisions than amounts of money. It also ignores the absolute, perhaps tragic nature of the losses involved in such trade-offs. This is masked by the language of dollar-amount cost–benefit, which makes it appear that what is at stake is simply commensurate units of cash, each of which can be substituted for the other. From the perspective of cost–benefit analysis, a rational decision, one that maximizes benefits in terms of the relevant units, is necessarily one in which any loss has been more than compensated. But once one looks behind the monist language and sees the actual goods 'represented' by the dollar amounts, one is obliged to acknowledge losses in terms of the goods themselves. As Walzer writes: 'Often enough money fails to represent value; the translations are made, but as with good poetry, something is lost in the process. Hence we can buy and sell universally only if we disregard real values; while if we attend to values, there are things that cannot be bought and sold' (ibid.: 97). Where the goods in question are incommensurable, there can be no complete compensation. Such losses are final, and cannot be made good by 'representing' them in other terms. Laissez-faire, in its acceptance of market-based measurements of goods and cost–benefit analysis, tends to gloss over the true character of trade-offs that value pluralism bids us take more seriously.[4]

The fifth and final respect in which laissez-faire fails to satisfy the principles implied by the pluralist outlook concerns the perfectionist or *virtues*-based strand in the pluralist case for liberalism (Chapter 8). Pluralism implies that certain personal capacities or virtues are part of the best lives for all persons, since those capacities are necessary for making rational choices among conflicting plural values. But under a regime of laissez-faire those virtues are unlikely to be widely realized.

The capacities in question are generosity, realism, attention and flexibility (implying personal autonomy) (8.1). First, a generous appreciation of the range and variety of human values is rendered unlikely by the relative narrowness of laissez-faire, under which the ends of the market force other values to the margins. Second, realistic acknowledgement of the nature of trade-offs among competing values depends on an acceptance of value incommensur-

PLURALIST LIBERALISM

ability, but as we have just seen this is likely to be papered over by the specious commensuration offered by money, commodification and cost–benefit analysis. Third, attention to particularities will also be at a premium. Attention to the particularities of human goods is blunted by the tendency to commensuration just mentioned. Attention to the particularities of situations is likely to be wanting for much the same reason. If values can be commensurated, then it should be possible to formulate a rule applicable to a generality of situations according to which conflicts can be decided by maximizing the commensurating unit, for example a form of utilitarianism or cost–benefit calculation. Attention to persons is also inadequately served by the laissez-faire outlook, which interprets the fundamental liberal commitment to equal concern and respect for all persons as satisfied by a regime of identical rights of a strictly negative character regardless of differences in circumstances. The fate of those who lack the resources or good fortune with which to exploit such rights is a matter of indifference, or at any rate is treated as beyond the concern of a just public policy. For the same reason, laissez-faire will be an unreliable promoter of the fourth of the pluralist virtues, flexibility, and its liberal counterpart, personal autonomy. To be capable of responding flexibly to different and perhaps rapidly changing situations requires access to real opportunities, options and resources. But these will not be available to those who, for whatever reason, fail in the market. The pluralist outlook implies that flexibility, and therefore personal autonomy, is required for the best human lives, but autonomy will be a realistic possibility only for some under laissez-faire.

I conclude that although value pluralism implies a case for liberalism, this is unlikely to be the classical or laissez-faire form of liberalism. Laissez-faire is open to serious criticism on the ground of each of the five pluralist principles I have identified. It remains to mount a positive case for the 'social' or 'egalitarian' alternative. Such a case can be briefly outlined, since it is implicit in the shortcomings of laissez-faire already discussed. The most general of these shortcomings is, of course, the reliance placed by laissez-faire on the distribution of goods and opportunities through the market alone. It follows that the kind of liberalism that fits best with the pluralist outlook will be, at least in some degree, interventionist in the field of economic distribution. That is, the liberal regime sanctioned by the pluralist outlook will be broadly

235

FROM PLURALISM TO LIBERALISM

redistributive: it will be prepared to intervene positively to correct or qualify or balance the effects of distribution through the market.[5]

From a pluralist point of view, state intervention will be required on the ground of each of the five principles mentioned. First, intervention is required in order to promote a diversity of goods, since the market alone cannot be relied upon to provide opportunities to enjoy 'non-market' goods. Second, the same case can be made with respect to the diversity of ways of life implied by reasonable disagreement about the good. Third, since some non-market goods contribute to the good life for any human being, state intervention will also ensure respect for universal values. Fourth, intervention is necessary to sustain people's sense of the incommensurability of values, and hence of the true nature of trade-offs. In Walzer's terms, the market cannot be relied upon to keep the different spheres of distributive justice separate, its constant tendency being towards commodification of all goods. Intervention is therefore required to maintain the boundaries around 'blocked exchanges', or rules forbidding the purchase of certain kinds of goods (Walzer, 1983: 100–3). Finally, intervention is also required in order to secure adequate opportunities for all persons to acquire the virtues necessary for good practical reasoning, and therefore a good life, under pluralism. The attainment of personal flexibility and autonomy in particular is possible only on a foundation of material resources, services and education which the market alone does not supply at an adequate level to everyone.

9.3 Cultural Minorities

The second public policy issue I want to consider from a pluralist–liberal point of view is that of the proper approach to cultural identifications and practices, especially those of minority cultures. This was noted in Chapter 2 as the second major source of disagreement within contemporary liberal theory, adding to the split between supporters of economic laissez-faire and redistribution. The latter debate is to some extent reflected in the cultural field, since one important sub-issue is whether the correct liberal attitude should be one of laissez-faire or 'indifference' to cultural affiliation, or whether liberal policy should involve state intervention. Supposing the liberal state does have an active role in the cultural field, a second sub-issue is whether its intervention should

236

PLURALIST LIBERALISM

favour the dominant or mainstream culture, or whether the proper liberal policy is some form of multiculturalism or official support for several different cultures. How should these questions be answered from a pluralist point of view?

As a first step, it will be helpful to gather together what has already been said about cultures in the course of the previous chapters. Taken together, these disparate strands show the pluralist attitude to culture to be complex. First, pluralism has important implications for the claims of culture as a moral authority. Recall that the conservative pluralist critics of liberalism, Kekes and (in his middle phase) Gray, argued that cultural tradition is the primary guide for the making of choices among competing plural and incommensurable values (Chapter 5). The element of truth in this claim is that choices among plural values are hard choices and that cultural traditions provide welcome signposts to their resolution. But we also saw that from a pluralist point of view the authority of local tradition is not exhaustive or decisive: pluralism must be distinguished from relativism. Contextual factors other than tradition may also help to guide choice among incommensurables. Moreover, the concept of value pluralism itself implies normative principles that apply universally. Culture makes an important contribution to moral decision making under pluralism, but that contribution needs to be balanced – indeed in some cases overridden – by other considerations.

Second, the pluralist argument for liberalism by way of neutrality rests on a commitment to diversity and on the accommodation of reasonable disagreement about the good life (Chapters 6 and 7). As we saw, pluralism requires in the first place a diversity of goods rather than cultures, but the former will to some considerable extent lead to the latter. Consequently, pluralism implies the valuing of cultural diversity, and a corresponding acceptance of reasonable disagreement among cultural outlooks concerning the nature of the good. It should be recalled, however, that 'diversity' here includes an element of 'coherence' or balance as well as sheer multiplicity (6.2). To promote a diversity of cultures is not simply to tolerate or encourage as many as possible without regard to their content and interrelationships, since some cultures are hostile to others and to cultural multiplicity. Pluralist support for a multiplicity of cultures within the same political society will therefore be tempered by the insistence that these be contained within a limiting framework, and I argued in Chapter 6 that the best framework will be a liberal one.

FROM PLURALISM TO LIBERALISM

Similarly, although pluralism supports the accommodation of reasonable disagreement concerning the good, this will be an accommodation, as I argued in Chapter 7, within liberal limits.

Third, a similar balance of considerations emerges from the perfectionist or virtues-based strand of the pluralist case for liberalism (Chapter 8). At the centre of that line of argument is a commitment to personal autonomy, which follows from the demanding nature of pluralist choice-making. At first sight an emphasis on individual autonomy may seem to weigh against the claims of culture: Mill, for example, defines autonomy in part as resistance to 'the despotism of custom'. But contemporary liberals like Raz (1986, 1995) and Kymlicka (1989, 1995) have shown that autonomy and culture are not wholly opposed, since autonomy itself requires a cultural basis. To begin with, any coherent life depends on the availability to the person living that life of a cultural map with which to make sense of the choices (including pluralist choices) facing her – thus far, Kekes and Gray are on firm ground in their stress on tradition. A liberal form of life, based on autonomy, is no exception. As Kymlicka argues:

> Liberals should be concerned with the fate of cultural structures, not because they have some moral status of their own, but because it's only through having a rich and secure cultural structure that people can become aware, in a vivid way, of the options available to them, and intelligently examine their value. (1989: 165)

Membership of a flourishing culture is valuable as a necessary condition for making autonomous choices. Since autonomous choices are required of us by a recognition of value pluralism, it follows that pluralism implies a case for the value of cultural membership.

Again, however, there are limits or qualifications to such a case. It is not just any culture that can be defended in this way. Cultural membership as such is a necessary but not a sufficient condition for autonomy, since autonomy is not valued highly or at all by some cultures. As Raz says, a particular culture may or may not be 'autonomy-supporting' (1986: 391). Consequently, the pluralist argument for the value of cultural membership by way of personal autonomy cannot be an argument in favour of cultures or particular cultural practices that are themselves opposed to the value of personal autonomy or individual choice. At this point the pluralist

238

view of cultural claims coincides with that of Kymlicka: 'Supporting the intolerant character of a cultural community undermines the very reason we had to support cultural membership – that it allows for meaningful individual choice' (1989: 197). The pluralist argument for liberal autonomy thus implies a case for the value of cultural membership, but this will be a case couched within liberal limits.

These various points can be integrated as follows. Pluralism implies a need to balance several different considerations when it comes to the claims of culture. On the one hand, the pluralist outlook suggests that cultures must be respected as, first, sites of value diversity and reasonable disagreement, and second, contexts for reasoned and autonomous choice among conflicting incommensurables. On the other hand, those same reasons for respecting cultures also imply limits to the authority of cultural claims. 'Diversity' involves coherence as well as multiplicity, and personal autonomy cannot be a reason for supporting cultures or practices that deny autonomy. Reasonable disagreement about the good life is similarly circumscribed by the limits of a liberal framework. Moreover, cultural traditions are not the sole or final ethical court of appeal from a pluralist point of view, but are themselves subject to critical assessment on the basis of key pluralist values such as diversity and autonomy.

Given these general pluralist attitudes to culture, how should the pluralist liberal answer the two policy issues raised at the start of this section? The first of these was whether the pluralist approach to culture requires laissez-faire or intervention.

The case for a laissez-faire cultural policy has been prominently argued by Chandran Kukathas (1992, 1997, 1998). Kukathas agrees with Kymlicka that cultural membership is an important human value. But he denies that the members of a particular culture within a liberal democracy have special rights to have their culture preserved or supported by the state. The proper liberal attitude to cultures is one of 'indifference' (1998: 691). Cultures rise and fall, flourish and decay: that is the way the world goes. Liberal governments should not attempt to interfere in this natural process either to retard or advance it, because the fundamental liberal commitment is to the well-being of the individual person. The claims of culture are morally significant only so far as they serve that basic end. 'Liberal theory looks at fundamental political questions from the perspective of the individual rather than that of the group

FROM PLURALISM TO LIBERALISM

or culture or community. Such collectives matter only because they are essential for the well-being of the individual' (1992: 112). The standard principles of the classical liberal tradition, in particular toleration and freedom of association, are sufficient to provide for cultural membership so far as it ought to be provided for. The argument 'is not that groups do not matter but rather that there is no need to depart from the liberal language of individual rights to do justice to them' (ibid.: 107). Freedom of association includes the right of the individual to adopt any cultural identification he or she pleases. How people choose to exercise that right is no business of the liberal state, the chief commitment of which is to individual liberty. With regard to the fate of particular cultural affiliations, liberalism recommends, in short, 'doing nothing' (1998: 687).

The problem with cultural laissez-faire from a pluralist point of view echoes the pluralist objection to economic laissez-faire in the previous section. Although such a policy gives the appearance of even-handedness or neutrality, it conceals a bias in favour of certain goods and ways of life rather than others. Moreover, the favoured range of goods and lives does not do justice to the general principles implied by the pluralist outlook. As Kymlicka points out, the bias in cultural laissez-faire is a bias in favour of the culture of the majority in a particular society and against minority cultures. There are two principal aspects to this. The more general is that 'benign neglect', as Kymlicka calls it, *cannot* be even-handed indifference, because even a minimal state cannot avoid making decisions that favour certain cultures against others. 'Government decisions on languages, internal boundaries, public holidays, and state symbols unavoidably involve recognizing, accommodating and supporting the needs and identities of particular ethnic and national groups. The state unavoidably promotes certain cultural identities, and thereby disadvantages others' (1995: 108). Even 'doing nothing' – that is, refraining from offering official support to any culture – amounts to favouring certain cultures over others, namely those with less need of state assistance to survive. This point is endorsed by the pluralist outlook which, as we have seen, acknowledges the inevitability of our having to rank goods when they conflict, and therefore the impossibility of any state neutrality that is more than 'approximate'.

Could Kukathas reply that cultural laissez-faire is, if not completely even-handed in its effects, at least approximately neutral, that is, more accommodating to diversity than alternative

240

PLURALIST LIBERALISM

arrangements? I believe the answer is no, because of a second, more specific aspect of the bias in cultural laissez-faire. This problem is evident from the last section: to rely on the strictly negative liberties of classical laissez-faire is in effect to privilege the goods of the market. In the cultural field it is to make cultural survival dependent on success in the market, thus to render cultural membership subject to the same market lottery. In pluralist terms this will be undesirable for two reasons. First, it is likely to lead to a reduction of cultural diversity and of the extent to which reasonable disagreement is properly accommodated. Second, partly as a consequence, it will undermine the capacity of many people for choice, especially autonomous choice, because it will undermine the cultural conditions for choice.

Recall that cultural diversity is a pluralist value so far as it serves the diversity of goods. Laissez-faire will tend to reduce cultural diversity because it will tend to work against minority cultures. Minority tastes and interests are in general ill-served by market-based institutions, which naturally answer best to demand that is sufficient to generate profit. A related problem is identified by Kymlicka (1989: Chapter 9; 1995: Chapter 6). Members of minority cultures, he argues, are at a natural disadvantage in cultural terms compared with members of a majority or dominant culture. The latter enjoy their culture 'for free', since the mainstream culture of a society is by definition pervasive. Minority cultural groups, however, must exert themselves to maintain their heritage. Where this requires access to relatively scarce resources such as land (especially important in the case of many indigenous groups), minorities typically find themselves having to 'bid' for those resources against members of the majority. What the mainstream gets for free, minorities must pay for, using up economic resources the majority can employ in other ways. Under a laissez-faire regime there would be no compensation for this disadvantage, and no means of preserving a group's cultural resources other than through whatever weight they could bring to bear in the market. The likely result is that some cultural identifications will be marginalized and will ultimately disappear simply through the economic weakness of their members.

Cultural laissez-faire will also be harmful in pluralist terms because of its effect on people's capacity for individual choice and autonomy, the latter required for practical reasoning under personal pluralism. Choice and autonomy are adversely affected by the decay of minority cultures in two ways. First, the members of those cultures will be deprived of the cultural map with which they make sense of the world and therefore of their options in it. Second, members of other cultures, including the mainstream, will be denied access to, or at least knowledge of, alternatives from which they could learn. Moreover, even mainstream culture is not available entirely for free even to its own members. Many cultural experiences, by no means only those at the 'high' end of culture, are accessible only through the market: books, cinema, sports and so on. Under laissez-faire, access to one's own culture, even if that happens to be the mainstream culture, is thoroughly dependent on one's success or failure in the market. Consequently, the opportunities a person has to exercise real choice or to develop a degree of personal autonomy are correspondingly at the mercy of market fortune. For the less fortunate, a laissez-faire approach to culture affords little prospect of living a good life in pluralist terms.

The pluralist outlook will not recommend laissez-faire in the cultural field any more than in economic distribution, and for similar reasons. It follows that, again, some degree of intervention is called for, probably through the agency of the state. The next question is, intervention of what kind, with what goals in mind? The answer is to some extent already implicit in the case against cultural laissez-faire. State intervention is needed to remedy the ill effects of market-based benign neglect. That is, the liberal state should take as a positive goal the promotion of cultural diversity in order to promote a diversity of goods and ways of life, to accommodate reasonable disagreement and to secure the conditions for personal autonomy. This will involve the recognition of special rights to compensate members of those minority groups suffering from undeserved cultural disadvantage – that is, lack of access to membership of a flourishing culture. In particular, indigenous minorities in 'settler societies' will be likely beneficiaries, since they generally have the clearest claim both to cultural disadvantage and to that disadvantage having been unchosen.[6]

This suggests an answer to the second of the policy issues listed earlier: supposing that the pluralist–liberal state ought to intervene in the cultural field, should its goal be multiculturalism or monoculturalism? The pluralist–liberal state will intervene to promote more than one culture within its jurisdiction, for two reasons. First, the pluralist commitment to cultural diversity and the accommodation of reasonable disagreement about the good clearly points towards multiculturalism. This is the conclusion drawn by Raz, for whom 'value pluralism is the view that many different activities and forms of life which are incompatible are valuable' (1995: 179). Although 'theoretically, the plurality of valuable ways of life asserted by pluralism need not manifest itself in the same society ... typically in our day and age, pluralism exists within every society, indeed within every culture' (ibid.: 179–80).

Second, multiculturalism is implied by the pluralist commitment to personal autonomy. Autonomy presupposes, in Raz's phrase, 'an adequate range of options' from which to choose. A multicultural society will, almost as a matter of necessity, provide a greater range of cultural options than a monocultural society. Moreover, in order to have an adequate range of options, *one's own* culture must be a flourishing one. In principle, what matters for liberal autonomy is membership of *some* thriving cultural group but not any such group in particular. In practice, however, most people will have the best chance of making sense of their lives in terms of the culture within which they were brought up. As Kymlicka writes: 'People are bound, in an important way, to their own cultural community. We can't just transplant people from one culture to another' (1989: 175). If that is the case, a state committed to promoting personal autonomy will also be committed to promoting more than one cultural identification, given the de facto multiplicity of such identities in modern societies.

But how far does pluralist multiculturalism extend, what are its limits? In particular, does pluralist multiculturalism require the state to tolerate, even to promote, minority cultures or practices that are illiberal? Many fundamentalist religious groups, for example, identify themselves with practices that are strongly patriarchal or that involve the inculcation of unquestioned orthodoxy rather than education for autonomy. Must groups and practices such as these be accommodated by pluralist liberalism? If, as I have argued, the pluralist case for liberalism gives priority to personal autonomy, the answer would seem to be, no. As Kymlicka points out, if the fundamental reason for valuing cultural membership is its role in the enabling of autonomous choice, then multiculturalism cannot extend to the promotion of cultures or particular cultural practices that deny or severely restrict choice.[7]

An alternative view has been put forward by William Galston (1999a). From an explicitly value-pluralist starting point, Galston argues that the paramount commitment of the liberal state should

FROM PLURALISM TO LIBERALISM

not be to autonomy but rather to the toleration of cultural diversity, including cultures and practices that are clearly illiberal. For Galston, personal autonomy is too sectarian a goal for either pluralism or liberalism. Instead, pluralism implies the valuing of many different ways of life and practices, excluding only those that violate 'the minimal content of the human good' (ibid.: 895). Above that threshold, which excludes practices such as human sacrifice, pluralist liberalism should tolerate and defend people's 'expressive liberty', or freedom to live in a way that expresses their deepest beliefs and identifications, even if that involves the denial of personal autonomy as a human good. He concludes that

> a liberal polity guided (as I believe it should be) by a commitment to moral and political pluralism will be parsimonious in specifying binding public principles and cautious about employing such principles to intervene in the internal affairs of civil associations. It rather will pursue a policy of *maximum feasible accommodation*, limited only by the core requirements of individual security and civic unity. (ibid.: 875)

Galston's conclusion should be rejected from a pluralist point of view. First, his dismissal of autonomy on the ground of pluralism is mistaken. At first sight it may seem that pluralism reduces autonomy to the status of merely one incommensurable good among others, but I have argued that pluralism accords a special role to autonomy as a key virtue required for pluralist practical reasoning (Chapter 8). Indeed, in my view the autonomy-based route from pluralism to liberalism takes precedence over the neutrality or accommodation route (9.1). Once personal autonomy is restored to its proper place at the centre of pluralist liberalism, the 'expressive liberty' of illiberal groups will be severely curtailed, at least in principle.[8]

Second, even on the ground of toleration and diversity Galston's position is not supported by the pluralist outlook. In effect, Galston acknowledges only one limitation on the claims of culture, namely 'the minimal content of the human good' or respect for universal values. Beyond that shallow threshold he assumes that value pluralism implies a degree of support for cultural diversity that is quite unrestricted. But I have argued that the pluralist view of culture is much more complex than this. Pluralist support for the claims of culture is in fact subject to a series of major qualifications

244

PLURALIST LIBERALISM

corresponding to the general principles implied by the notion of pluralism itself. The same qualifications apply to any pluralist policy of multiculturalism. Respect for universal values is only the first of these. A second qualification is implied by recognition of the incommensurability of values, which ruled out certain utopian forms of politics (Chapter 4). Most important for present purposes, however, because imposing very significant restrictions on the claims of culture, are the qualifications implied by the remaining three general norms of pluralism: promotion of diversity, accommodation of reasonable disagreement, and exercise of the pluralist virtues, especially autonomy. Once more, the kind of diversity to which pluralists are committed is not, as Galston supposes, a simple multiplicity regardless of the content of, and relations among, the goods and cultures concerned. Rather, to be endorsed from a pluralist viewpoint cultural identifications must themselves be sufficiently tolerant of other cultures to present a realistic prospect of coexistence within a minimally coherent social order – the 'coherence' element of pluralist diversity. A multiculturalism based on pluralist diversity cannot support cultures or practices that themselves oppose that diversity. This parallels Kymlicka's point about the limitations of a case for cultural rights based on autonomy. Moreover, if pluralist diversity involves, as I have argued, a balance between multiplicity and coherence that is best achieved within a liberal political framework, then pluralist multiculturalism must be multiculturalism within liberal limits. Second, similar considerations apply to the pluralist injunction to accommodate reasonable disagreement. Not all disagreements about the good are to be accommodated, but only those that are both 'reasonable' in Rawlsian terms, and consistent with pluralism. Third, to be included within pluralist multiculturalism, groups must be at least sufficiently tolerant of the personal autonomy of their own members and of other people to contribute to a cultural basis supportive of choice and autonomy in the society overall – perhaps the chief condition for a good life under pluralism.

The multiculturalism sanctioned by the pluralist outlook will not, then, be as extremely accommodating as that proposed by Galston. Rather, it will take a more qualified or moderate form in the sense that it will be hedged about by the basic principles of liberalism, in particular that of personal autonomy. Pluralist multiculturalism will have much the same limits as those proposed by Kymlicka. It will 'accord substantial civil rights to the members

245

of minority cultures', that is, rights not to be mistreated (in liberal terms) by those cultures (Kymlicka, 1995: 164).

Will this not involve wholesale and heavy-handed state interference with such groups? Kymlicka rightly replies that it need not, if we distinguish between the principles or ends of policy and the means used to pursue those ends. A liberal state should secure the civil rights of all its citizens, including those who are members of minority cultural groups. It does not follow that the only or best way of securing civil rights in such cases is coercive interference. Alternatives mentioned by Kymlicka include 'speaking out' (information and advocacy), incentives of various kinds, and 'international mechanisms' such as judicial review by courts other than those of the domestic majority culture (*ibid.*: 171). Still, this more cautious approach to the means by which policy ends are pursued does not detract from the importance of identifying those ends clearly. 'Liberals have no automatic right to impose their views on non-liberal national minorities. But they do have the right, and indeed the responsibility, to identify what those views actually are (*ibid.*).' In the case of a liberalism based on value pluralism, it is important to see that the implications of pluralism are less permissive towards illiberal cultures than some writers have supposed.

9.4 Constitutionalism and Politics

In the two preceding sections I dealt with issues concerning the *content* of public policy under pluralist liberalism: what should the goals and principles of policy be in relation to economic distribution and cultural minorities? My final question addresses the *process* by which policy should be decided: how and by whom? More specifically, should the emphasis in pluralist liberalism be on appeals to principles entrenched in a constitution above the political fray, or on decision-making processes that are part of political negotiation? I shall argue that value pluralism gives us reason to be wary of abandoning constitutionalism for politics, but also that pluralism implies an important role for political compromise together with a principled approach to such compromise.

The issue between constitutionalism and politics has been much discussed in recent years, in particular by thinkers who see a close connection between the content of justice and the process by which

PLURALIST LIBERALISM

just public policy is formulated. They argue that under modern conditions of pervasive plurality of belief it is no longer clear that the standard principles and institutions of liberal democracy can be relied upon to reflect fairly the beliefs and values of different groups. The standard liberal-democratic response to difference is to accommodate it by clearing areas within which individuals are at liberty to live as they please. Those areas are marked by individual rights that are, in various ways including constitutionally entrenched bills of rights, marked off from interference by political majorities – the legal and political expression of the idea captured in Ronald Dworkin's phrase, 'rights as trumps' (Dworkin, 1977). But the critics question whether any scheme of rights, no matter how generous or well-intentioned, can be adequate if it does not emerge from the voices of those it affects. Advocates of the 'politics of identity', for example, deny that any perspective on justice can be wholly impartial, and insist that genuine justice requires more strongly democratic approaches such as group representation (Young, 1990). Another group of critics are the proponents of 'deliberative democracy', who argue that liberal–democratic reliance on judicial review of entrenched rights amounts to the usurpation by an elite forum of moral questions that ought to be deliberated by citizens, resulting in the weakening of democratic citizenship and legitimacy (Macedo, 1999). It is this second line of argument that I shall focus on in what follows. That is because while much of the politics of identity is argued from a relativist or postmodernist perspective that is opposed by value pluralism, the pluralist outlook has been interestingly linked with the literature of deliberative democracy.

What lessons does the pluralist outlook have for the issue of constitutionalism versus politics? We have already seen one answer, that of Gray (Chapter 5). For Gray, a liberal account of justice or rights is just one possible ranking of plural values with no inherent or universal superiority to the alternatives. Contrary to liberal neutralists like Rawls, Gray argues that there is no reason to place liberal rights in a separate category from any other moral or political claim, therefore no reason to insulate such rights from the political process. Rather, when plural and incommensurable values collide, the only solution is to reach an accommodation or compromise appropriate to the circumstances, a modus vivendi, which must always be the product of a political process of accommodation and bargaining. For Gray, then, value pluralism implies the impossi-

247

FROM PLURALISM TO LIBERALISM

bility of liberal constitutionalism and the pervasiveness of politics. Moreover, pluralist politics may or may not be liberal, depending on the context. But we have also seen that Gray's argument from pluralism to modus vivendi suffers from several difficulties, the central problem being its sheer vagueness. Gray nowhere clarifies what he means by 'compromise' or 'accommodation' among rival views, or how such settlements are to be achieved. In fact, his notion of modus vivendi is so empty of structure or principle that it amounts to a monist privileging of either self-interest or peace at any price (5.2).

A more fully developed argument from pluralism to democratic politics can be found in the work of Richard Bellamy (1999, 2000). Bellamy's view is in some respects similar to Gray's, in that he sees pluralism as implying the need for abandoning pre-political constitutions in favour of looser political accommodations. Pluralism undermines the possibility of the reasoned consensus necessary to ground constitutions, 'and creates clashes of principles, values and interests that can be defused only through political compromise' (1999: 93). However, Bellamy gives a more careful and nuanced account of such compromises than that offered by Gray, and he presents his theory as a liberal one. He describes his 'democratic liberalism' as 'a form of politics that makes liberalism an aspect of the democratic process itself, rather than a normative constraint on the scope of democracy' (ibid.). The basic idea is that just outcomes will be arrived at solely through political negotiation reflecting the views of all concerned. However, these accommodations will not usually be the result of mere self-interested bargaining, but of principled negotiation structured by moral limits that are intrinsic to the process (ibid.: 106).

Bellamy's position is thus a version of deliberative democracy in the manner of Amy Gutmann and Dennis Thompson (1996). Following them, he sees the chief moral limit on deliberative negotiation as the principle of 'reciprocity'. Deliberation is reciprocal when each party tries to justify its view in terms that are acceptable to the other (ibid.: Chapter 2). Reciprocity therefore rules out justifications that depend on self-interest or which rely on implausible empirical claims or claims of value that can only be accepted by those who subscribe to a particular conception of the good. Certain arguments put forward by religious fundamentalists, for example, would be excluded on these last grounds. The precise terms of a deliberative accommodation would depend on the particular case. Bellamy departs somewhat from Gutmann and Thompson in emphasizing the frequency with which accommodation is unlikely to take the form of consensus. For Bellamy, disagreement is the more probable outcome, calling for compromises which may take various forms in different circumstances. Bargaining may be appropriate in some cases, other forms of compromise elsewhere (Bellamy, 1999: 103–5).

Bellamy's view has much to recommend it, but it is open to two main lines of objection, respectively liberal and pluralist. First, an obvious source of concern for liberals will be that a scheme like this, which makes all claims subject to democratic politics, will provide inadequate protection for individuals and minorities. How, for example, will democratic liberalism secure the traditional liberal right of free expression? One answer might be that freedom of expression is required as a precondition for democratic deliberation (Cohen, 1989). But then, in the absence of constitutional safeguards, what is there to prevent freely expressive deliberation from issuing in illiberal outcomes, including restrictions on future expression? The deliberative response would be that such outcomes are less likely where deliberation is properly reciprocal. But although reciprocity rules out self-interested, implausible and morally inaccessible claims, the exclusion of these does not guarantee decisions that respect freedom of expression as an outcome. Moreover, in ruling out certain sorts of claim, reciprocity imposes its own restrictions on expression at the level of process.[9] Overall, Bellamy's democratic liberalism and other versions of deliberative democracy tread a fine line between, on the one hand, accommodating views hostile to liberalism and so allowing illiberal outcomes, and on the other, providing adequate protection for liberal concerns but at the price of imposing procedural restrictions on deliberation that tend to nullify its democratic purpose.

This tension in deliberative-democratic theories is essentially a tension between their democratic and liberal elements, and it suggests a second question: does deliberative democracy sufficiently acknowledge the implications of value pluralism? First, a value pluralist may doubt that democratic liberalism does justice to the distinctness and incommensurability of personal freedom and collective self-government when it tries to bring these together by harmonizing them within the same political process. That the promotion of democracy does not necessarily serve the value of individual liberty, and often has the opposite effect, is the heart of

FROM PLURALISM TO LIBERALISM

Berlin's critique of those conceptions of positive liberty that purport to see these as identical. Bellamy's attempt to reconcile the two values by contouring their definitions – democracy becoming reciprocity and liberty 'non-domination' (1991: 120) – is the kind of manoeuvre that Berlin counsels us to be wary of. Such conceptual moves, even when well-intentioned, are apt to blind us to the reality of hard choices and the costs these entail. Bellamy runs this risk when he tries to persuade us that democratic politics will itself preserve personal liberty. The risk is lessened in a political system where the democratic process is seen to be checked and balanced by a consititution in some degree insulated from quotidian politics. The distinct values at stake are then seen more clearly for what they are.

Bellamy would perhaps reply that individual rights are best protected through the democratic process because they are best protected by giving a political voice to those whose rights they are. 'Domination,' he writes, 'most commonly manifests itself through inhibiting or preventing groups or individuals from having a voice in the decisions governing their lives ... Typically, oppression has manifested itself indirectly through the mechanisms of hegemony' (1999: 122). But this reply rests on two contestable assumptions. First, when it comes to tackling hegemony it is not obvious that political accommodation will be more effective than constitutional guarantees. The kind of coalition-building that is the stuff of democratic politics does not always preserve a robust freedom of expression for unpopular views. Second, while hegemony should certainly not be underrated as a source of oppression and the denial of rights, the assumption that it is the principal source is both unwarranted in general and un-pluralist in particular.

The assumption is unwarranted and at odds with pluralism because there is no good reason to regard hegemony as always or generally more significant than other sources of oppression. On the pluralist view, just as there is no *summum bonum*, so there is no *summum malum*: that role cannot be played by hegemony any more than by other candidates.[10] Consider, for example, the 'five faces of oppression' identified by Iris Marion Young (1990): exploitation, marginalization, powerlessness, cultural imperialism and violence. Of these, the only one clearly identical with or reducible to hegemony is 'cultural imperialism'. Cultural imperialism is experienced when (in the relevant part of Young's definition) 'the dominant meanings of a society render the particular perspective of one's own group invisible' (*ibid.*: 58–9). It is true that cultural

250

imperialism or hegemony often prevents us from *recognizing* instances of other kinds of oppression, for example where unfairly low wages are not seen to be exploitative because defended by a rhetoric of 'voluntary contract' that reflects only the perspective of employers yet is widely accepted. But that is not to say that hegemony is the cause of the exploitation or a more significant evil. Even if hegemonic acceptance of it is dissolved, the exploitation itself may continue. To give a voice to those hitherto silenced or ignored is a step in the right direction, since it is likely to introduce into the debate important considerations that were previously excluded. But that is not the whole story, because even when all the relevant groups have spoken it remains to weigh their respective claims. Pluralists can accept that hegemony is a serious obstacle to justice and that having a voice is a vital political good, but they should beware of supposing that hegemony is the worst political evil and that removing it is a panacea. Even supposing that the evil of hegemony is best combated and the good of collective self-expression served in the arena of democratic politics, it does not follow that the same is true of other incommensurably important goods and evils. For them, constitutional protection may be equally appropriate if not more so.

Bellamy might further reply that an entrenched constitution requires a degree of consensus which political compromise does not, a degree of consensus impossible in the face of pluralism (plurality of belief and the value pluralism underlying it). The problem with this claim is the same as the most fundamental problem with the position taken by Gray: it overestimates the extent to which value pluralism implies reasonable disagreement. Of course, value pluralism does imply reasonable disagreement, in particular about substantial conceptions of the good life (Chapter 7). But I have also argued that pluralism implies the possibility, at least in principle, of reasoned agreement in several key areas, including the political framework for a society characterized by widespread plurality of belief (and even an ethical framework for the best human lives). That is, pluralism implies a set of compelling reasons for agreeing on the terms of a (liberal) constitution. Again, this is not to deny that there will be very considerable areas of reasonable disagreement and so a substantial role for compromise under pluralist liberalism, as I shall discuss in a moment. It is to say that the concept of value pluralism itself generates principles sufficient to mandate reasoned agreement on a constitution.

FROM PLURALISM TO LIBERALISM

No doubt there is more to be said on this issue, but I postpone a more thorough investigation to another time. For my purposes here enough has been said to warrant a tentative conclusion, namely that the claim that pluralism requires appeal to political negotiation (or deliberative democracy) rather than constitutional principle has not yet been fully made out. On the face of it, the liberal political framework indicated by pluralism might be conceived as taking either a constitutional or a negotiated form. Indeed, so far as pluralism implies the possibility of reasonable disagreement, it might be thought (as by Gray and Bellamy) to favour political compromise over constitutional consensus. On reflection, however, there is reason to doubt that a political process alone, even modified in a deliberative direction (supposing that were practicable), would adequately respect either the fundamental values of liberalism or the outlook of value pluralism. On the contrary, the pluralist outlook suggests reasons to commend a system under which democratic processes are checked and balanced by constitutional entrenchment and judicial review. From a pluralist perspective, such a system highlights the incommensurability of personal liberty and collective self-government, and the potential for conflict between the two. Its mix of institutions reflects an appropriate mix of distinct values.

Even if political accommodation is rejected as an adequate *substitute* for constitutional protection, however, that does not exclude an important role for a politics of compromise *within* a constitutional framework. Moreover, the pluralist outlook makes a significant contribution to the proper regulation of such compromises. Through much of this book my emphasis has been on the extent to which reasoned *agreement* is possible in the face of value pluralism – since I have been principally concerned to provide a pluralist case for liberal universalism and to argue against more sceptical or narrowly particularist readings of pluralism. But the lines of agreement I have indicated still leave very considerable spaces in which reasonable disagreement is likely and therefore (given the need for a decision) some kind of compromise necessary.

The existence of such spaces of disagreement was indicated most explicitly in my discussion of the link between pluralism and reasonable disagreement about the nature of the good life (Chapter 7), but it extends much further than this. I have argued that under value pluralism reasoned agreement is possible in principle, despite value conflict, in two main areas. First, reasoned agreement is compatible with pluralism in cases of conflict among plural values

252

PLURALIST LIBERALISM

where choice can be guided by a sufficiently specified context (Chapters 3 and 5). Second, pluralism itself gives us reason to agree on the principles of liberalism (in a perfectionist, redistributive and moderately multicultural version) as the political framework for a given society (Chapters 6–9), and as the ethical framework for the best lives (Chapter 8). But beyond these areas of potential agreement lie all those instances in which conflicts among plural values can be decided neither by reference to context nor to liberal principles. Examples include (but are by no means limited to) notoriously intractable questions like the moral permissibility of abortion or of capital punishment. Issues such as these remain sites of sharp disagreement within most specifications of context and most accounts of liberalism. Here the value pluralist should join hands with the deliberative democrat in recognizing that in such cases views on both sides may be equally – or incommensurably – reasonable. Yet given that these are unavoidably matters of public policy and that a decision must be made one way or the other, how should that decision be made? In particular, does the pluralist outlook provide any guidance in such cases?

The pluralist outlook does indeed remain instructive even in cases where agreement is not possible and the best that can be achieved is accommodation or compromise. Accommodation still ought to be guided by principle if it is not to become a mere 'compromise' in the worst sense of the word – the abandonment of principle – or a monist modus vivendi, such as that supported by Gray, understood as a balance of power or the pursuit of peace at any price. The pluralist outlook suggests what some of those guiding principles should be. The pluralist virtues provide an especially pertinent focus, since these are the qualities of mind necessary to choose rationally among conflicting plural values in particular cases. A principled approach to particular cases of deep and continuing disagreement is one that receives guidance from the four pluralist virtues developed in Chapter 8: generosity, realism, attentiveness and flexibility.

My claim here overlaps a similar point made by some of the theorists of deliberative democracy. Gutmann and Thompson, for example, argue that deliberative reciprocity requires the support of certain 'civic virtues' or favourable dispositions of character (1996: 79–91). These are important for all deliberation, but become crucial in maintaining a deliberative, mutually respectful approach to cases where agreement is impossible. There are two main families of civic

FROM PLURALISM TO LIBERALISM

virtues along these lines, the first being that of 'civic integrity', dealing with the proper attitude to one's own arguments. One's arguments should be justified morally rather than based on self-interest, they should be acted on consistently as a sign of sincerity, and one should also be consistent in accepting their broader implications. Corresponding to these elements of civic integrity are the components of 'civic magnanimity', the second family of civic virtues, which apply to our proper attitude towards the arguments of others. It is this second set of virtues that is so resonant of the virtues implied by value pluralism.

Gutmann and Thompson's civic magnanimity consists of three elements, each of which has its pluralist counterpart. First, in cases of deliberative disagreement we should be prepared to acknowledge that not only we but also our opponents are making a moral case in which legitimate values are at stake. This corresponds to the pluralist virtue of 'generosity' (and its liberal equivalent, broad-mindedness), which involves acknowledgement of something of the full range of human values, including the validity and weight of values and ways of life other than our own. Second, we should adopt an attitude of 'open-mindedness', or willingness to change our minds given good reason to do so. Here the pluralist will similarly commend the virtue of 'flexibility', or responsiveness to context as against the rigid application of general rules. The third component of civic magnanimity is what Gutmann and Thompson call 'the economy of moral disagreement', which bids citizens 'seek the rationale that minimizes rejection of the position they oppose' (ibid.: 84–5). Even where we decide against a view, we should concede as much to it as we can in the knowledge that it expresses a set of genuine values that ought to be taken seriously, even if we must place our priorities elsewhere. This idea echoes the pluralist virtue of 'realism', which requires us to reflect that value trade-offs among incommensurables always involve genuine, perhaps tragic, loss. The remaining pluralist virtue of attentiveness to the particularity of values, situations and persons is echoed by the emphasis placed by deliberative democrats on discussion of actual cases as against attempts to resolve questions solely by way of abstract rules (ibid.: 5–6).

Pluralist liberals will thus seek, in a case of indefeasible disagreement, a principled accommodation which pays due regard to the values at stake. The principles in question will not be abstract rules to be applied mechanically, but dispositions of character implied by the elements of value pluralism itself. To achieve a principled compromise under pluralism is to negotiate in the spirit of the pluralist virtues. While reflection on the elements of pluralism suggests the possibility of reasoned agreement to a greater extent than allowed by most interpretations of pluralism, it also helps to deal constructively with cases of disagreement.

Notes

1. See Chandran Kukathas (1989), who argues that an unresolved tension runs throughout Hayek's thought between, on one hand, a Humean scepticism about the scope of human knowledge and, on the other, a Kantian objectivism when it comes to the value of freedom.
2. For a similar value-pluralist critique of the market, see Bellamy (2000: 190–1).
3. It might be objected that the 'pluralism' on which Walzer bases his argument is not on all fours with my own because Walzer appeals more to an empirical pluralism of belief than to a fully fledged value pluralism in Berlin's sense. Thus he conceives of the goods with which distributive justice is concerned as 'social goods' (1983: 7), meaning that they count as goods not because of any inherent qualities but because they happen to be understood as goods by a particular society. It is the particular, local, social meaning ascribed to a good that determines its legitimate distribution: 'Distributive criteria and arrangements are intrinsic not to the good-in-itself but to the social good' (ibid.: 8–9). Social meanings, and therefore conceptions of the just distribution of goods, vary with time and place. This aspect of Walzer's theory seems to rest on an account of plurality of belief, or cultural relativism, rather than value pluralism. Although this is indeed Walzer's official doctrine, it is arguable that his case depends (like Rawls's) on a partially submerged pluralism of value in the deeper, Berlinian sense. In particular, without a notion of value pluralism it is hard to make sense of Walzer's advocacy of 'complex equality'. Walzer argues that most conceptions of distributive justice have aimed at 'simple equality', namely the more equal distribution of some particular 'dominant' good, e.g. money. For Walzer, this is futile because some people are always naturally better than others at monopolizing certain goods. Rather, policies aiming at justice in distribution should address the deeper problem, namely 'dominance', where 'one good or one set of goods is dominant and determinative of value in all spheres of distribution' (ibid.: 10). Walzer therefore recommends 'complex equality', under which 'no particular good is generally convertible' and each sphere remains autonomous (ibid.: 17). People naturally successful in one sphere will not

FROM PLURALISM TO LIBERALISM

necessarily be able to dominate in another. It is complex rather than simple equality that comes nearer to an adequate understanding of justice (ibid.: 13). However, this view seems to cut across the relativist aspect of Walzer's view according to which 'justice is relative to social meanings' (ibid.: 312). Complex equality would seem to have no place in a society in which shared understandings favoured the dominance of a particular good. In such a society, what reason would there be to maintain the autonomy of the different spheres, or even to acknowledge that there are such separate spheres? My suspicion is that Walzer's theory is an unstable combination of cultural relativism and value pluralism. He appeals to relativism when stressing cultural and historical variety, but relies on a tacit value pluralism when distinguishing among different goods and their 'spheres' and advancing complex equality as a normative standard. So far as he is doing the latter, Walzer is a value pluralist in the Berlinian sense, and thus far a universalist and metaphysician after all.

4. For recent value-pluralist criticisms of cost–benefit analysis, see Nussbaum (2000a), Richardson (2000) and Sen (2000).

5. The question of the best agency for pluralist liberal intervention, whether the institutions of the state or of civil society, is not one I shall pursue here. I assume that some combination of the two will be required, with the state as the more active and reliable partner. Consequently I shall refer to the liberal state as the chief counterweight to the market both here and in the following section, while recognizing that this is a contentious issue. For an account of the so-called 'third way' approach, in which social–democratic goals are pursued through the institutions of civil society rather than the state, see Giddens (1998, 2000).

6. See Kymlicka (1995) for a distinction between the claims to group-differentiated rights of 'national' (i.e. indigenous) minorities and those of 'ethnic' (i.e. immigrant) minorities. On Kymlicka's account both kinds of group have legitimate claims to special rights, but those of national minorities are more extensive.

7. Similar liberal limits to pluralist multiculturalism are advocated by Raz, who argues that liberal 'multiculturalism urges respect for cultures which are not themselves liberal cultures – very few are . . . [But] it does so while imposing liberal protection of individual freedom on those cultures. This in itself brings it into conflict with the cultures it urges governments to respect. The conflict is inevitable because liberal multiculturalism recognizes and respects those cultures because and to the extent that they serve true values' (1995: 182–3).

8. Galston also rejects autonomy as the chief basis for liberalism on the ground of liberal tradition, and this too seems to me to be mistaken. See Kymlicka (1995: 152–8), who points out that the distinctively liberal conception of toleration is toleration of individual conscience. There are other, non-liberal forms of toleration, such as the Ottoman millet system

256

PLURALIST LIBERALISM

which conceded limited self-government to religious minorities, who were thus empowered to impose their own orthodoxy on their own people. But on the distinctively liberal view of toleration, it is the conscience and judgement of the individual that is paramount. For liberals, then, toleration is secondary to personal autonomy.

9. Gutmann and Thompson expressly allow that reciprocity may require restrictions on 'conventional liberal doctrines of free speech' (1996: 91), for example to prevent non-reciprocal imputations of ulterior or self-interested motives in the making of arguments. See also William Galston (1999c), who sees reciprocity, as interpreted by Gutmann and Thompson, as wrongly excluding from deliberation the legitimate beliefs of religious fundamentalists. Compare Joshua Cohen (1996), who argues that deliberative democracy is itself sufficient to protect civil liberties.

10. Kekes (1996) makes this point as the basis of his argument against the claim, made by Judith Shklar and others, that for liberals 'cruelty' is the greatest evil.

CHAPTER 10

Conclusion

I have tried in this book to steer a course between the inadequacy of past attempts to argue from pluralism to liberalism and the precipitancy of recent claims that deny the possibility of such an argument altogether. On the one hand, the claim that value pluralism endorses liberalism has often been simply assumed to be true, or else supported by arguments that collapse on inspection. In some cases the argument turns out to be based not on Berlinian value pluralism at all but rather on de facto plurality of belief, which is in any case consistent not only with liberalism but also with its denial. A more sophisticated version of the argument from plurality of belief is presented by Rawls, but this works only to the extent that it depends on an implicit appeal to value pluralism after all. When value pluralism is taken as the explicit starting point, the results are often no better, as in the 'argument from indeterminacy'. There, pluralism is mistakenly said to yield a radical or unrestricted indeterminacy, which again cannot justify liberalism anyway. The arguments sketched by Berlin, too, are flawed or limited in the form in which he presents them.

The failure of these arguments does not, however, mean that no route from pluralism to liberalism is navigable, still less that pluralism rules out the reasoned justification of liberalism. The recent pluralist critics of liberalism are no less mistaken than the liberals they criticize. At their most extreme, the anti-liberal critics interpret pluralism as implying that there can be no reason to justify liberal rankings ahead of others because choices among conflicting

258

CONCLUSION

plural values must be non-rational. That claim is refuted by the more considered, particularist view that allows rational choice among plural values in context. But this too is often given an unduly narrow interpretation such that context is identified wholly or decisively with local tradition. An alternative anti-liberal position, Gray's advocacy of a pragmatic modus vivendi, widens the context for pluralist choice but proposes no principle that would prevent such choices from being mere assertions of self-interest or exercises in appeasement. In response to these views, I have argued that so far as pluralist choice must be particularist, reasons for liberal rankings may be generated by contexts wider than the strictly traditional. Moreover, beyond participation reasons for liberal rankings are implicit in a set of notion of value pluralism itself, that is, in a set of general principles that follow from the constituent elements of pluralism. This brings me to my own pluralist case for liberalism.

My argument is directed towards establishing three principal claims. First, a case for liberalism is, contrary to some views, compatible with value pluralism. Second, more controversially still, pluralism itself generates a case for liberalism, a case that is universal in reach. Third, the kind of liberalism justified by the pluralist outlook is broadly perfectionist or autonomy-based in its general character, redistributive rather than laissez-faire in its attitude to distributive justice, multicultural within liberal limits, and democratic within constitutional limits. Let me now draw together the main lines of argument for these claims.

First, liberalism is compatible with value pluralism at least in virtue of the possibility of a particularist case for liberalism. The idea of value pluralism comprises four main elements: (1) some generic values at least are universal, or regarded by all human beings as contributing to a good life; (2) genuine values, including both universal and local values, are plural; (3) many such values are incommensurable with one another, or radically distinct; (4) values conceived as plural and incommensurable in this way may, and often do, come into conflict with one another. In cases of conflict among plural and incommensurable values, we are faced with choices that are 'hard' in two senses. First, they involve losses in terms of one value that cannot be wholly compensated by gains in terms of another. Second, they cannot be resolved by the application of any single, straightforward rule for ranking values in all cases (e.g. utilitarianism), since the possibility of such a rule is excluded by

259

CONCLUSION

value incommensurablity. But although such choices are hard, they may still be rational. Although pluralism makes more abstract rankings problematic, there may be good reason for particular rankings in particular contexts. It follows that a reasoned case for liberalism is compatible with pluralism if suitably particularist.

The second of my three principal claims is that a case for liberalism is not merely compatible with pluralism but can be generated by it. This is possible in either of two ways. First, a particularist case for liberalism is implied by pluralism so far as pluralism invites attention to context (supposing that the relevant context happens to be favourable to liberalism). However, although particularist arguments for liberalism are possible, they fail to live up to the traditionally universalist aspirations of the liberal project. Liberals might then look to another route to rational choice under pluralism, namely reflection on the implications of the concept of pluralism itself. The elements of pluralism imply a set of five principles that are capable of grounding universalist case for liberalism. Some of these principles have the effect of ruling out liberalism's ideological rivals. First, the principle of respect for generic universal values rules out conservative (or strong communitarian) views that rely conclusively on the moral authority of local tradition. Second, recognition of value incommensurability tells against utopian views such as classical Marxism and anarchism, which look forward to a perfected society in which all significant moral and social conflicts have been resolved. The other three principles implied by pluralism go beyond the elimination of non-liberal competitors and provide liberalism with a set of positive justifications. First, the plurality and incommensurability of values imply a commitment to value diversity, which is in turn best satisfied by liberalism's 'approximate neutrality' or superior capacity for accommodating different goods and ways of life. Second, that same capacity for accommodation also enables liberalism to satisfy another pluralist principle, corresponding in particular to the elements of incommensurability and conflict, namely acknowledgment of reasonable disagreement among conceptions of the good. Pluralism is itself a conception of the good in a sense, but not one on all fours with those conceptions that are typically subject to reasonable disagreement. Third, practical reasoning under pluralism requires the exercise of certain attributes of character or virtues, in particular that of personal autonomy, which again are best developed and promoted within a liberal form of politics.

CONCLUSION

My third principal claim is that in this way value pluralism implies a case for a particular kind of liberalism. This will be a universalist liberalism, since it is justified by principles that are not merely particularist but universal. In addition, the pluralist approach enables liberals to take a position on the question of the relative priority of the neutralist and perfectionist strands within the liberal tradition. The pluralist outlook suggests that although both are important, it is the perfectionist or autonomy-based strand that has priority. Pluralist liberalism will therefore be broadly universalist and perfectionist in character. In economic distribution it will favour redistributionist policies as against pure laissez-faire, and in the cultural field it will endorse a degree of multiculturalism but within the limits implied by a commitment to personal autonomy. The process by which the pluralist–liberal polity arrives at such policies will be broadly democratic, but is likely to be subject to constitutional constraints entrenching civil liberties. Within the constitutional framework there will be many cases where reasoned agreement is not possible and compromise is required. Such compromises will be principled, however, structured by exercise of the pluralist–liberal virtues.

The case I have constructed is bound to attract objections, and I have tried to anticipate and reply to these in the course of the argument. Perhaps the most basic question is whether, in linking value pluralism and liberalism, I have distorted the basic character of both. First, the idea of value pluralism emphasizes the plurality of legitimate values and (to a lesser extent) conceptions of the good. Yet I have concluded that the political implications of pluralism favour liberal perfectionism, the view that the best political system is one that promotes a single conception of the good, or family of conceptions, namely that of liberalism. If not an outright contradiction, is this not a denial of the underlying spirit of the pluralist outlook? Second, on the pluralist view no single value overrides all others in all cases; rather, each is (outside of a particular context) 'equally ultimate'. By seeking to ground liberalism in value pluralism, have I not departed from a fundamental liberal insight, namely that there is an overriding value, namely respect for the human individual?

My reply to the first question is that value pluralism is not as rationally and ethically open-ended as is often assumed, and liberalism is not as narrow. Pluralism is not to be confused with either subjectivism or relativism. Rather, it implies a particular set

261

CONCLUSION

of objective norms that ought to guide moral and political choices universally. Choices are unavoidable under pluralism because there is never enough space in the life of a person or a society for us to enjoy, equally, all human values. Any ethical or political system must emphasize some goods at the expense of others. That is, any ethical or political system will be informed by a certain general ranking of values, a conception of the good. The liberal conception of the good is simply the most capacious that we know of, making room for the pursuit of a greater range of values and ways of life than is possible under rival systems. In addition, the liberal virtues are those which best fit us for coping well with the exigencies of choice among incommensurables, and so for living the best lives possible under pluralism. The underlying spirit of value pluralism is thus expressed rather than denied by liberalism.

As to the second question, the many different goods that are equally ultimate on the pluralist view count as goods only because they contribute to the well-being of actual persons. Rather than sources of value that rival the claims of the individual, the goods with which pluralists are concerned are goods in virtue of their role in the lives of individuals. Recall the distinction between the pluralist commitment to promoting the diversity of goods and the relativist or conservative stress on the value of forms of life independent of the fate of their individual members (5.3, 6.3). Recall, too, that attention to persons was one of the characteristic virtues required for practical reasoning under pluralism (8.1.3). The ethical individualism fundamental to liberalism is not at all foreign to the pluralist outlook.

It is also true, however, that value pluralism offers an approach to liberal argument that distinguishes it from others such as utilitarianism and Kantianism. The difference at its broadest is that the pluralist perspective is wider than these, indeed embracing them along with other ethical perspectives. Rather than resting the case for liberalism on some one or a few values – utility or Kantian respect for rational agency – the pluralist must take seriously the whole range of human goods. This is at once the great challenge the pluralist outlook faces, and the source of its strength.

References

Archard, D. (ed.) (1996) *Pluralism and Philosophy*. Cambridge: Cambridge University Press.

Barber, B. (1995) *Jihad vs McWorld*. New York: Ballantine.

Barker, C. (1999) *Television, Globalization and Cultural Identities*. Buckingham: Open University Press.

Barry, B. (1991) 'How not to defend liberal institutions', *British Journal of Political Science*, 20, 1–14.

Bellamy, R. (1999) *Liberalism and Pluralism: Towards a Politics of Compromise*. London and New York: Routledge.

Bellamy, R. (2000) 'Liberalism and the challenge of pluralism', in *Rethinking Liberalism*. London and New York: Pinter.

Benn, S.I. (1976) 'Freedom, autonomy, and the concept of a person', *Proceedings of the Aristotelian Society*, New Series, 76, 109–30.

Benn, S.I. (1988) *A Theory of Freedom*. Cambridge: Cambridge University Press.

Berkowitz, P. (1999) *Virtue and the Making of Modern Liberalism*. Princeton, NJ: Princeton University Press.

Berlin, I. (1963) *Karl Marx: His Life and Environment*, 3rd edn. London: Oxford University Press.

Berlin, I. (1969) *Four Essays on Liberty*. London: Oxford University Press.

Berlin, I. (1980) *Concepts and Categories: Philosophical Essays*, ed. H. Hardy. Oxford: Oxford University Press.

Berlin, I. (1981) *Against the Current: Essays in the History of Ideas*, ed. H. Hardy. Oxford: Oxford University Press.

REFERENCES

Berlin, I. (1992a) *The Crooked Timber of Humanity: Chapters in the History of Ideas*, ed. H. Hardy. New York: Vintage.

Berlin, I. (1992b) 'Reply to Ronald H. McKinney, "Towards a postmodern ethics: Sir Isaiah Berlin and John Caputo"', *Journal of Value Inquiry*, 26, 257–60.

Berlin, I. (1996) *The Sense of Reality: Studies in Ideas and their History*, ed. H. Hardy. London: Chatto & Windus.

Berlin, I. (1997) *The Proper Study of Mankind: An Anthology of Essays*, eds H. Hardy and R. Hausheer. London: Chatto & Windus.

Berlin, I. (1998) *The First and the Last*, ed. H. Hardy. New York: New York Review Books.

Berlin, I. (2000) *Three Critics of the Enlightenment: Vico, Hamann, Herder*, ed. H. Hardy. Princeton, NJ, and Oxford: Princeton University Press.

Berlin, I. and Jahanbegloo, R. (1991) *Conversations with Isaiah Berlin*. New York: Charles Scribner's Sons.

Berlin, I. and Williams, B. (1994) 'Pluralism and liberalism: a reply', *Political Studies*, 42, 306–9.

Blokland, H. (1999) 'Berlin on pluralism and liberalism: a defence', *European Legacy*, 4, 1–23.

Bock, P.K. (1974) *Modern Cultural Anthropology: an Introduction*, 2nd edn. New York: Alfred A. Knopf.

Bullock, A. and Shock, M. (eds) (1967) *The Liberal Tradition*. Oxford: Clarendon Press.

Burke, E. (1968) *Reflections on the Revolution in France*, ed. C. O'Brien. Harmondsworth: Penguin.

Casey, J. (1990) *Pagan Ethics*. Oxford: Clarendon Press.

Chang, R. (1997) 'Introduction', in R. Chang (ed.), *Incommensurability, Incomparability, and Practical Reason*. Cambridge, MA: Harvard University Press.

Christman, J. (1991) 'Liberalism and individual positive freedom', *Ethics*, 101, 343–59.

Cohen, J. (1989) 'Deliberation and democratic legitimacy', in A. Hamlin and P. Pettit (eds), *The Good Polity*. Oxford: Blackwell, 17–34.

Cohen, J. (1996) 'Procedure and substance in deliberative democracy', in S. Benhabib (ed.), *Democracy and Difference: Contesting the Boundaries of the Political*. Princeton, NJ: Princeton University Press, 95–119.

Colls, R. (1998) 'Ethics man: John Gray's new moral world', *Political Quarterly*, 69, 59–71.

REFERENCES

Constant, B. (1988) *Political Writings*, ed. B. Fontana. Cambridge: Cambridge University Press.

Crick, B. (1987) *Socialism*. Minneapolis, IN: University of Minnesota Press.

Crisp, R. (ed.) (1996) *How Should One Live? Essays on the Virtues*. Oxford: Clarendon Press.

Crowder, G. (1988) 'Negative and positive liberty', *Political Science*, 40, 57–73.

Crowder, G. (1991) *Classical Anarchism: The Political Thought of Godwin, Proudhon, Bakunin, and Kropotkin*. Oxford: Clarendon Press.

Crowder, G. (1994) 'Pluralism and liberalism', *Political Studies*, 42, 293–305.

Crowder, G. (1996) 'Communication: Isaiah Berlin and Bernard Williams, "Pluralism and liberalism"', *Political Studies*, 44, 649–50.

Crowder, G. (1998) 'John Gray's pluralist critique of liberalism', *Journal of Applied Philosophy*, 15, 287–98.

Crowder, G. (1999) 'From value pluralism to liberalism', in R. Bellamy and M. Hollis (eds), *Pluralism and Liberal Neutrality*. London: Frank Cass.

Crowder, G. and Griffiths, M. (1999) 'Postmodernism and international relations theory: a liberal response', in J. Brookfield *et al.* (eds), *Proceedings of the 1999 Conference of the Australasian Political Studies Association*, vol. 1. Sydney: University of Sydney, 135–45.

Douglass, R.B., Mara, G. and Richardson, H.S. (eds) (1990) *Liberalism and the Good*. New York: Routledge.

Doyle, M. (1983) 'Kant, liberal legacies, and foreign affairs: Part 1', *Philosophy and Public Affairs*, 12, 205–34.

Dworkin, G. (ed.) (1992) 'Symposium on pluralism and ethical theory', *Ethics*, 102.

Dworkin, R. (1977) *Taking Rights Seriously*. London: Duckworth.

Dworkin, R. (1985) *A Matter of Principle*. Cambridge, MA: Harvard University Press.

Dzur, A. (1998) 'Value pluralism versus political liberalism?', *Social Theory and Practice*, 24, 375–92.

Evans, M. (1975) *Karl Marx*. London: George Allen & Unwin.

Finnis, J. (1980) *Natural Law and Natural Rights*. Oxford: Clarendon Press.

Foot, P. (1978) *Virtues and Vices*. Oxford: Blackwell.

REFERENCES

Friedman, M. (1982) *Capitalism and Freedom*. Chicago: University of Chicago Press.

Fukuyama, F. (1992) *The End of History and the Last Man*. Harmondsworth: Penguin.

Galipeau, C. (1994) *Isaiah Berlin's Liberalism*. Oxford: Oxford University Press.

Galston, W. (1991) *Liberal Purposes: Goods, Virtues, and Diversity in the Liberal State*. Cambridge: Cambridge University Press.

Galston, W. (1995) 'Two concepts of liberalism', *Ethics*, 105, 516–34.

Galston, W. (1999a) 'Expressive liberty, moral pluralism, political pluralism: three sources of liberal theory', *William and Mary Law Review*, 40, 869–907.

Galston, W. (1999b) 'Value pluralism and liberal political theory', *American Political Science Review*, 93, 769–78.

Galston, W. (1999c) 'Diversity, toleration, and deliberative democracy: religious minorities and public schooling', in S. Macedo (ed.), *Deliberative Politics: Essays on Democracy and Disagreement*. New York and London: Oxford University Press, 39–54.

Giddens, A. (1998) *The Third Way: The Renewal of Social Democracy*. Cambridge: Polity.

Giddens, A. (2000) *The Third Way and its Critics*. Cambridge: Polity.

Godwin, W. (1976) *Enquiry Concerning Political Justice*, ed. I. Kramnick. Harmondsworth: Penguin.

Gray, J. (1986) *Liberalism*. Milton Keynes: Open University Press.

Gray, J. (1989) *Liberalisms: Essays in Political Philosophy*. London: Routledge.

Gray, J. (1993a) *Beyond the New Right: Markets, Government and the Common Environment*. London: Routledge.

Gray, J. (1993b) *Post-Liberalism: Studies in Political Thought*. London: Routledge.

Gray, J. (1995a) *Berlin*. New York: HarperCollins.

Gray, J. (1995b) *Enlightenment's Wake: Politics and Culture at the Close of the Modern Age*. London: Routledge.

Gray, J. (1995c) 'Why irony can't be superior', *Times Literary Supplement*, 3 November.

Gray, J. (1997) *Endgames: Questions in Late Modern Political Thought*. Cambridge: Polity.

Gray, J. (1998) 'Where pluralists and liberals part company', *International Journal of Philosophical Studies*, 6, 17–36.

REFERENCES

Gray, J. (2000a) 'Pluralism and toleration in contemporary political philosophy', *Political Studies*, 48, 323–33.

Gray, J. (2000b) *Two Faces of Liberalism*. Cambridge: Polity.

Grisez, G. (1970) *Abortion: The Myths, the Realities, and the Arguments*. New York: Corpus Books.

Gutmann, A. and Thompson, D. (1996) *Democracy and Disagreement*. Cambridge, MA: Belknap.

Hampshire, S. (1983) *Morality and Conflict*. Cambridge, MA: Harvard University Press.

Hampton, J. (1989) 'Should political philosophy be done without metaphysics?', *Ethics*, 99, 791–814.

Harbour, W.R. (1982) *The Foundations of Conservative Thought*. Notre Dame, IN: University of Notre Dame Press.

Hardy, H. (2001) *The Isaiah Berlin Virtual Library*, http://berlin.wolf.ox.ac.uk

Harris, I. (1996) 'Isaiah Berlin: two concepts of liberty', in M. Forsyth and M. Keens-Soper (eds), *The Political Classics: Green to Dworkin*. Oxford: Oxford University Press, 121–42.

Hart, H.L.A. (1979) 'Between utility and rights', in A. Ryan (ed.), *The Idea of Freedom*. Oxford: Clarendon Press.

Hayek, F. (1944) *The Road to Serfdom*. London: Routledge.

Hayek, F. (1960) *The Constitution of Liberty*. London: Routledge.

Hayek, F. (1967) 'The principles of a liberal social order', in *Studies in Philosophy, Politics and Economics*. London: Routledge.

Hegel, G.W.F. (1962) *On Tragedy*, ed. A. and H. Paolucci. Garden City, NY: Anchor Books.

Holton, R. (1998) *Globalization and the Nation-State*. New York: St Martin's Press.

Hume, D. (1978) *A Treatise of Human Nature*, ed. L.A. Selby-Bigge, revised by P.H. Nidditch. Oxford: Oxford University Press.

Huntington, S. (1996) *The Clash of Civilizations and the Remaking of World Order*. New York: Simon & Schuster.

Hurka, T. (1996) 'Monism, pluralism, and rational regret', *Ethics*, 106, 555–75.

Ignatieff, M. (1998) *Isaiah Berlin: A Life*. London: Chatto & Windus.

Johnston, D. (1994) *The Idea of a Liberal Theory: A Critique and Reconstruction*. Princeton, NJ: Princeton University Press.

Jones, P. (1995) 'Review article: two conceptions of liberalism, two conceptions of justice', *British Journal of Political Science*, 25, 515–50.

REFERENCES

Kant, I. (1956) *The Moral Law*, ed. H.J. Paton, 3rd edn. London: Hutchinson.

Kant, I. (1991) *Political Writings*, ed. H. Reiss. Cambridge: Cambridge University Press.

Katznelson, I. (1994) 'A properly defended liberalism: John Gray on the filling of political life', *Social Research*, 61, 611–30.

Kekes, J. (1993) *The Morality of Pluralism*. Princeton, NJ: Princeton University Press.

Kekes, J. (1996) 'Cruelty and liberalism', *Ethics*, 106, 834–44.

Kekes, J. (1997) *Against Liberalism*. Ithaca: Cornell University Press.

Kekes, J. (1998) *A Case for Conservatism*. Ithaca: Cornell University Press.

Kenny, M. (2000) 'Isaiah Berlin's contribution to modern political theory', *Political Studies*, 48, 1026–39.

Kluckhohn, C. (1965) 'Universal categories of culture', in A. Kroeber (ed.), *Anthropology Today*. Chicago: University of Chicago Press.

Kocis, R. (1989) *A Critical Appraisal of Sir Isaiah Berlin's Political Philosophy*. Lewiston, NY: Edwin Mellen Press.

Kukathas, C. (1989) *Hayek and Modern Liberalism*. Oxford: Clarendon Press.

Kukathas, C. (1992) 'Are there any cultural rights?', *Political Theory*, 20, 105–39.

Kukathas, C. (1997) 'Liberalism, multiculturalism and oppression', in A. Vincent (ed.), *Political Theory: Tradition and Diversity*. Cambridge: Cambridge University Press, Chapter 6.

Kukathas, C. (1998) 'Liberalism and multiculturalism: the politics of indifference', *Political Theory*, 26, 686–99.

Kymlicka, W. (1989) *Liberalism, Community, and Culture*. Oxford: Clarendon Press.

Kymlicka, W. (1990) *Contemporary Political Philosophy*. Oxford: Clarendon Press.

Kymlicka, W. (1995) *Multicultural Citizenship*. Oxford: Clarendon Press.

Larmore, C. (1987) *Patterns of Moral Complexity*. Cambridge: Cambridge University Press.

Larmore, C. (1996) *The Morals of Modernity*. Cambridge: Cambridge University Press.

Larmore, C. (1997/8) Review of Isaiah Berlin, *The Sense of Reality*, *Boston Review of Books*.

REFERENCES

Legutko, R. (1994) 'On postmodern liberal conservatism', *Critical Review*, 8, 1–22.

Lessnoff, M. (1999) *Political Philosophers of the Twentieth Century*. Oxford: Blackwell.

Locke, J. (1988) *Two Treatises of Government*, ed. P. Laslett. Cambridge: Cambridge University Press.

Locke, J. (1991) *A Letter Concerning Toleration: in focus*, ed. J. Horton and S. Mendus. London and New York: Routledge.

Lukes, S. (1985) *Marxism and Morality*. Oxford: Clarendon Press.

Lukes, S. (1991) 'Making sense of moral conflict', in *Moral Conflict and Politics*. Oxford: Clarendon Press.

Lukes, S. (1993) 'Five fables about human rights', in S. Shute and S. Hurley (eds), *On Human Rights: the Oxford Amnesty Lectures 1993*. New York: Basic Books.

Lukes, S. (1994) 'The singular and the plural: on the distinctive liberalism of Isaiah Berlin', *Social Research*, 61, 687–717.

Lyotard, J.-F. (1984) *The Postmodern Condition: A Report on Knowledge*. Minneapolis, IN: University of Minnesota Press.

Macedo, S. (1990) *Liberal Virtues: Citizenship, Virtue, and Community in Liberal Constitutionalism*. Oxford: Clarendon Press.

Macedo, S. (1999) Introduction to S. Macedo (ed.), *Deliberative Politics: Essays on Politics and Disagreement*. New York and Oxford: Oxford University Press.

MacIntyre, A. (1985) *After Virtue*, 2nd edn. London: Duckworth.

MacIntyre, A. (1988) *Whose Justice? Which Rationality?* Notre Dame, IN: University of Notre Dame Press.

Mack, A. (ed.) (1994) 'Liberty and pluralism' issue, *Social Research*, 66.

MacKenzie, I. (1999) 'Berlin's defence of value-pluralism: clarifications and criticisms', *Contemporary Politics*, 5, 325–37.

Manning, D.J. (1976) *Liberalism*. London: Dent & Sons.

Margalit, E. and A. (eds) (1991) *Isaiah Berlin: A Celebration*. London: Hogarth.

Marx, K. (1977) *Karl Marx: Selected Writings*, ed. D. McLellan. Oxford: Oxford University Press.

McKinney, R.H. (1992) 'Towards a postmodern ethic: Sir Isaiah Berlin and John Caputo', *Journal of Value Inquiry*, 26, 395–407.

Mill, J.S. (1974) *On Liberty*, ed. G. Himmelfarb. Harmondsworth: Penguin.

Miller, D. (1984) *Anarchism*. London: Dent.

Mulhall, S. and Swift, A. (1996) *Liberals and Communitarians*, 2nd

REFERENCES

edn. Oxford: Blackwell.

Murdoch, I. (1970) *The Sovereignty of Good*. London: Routledge.

Murdock, G.P. (1945) 'The common denominators of culture', in R. Linton (ed.), *The Science of Man in the World Crisis*. New York: Columbia University Press.

Nagel, T. (1973) 'Rawls on justice', in N. Daniels (ed.), *Reading Rawls*. New York: Basic Books.

Nagel, T. (1991) 'The fragmentation of value', in *Mortal Questions*. Cambridge: Canto.

Neal, P. (1997) *Liberalism and its Discontents*. New York: New York University Press.

Newey, G. (1998) 'Value-pluralism in contemporary liberalism', *Dialogue*, 37, 493–522.

Nozick, R. (1974) *Anarchy, State, and Utopia*. New York: Basic Books.

Nussbaum, M. (1986) *The Fragility of Goodness: Luck and Ethics in Greek Tragedy and Philosophy*. Cambridge: Cambridge University Press.

Nussbaum, M. (1990) 'Aristotelian social democracy', in R.B. Douglass, G. Mara and H.S. Richardson (eds), *Liberalism and the Good*. New York: Routledge.

Nussbaum, M. (1992a) 'Human functioning and social justice: in defense of Aristotelian essentialism', *Political Theory*, 20, 202–46.

Nussbaum, M. (1992b) *Love's Knowledge: Essays on Philosophy and Literature*. Oxford: Oxford University Press.

Nussbaum, M. (1993) 'Non-relative virtues: an Aristotelian approach', in M. Nussbaum and A. Sen (eds), *The Quality of Life*. Oxford: Clarendon Press.

Nussbaum, M. (1995) 'Aristotle on human nature and the foundation of ethics', in J. Altham and R. Harrison (eds), *World, Mind and Ethics*. Cambridge: Cambridge University Press.

Nussbaum, M. (2000a) 'The costs of tragedy: some moral limits of cost–benefit analysis', *Journal of Legal Studies*, 29, 1005–36.

Nussbaum, M. (2000b) *Women and Human Development: the Capabilities Approach*. Cambridge: Cambridge University Press.

Rawls, J. (1971) *A Theory of Justice*. Oxford: Oxford University Press.

Rawls, J. (1985) 'Justice as fairness: political not metaphysical', *Philosophy and Public Affairs*, 14, 223–51.

Rawls, J. (1993) *Political Liberalism*. New York: Columbia University Press.

REFERENCES

Raz, J. (1986) *The Morality of Freedom*. Oxford: Clarendon Press.

Raz, J. (1995) 'Multiculturalism: a liberal perspective', in *Ethics in the Public Domain: Essays in the Morality of Law and Politics*. Oxford: Clarendon Press, 170–91.

Richardson, H. S. (1997) *Practical Reasoning about Final Ends*. Cambridge: Cambridge University Press.

Richardson, H. S. (2000) 'The stupidity of cost–benefit analysis', *Journal of Legal Studies*, 29, 971–1003.

Riley, J. (2000) 'Crooked timber and liberal culture', in M. Baghramian and A. Ingram (eds), *Pluralism: The Philosophy and Politics of Diversity*. London and New York: Routledge, 120–55.

Rorty, R. (1989) *Contingency, Irony, and Solidarity*. Cambridge: Cambridge University Press.

Rorty, R. (1991) *Objectivity, Relativism, and Truth: Philosophical Papers Volume 1*. Cambridge: Cambridge University Press.

Rosenblum, N. (1989) 'Introduction', in N. Rosenblum (ed.), *Liberalism and the Moral Life*. Cambridge, MA: Harvard University Press.

Ruddick, S. (1980) 'Maternal thinking', *Feminist Studies*, 6, 342–67.

Ryan, A. (ed.) (1979) *The Idea of Freedom: Essays in Honour of Isaiah Berlin*. Oxford: Clarendon Press.

Sandel, M. (1982) *Liberalism and the Limits of Justice*. Cambridge: Cambridge University Press.

Sandel, M. (1984) 'Introduction', in M. Sandel (ed.), *Liberalism and its Critics*. Oxford: Oxford University Press.

Sandel, M. (1991) 'Morality and the liberal ideal', in J. Arthur and W. Shaw (eds), *Justice and Economic Distribution*. Englewood Cliffs, NJ: Prentice Hall.

Sandel, M. (1994) 'Political liberalism', *Harvard Law Review*, 107, 1765–94.

Sandel, M. (1996) *Democracy's Discontent: America in Search of a Public Philosophy*. Cambridge, MA: Belknap.

Scanlon, T. (1988) 'The significance of choice', *Tanner Lectures on Human Values*, 8. Salt Lake City: University of Utah Press, 149–216.

Scheffler, S. (1994) 'The appeal of political liberalism', *Ethics*, 105, 4–22.

Schlesinger, A.M. (1992) *The Disuniting of America: Reflections on a Multicultural Society*. New York and London: Norton.

Scholte, J. (2000) *Globalization: A Critical Introduction*. Basingstoke: Palgrave.

REFERENCES

Sen, A. (2000) 'The discipline of cost–benefit analysis', *Journal of Legal Studies*, 29, 931–52.

Sheridan, G. (1999) *Asian Values, Western Dreams*. St Leonards, NSW: Allen & Unwin.

Shklar, J. (1989) 'The liberalism of fear', in N. Rosenblum (ed.), *Liberalism and the Moral Life*. Cambridge, MA: Harvard University Press.

Slote, M. (1992) *From Morality to Virtue*. New York: Oxford University Press.

Stocker, M. (1990) *Plural and Conflicting Values*. Oxford: Clarendon Press.

Strauss, Leo (1989) 'Relativism', in *The Rebirth of Classical Political Rationalism: An Introduction to the Thought of Leo Strauss*, selected and introduced by T. Pangle. Chicago: Chicago University Press.

Stretton, H. and Orchard, L. (1994) *Public Goods, Public Enterprise, Public Choice: Theoretical Foundations of the Contemporary Attack on Government*. New York: St Martin's Press.

Taylor, C. (1985) 'What is human agency?', *Philosophy and the Human Sciences: Philosophical Papers* vol. 1. Cambridge: Cambridge University Press.

Taylor, C. (1989a) 'Cross-purposes: the liberal–communitarian debate', in N. Rosenblum (ed.), *Liberalism and the Moral Life*. Cambridge, MA: Harvard University Press.

Taylor, C. (1989b) *Sources of the Self: The Making of the Modern Identity*. Cambridge, MA: Harvard University Press.

Taylor, C. (1994) 'The politics of recognition', in A. Gutmann (ed.), *Multiculturalism: Examining the Politics of Recognition*. Princeton, NJ: Princeton University Press.

Tronto, J. (1993) *Moral Boundaries: A Political Argument for an Ethic of Care*. New York and London: Routledge.

Turnbull, C. (1984) *The Human Cycle*. London: Jonathan Cape.

Vlastos, G. (1962) 'Justice and equality', in R.B. Brandt (ed.), *Social Justice*. Englewood Cliffs, NJ: Prentice Hall.

Waldron, J. (1987) 'Theoretical foundations of liberalism', *Philosophical Quarterly*, 37, 127–50.

Waldron, J. (1991) 'Locke: toleration and the rationality of persecution', in J. Horton and S. Mendus (eds), *A Letter Concerning Toleration: in focus*. London and New York: Routledge.

Walzer, M. (1983) *Spheres of Justice*. Oxford: Martin Robertson.

Walzer, M. (1990) 'The communitarian critique of liberalism', *Political Theory*, 18, 6–23.

REFERENCES

Walzer, M. (1995) 'Are there limits to liberalism?' *New York Review of Books*, 19 October, a review of J. Gray, *Berlin*.

Waters, M. (1997) *Globalization*. London: Routledge.

Weinstock, D. (1998) 'The Graying of Berlin', *Critical Review*, 11, 481–501.

White, S.K. (1991) *Political Theory and Postmodernism*. Cambridge: Cambridge University Press.

Williams, B. (1979) 'Conflicts of values', in A. Ryan (ed.), *The Idea of Freedom: Essays in Honour of Isaiah Berlin*. Oxford: Clarendon Press.

Williams, B. (1980) 'Introduction' to I. Berlin, *Concepts and Categories*, ed. H. Hardy. London: Oxford University Press.

Williams, B. (1985) *Ethics and the Limits of Philosophy*. London: Fontana.

Wintrop, N. (1993) 'Fukuyama's challenge to leftists', *Quadrant*, June.

Wolf, S. (1992) 'Two levels of pluralism', *Ethics*, 102, 785–98.

Wolff, R.P. (1970) *In Defense of Anarchism*. New York: Harper Torchbooks.

Yack, B. (ed.) (1996) *Liberalism without Illusions: Essays on Liberal Theory and the Political Vision of Judith N. Shklar*. Chicago: Chicago University Press.

Young, I.M. (1990) *Justice and the Politics of Difference*. Princeton, NJ: Princeton University Press.

Index

anarchism 12, 14, 78, 90–1, 96, 98, 156, 260
Aristotle 17 n.2, 58–9, 46, 49, 66, 70, 74 n.3, 187–8, 191, 221
attentiveness 191, 196–8, 235, 254, 262
autonomy, personal 7, 10, 11, 12, 16, 23, 24, 26, 27, 30, 35–40 *passim*, 113–14, 128–9, 182, 185, 186, 198–211, 217, 234–5
and culture 238–9, 243–5

Bakunin, Michael 90, 96
Bellamy, Richard 248–52
Bentham, Jeremy 50, 51, 52, 91
Berlin, Isaiah 2, 4–5, 8, 14, 46, 47, 54, 57, 61, 74 n.1, 78–102 *passim*, 104, 105, 115, 126, 130 n.6, 136, 138, 140, 148, 166, 168, 170, 173, 174, 175, 194, 197, 201, 210, 212, 250, 258
broad-mindedness 193–4
Burke, Edmund 106

capitalism 147–8, 228–36
see also laissez-faire
Chang, Ruth 59
communitarianism 26, 30–1, 140, 156
compromise 246–55
see also modus vivendi

conservatism 12, 14, 78, 99, 103–31 *passim*, 149, 156, 174, 198
Constant, Benjamin 113
constitutionalism 246–52
context *see* particularism
cost–benefit analysis 234
cultural relativism *see* relativism, ethical
cultures, minority 16, 236–46

democracy, deliberative 17, 246–55
disagreement, reasonable 158–84 *passim*
diversity 135–57 *passim*
and coherence 15, 139, 142–5
cultural 150–5
of goods 152–4
ethic of 135–8
and multiplicity 15, 139–142
Dworkin, Ronald 17 n.2, 22, 23, 24, 26, 28, 30, 31, 91, 105, 155, 247

equality 2, 3, 22, 26, 54, 55, 83, 89, 91, 105, 151, 230, 232

Finnis, John 129–30 n.3
flexibility 191–2, 254
freedom *see* liberty
Fukuyama, Francis 25

INDEX

Galston, William 5–6, 34, 37, 146, 183–4 n.4, 186, 193, 195, 218, 243–5, 256 n.8
generosity 188–90, 254
globalization, cultural 155
Godwin, William 90, 215–16 n.14
Gray, John 11, 14, 24, 46, 54, 75 n.8, 103–4, 115–31 *passim*, 140, 141, 146–56, 175, 186–7, 198, 216 n.15, 237, 238, 247–8, 251, 252, 253, 259
Green, T. H. 24
Gutmann, Amy 248–9, 253–4

Hampton, Jean 180
Hardy, Henry 74 n.2, 100 n.1
Hart, H. L. A. 229
Hayek, Friedrich 16, 24, 157 n.5, 227–8
Hegel, G. W. F. 71, 72, 86, 90, 91, 140
Herder, J. G. 17 n.2
Hobhouse, L. T. 24
Hume, David 17 n.2, 66, 74 n.1

incommensurability 2–3, 49–54, 69–73, 127, 223, 232, 249–50
indeterminacy, argument from 8–9, 79–80, 228

Johnston, David 154

Kant, Immanuel 22, 23, 35–7, 40
Kekes, John 11, 14, 40, 42 n.7, 46–9, 56, 61, 69, 103–31 *passim*, 139–42, 149, 156 n.2, 174–5, 186–7, 237, 238, 257 n.10
Kropotkin, Peter 90
Kukathas, Chandran 99, 239–40, 255 n.1
Kymlicka, Will 34, 231, 238, 239–46 *passim*, 256 n.8

laissez-faire
economic 24, 228–36
cultural 24–5
Larmore, Charles 15, 36–7, 98, 158–84 *passim*
liberalism
classical vs. social 24–5

elements 22–5
justificatory theories 26–42
pluralist 217–57
'political' 32–4, 158–84 *passim*
liberty 23, 250
negative vs positive 2, 3, 6, 86–90, 210–11, 249–50
Locke, John 23–4, 26, 35, 40, 91, 173
Lukes, Steven 93, 215 n.6
Lyotard, Jean-François 143

Macedo, Stephen 16, 150, 154, 188–9, 193, 195, 201, 205–7, 214 n.5
Machiavelli, Niccolò 17 n.2
MacIntyre, Alasdair 31, 140
Marx, Karl 55, 86, 90, 91, 92–5, 140, 233
Marxism 12, 14, 26, 78, 92–5, 98, 100, 115, 122, 129, 147, 149, 156, 174, 260
Mill, John Stuart 23, 28, 29, 35–6, 37, 38, 40, 46, 51, 87–8, 91, 125, 163, 198, 199, 214 n.5, 219, 231, 238
moderation 194–6
modus vivendi 11, 14, 99, 103, 119–22, 149, 152, 198, 216 n.15, 220, 248, 253, 259
monism, ethical 4–5, 65, 69–73, 84, 85–6, 88–97, 121–2, 173
Montaigne, Michel de 17 n.2

Nagel, Thomas 46, 168, 170
natural law 4, 66, 90–1, 110–11, 129 n.3
see also rights, natural
Neal, Patrick 34–5, 42 n.6
neutrality, liberal 8, 12, 13, 15, 16, 21, 27, 29–35, 38, 40–2, 108, 135–57 *passim*, 158–84 *passim*, 217–18, 220–6, 228, 237, 240, 260
approximate 15, 31, 42 n.7, 109, 138, 146, 161, 163, 179, 221
Nozick, Robert 16, 24, 105, 229
Nussbaum, Martha 45, 46, 47, 48–9, 54, 58–9, 62, 65, 66–7, 70–1, 73 n.1, 187–8, 190, 191–2, 197

Oakeshott, Michael 17 n.2

275

INDEX

particularism
 in liberal justification 12, 14, 21,
  26–7, 32–4, 38–42, 109–15,
  122–9, 259–60
 in practical reasoning 13, 57–62,
  103–31 *passim*, 185–216 *passim*
perfectionism, liberal 12, 15–16, 21,
 26–7, 34–43 *passim*, 185–216
 passim, 217–18, 220–6, 242–6,
 261
philosophy, political 179–82
Plato 52, 58, 86, 90, 91, 141
pluralism
 goods vs. cultures 54, 126–7
 plurality of belief 3, 9–10, 160,
  165–71 *passim*
 see also diversity; value pluralism
postmodernism 26, 143–5
practical reasoning *see* particularism
pragmatism 14, 78, 99, 174
 see also modus vivendi
property, private 24, 148
 see also capitalism
Proudhon, Pierre-Joseph 90

Rawls, John 3, 12, 15, 24, 28, 29–34,
 35, 36, 39, 66, 105, 108, 112,
 119, 120, 121, 128, 155, 158–84
 passim, 214 n.4, 218, 221, 222,
 230, 247, 258
Raz, Joseph 16, 34, 38–40, 61, 105,
 113–14, 119, 128–9, 200, 201–4,
 207, 208, 211, 218, 222, 238,
 243
realism, pluralist 190, 194, 254
relativism, ethical 3–4, 8, 38, 44, 48,
 65–8, 80, 123–7, 143–5, 153,
 197–8, 212, 219, 237, 255 n.3,
 261
respect for persons 22, 151, 197, 235,
 262
Richardson, Henry S. 50, 51, 61
rights
 individual 23, 105, 145–6, 196–7,
  229, 247
 cultural 16, 25, 238–46

natural 110–11
Riley, Jonathan 101 n.4
Rousseau, Jean-Jacques 86, 88, 90, 91

Sandel, Michael 30, 31, 42, 43, 79, 80,
 129
social democracy 147
socialism 147–8, 149
Strauss, Leo 101 n.3

Taylor, Charles 31
Thompson, Dennis 248–9, 253–4
toleration 9–10, 23, 28, 31, 256–7 n.8

United States of America 32, 111, 233
universal values 2, 26, 45–8, 65–9,
 73–4 n.1, 82–4, 101 n.4, 122–9,
 137, 153, 219–20, 232
utilitarianism 4, 50–1, 58, 91, 104,
 110, 115, 120, 138, 199, 209,
 217, 233, 235, 259, 262
utopianism 4, 78, 84–100 *passim*, 115,
 116, 122, 127, 135, 146, 147,
 149, 174, 194,
 231, 245, 260

value pluralism
 defenders 17 n.2
 definition 2
 elements 2–4, 45–56
 rational choice under 5–6, 56–64
 truth of 64–73, 170, 202–4
Vico, Giambattista 17 n.2
virtues 185–216 *passim*
 liberal 16, 192–200
 pluralist 16, 181–92

Walzer, Michael 9–10, 111, 112, 165,
 186–7, 188, 190, 232–3, 234,
 236, 255–6 n.3
Weber, Max 17 n.2
White, Stephen 143
Williams, Bernard 68, 136, 139, 181,
 216 n.17

Young, Iris Marion 250